Conflict
in Higher Education

State Government
Coordination Versus
Institutional Independence

John D. David Millett, 1912-

with the assistance of

Fred F. Harcleroad
Robert B. Mautz
T. Harry McKinney
Robert C. Wood
and Marcy Muringhan

Conflict
in Higher Education

State Government
Coordination Versus
Institutional Independence

Bec₃

Jossey-Bass Publishers

San Francisco • Washington • London • 1984

CONFLICT IN HIGHER EDUCATION
State Government Coordination Versus Institutional Independence
by John D. Millett

Copyright © 1984 by Jossey-Bass Inc., Publishers
433 California Street
San Francisco, California 94104

&

Jossey-Bass Limited
28 Banner Street
London EC1Y 8QE

Library of Congress Cataloging in Publication Data

Millett, John David
  Conflict in higher education.

  Bibliography: p. 267
  Includes index.
  1. Higher education and state — United States.
2. University autonomy — United States.   I. Title.
LC173.M54   1983   379.1'52   83-24806
ISBN 0-87589-589-1

Manufactured in the United States of America

The paper in this book meets the guidelines for
permanence and durability of the Committee on
Production Guidelines for Book Longevity of the
Council on Library Resources.

JACKET DESIGN BY WILLI BAUM

FIRST EDITION

Code 8403

The Jossey-Bass
Higher Education Series

Preface

THE AUTONOMY, or lack thereof, of public institutions of higher education has commanded a substantial amount of attention in the years since the end of World War II. This writing, forthcoming mostly from individuals with a campus base, is relatively more extensive on the evils of governmental encroachment and less so on the inadequacies of individual colleges and universities in responding to social concerns. Moreover, the discussion has not always made appropriate distinctions among the "villains" in the drama of curtailing institutional independence.

The expansion of federal government financial support of higher education after 1960 was quickly followed by restrictions on institutional independence in providing access to students, in determining programs to offer and support, in providing employment to faculty and staff, and in operating facilities. These federal government intrusions on institutional autonomy fell equally upon public and private colleges and universities. Public institutions were subject to a different set of restrictions in their relationship to state governments. Since public institutions, with few exceptions, are chartered by state governments and receive the major support for their instructional mission from state governments, from the public institutions' point of view state government control of university operations and of university governance is of primary concern.

The state government interest in state-sponsored institutions of higher education has been of two kinds. One interest we may label the administrative management concern, which grew up out of the governmental economy and efficiency movement starting early in this century. This concern was addressed to the issues of budgeting, accounting, financial management, purchasing, personnel, and construction. These issues were the subject of attention in a report by the Committee on Government and Higher Education sponsored by the Fund for the Advancement of Education of the Ford Foundation. The published report bore the intriguing title *The Efficiency of Freedom* (1959). These issues are still with us and have more recently been taken up in the Sloan Commission report (1980) and in a small report published by the Southern Regional Education Board, *Management Flexibility and State Regulation in Higher Education* (1983).

The second state government interest has been with state coordination of public institutions of higher education. This concern developed from two circumstances: the existence of multiple institutions of higher education in a state that after World War II evidenced similar aspirations in the expansion of instructional programs, and the competition of these institutions for ever-increasing financial support from state government. As a consequence, state governments found it essential to limit unplanned growth and to ensure an equitable distribution of available financial support. Necessarily, these actions constituted restrictions on the autonomy of public institutions of higher education.

Both public and private colleges and universities have been alarmed by federal government intrusions on institutional autonomy. Only slowly have they learned to live with the federal restrictions that express broad social concern over racial, sexual, and other factors affecting equality of opportunity in access, program offerings, and employment. Public colleges and universities have been alarmed by state government intrusions on their administrative management and on their program scope and financing. The intrusions in the name of statewide coordination have aroused the ire of faculty members and students as well as that of administrative leaders. Often the three constituencies have found a tenuous alliance in their opposition to a common enemy, state coordination. Unfortunately, private colleges and universities have been slow to recognize that they too have a stake in state coordination as well as in state government financial assistance programs. The welfare of privately sponsored higher education is also a concern of state government, but this fact has not always been appreciated as it should be by private colleges and universities.

Major Aims

This study is concerned with state government coordination of higher education. It is concerned with administrative arrangements whereby state governments have sought to identify and articulate a state government interest in higher education. In contrast with other studies, I have classified the basic organizational choices into three categories: the statewide governing board (at least for senior institutions), the state coordinating board, and the state advisory board. I have given definition to each type of organization and I have listed the relative advantages and disadvantages of each. In addition, I have pointed out one important recent development largely ignored in the literature up to the present time: the addition of state advisory boards in most of the states with a statewide governing board for senior institutions. I have not had the opportunity to examine this development in the depth it deserves. A state university president in a statewide governing structure said to me recently that the action in his state was now located in the state advisory board, not in the statewide governing board.

A major thesis of this study is that the state government interest in higher education is different from the campus and governing board interest in higher education. Faculty members, campus executives, and even governing board members are wont to declare that institutional interests and state government interests are one and the same. This identity of interest can only exist in a state government with unlimited financial resources and a willingness to expend a major proportion of those resources on higher education. In a state government with limited resources and with conflicting claims upon those resources there must be means whereby governors and legislatures can determine the urgent priorities of higher education in the light of state interests.

To be sure, the state government interests in higher education are not easy to determine. Political scientists have long argued about the definition of the public interest and of the public welfare in a mixed economy, a pluralistic society, and a liberal democracy. Yet the complexities of definition have by no means led to the abandonment of the standard of the public interest as an imprecise but nonetheless essential guide to the political process. State governments somehow must determine the public interest in higher education in an economy of scarce resources. Administrative agencies have been created to assist governors and legislatures in the process of such determination. It is an awesome task.

Contents and Organization

This volume begins with a discussion of the multiple institutions of higher education and their post-World War II development in the various states as the essential backdrop for the state government organizational concern with higher education. The second chapter reviews some of the major studies concerned with state governments in their relation to higher education. The third chapter considers the principal issues that constitute the state government agenda of the 1980s insofar as higher education is concerned. These are issues that governors and legislatures must resolve, and on which governors and legislatures seek assistance from state higher education boards in addition to assistance from campus executives and others.

Chapter Four defines the three major types of administrative organization at the state government level that are concerned with higher education. The next chapter reviews the two primary arrangements for full-time professional leadership to state higher education boards.

Chapters Six and Seven are devoted to a discussion of the two basic questions about public higher education that state governments must resolve: the differentiation of mission among multiple institutions of higher education and the allocation of available resources among public institutions and public programs. The essence of state government action in relation to higher education is to be found in these two areas of concern. Moreover, in the comparison of financial support for higher education among states there are intricacies of analysis that demand careful attention.

The final two chapters are devoted to a discussion of institutional autonomy in relation to state governments and to some speculation about the organizational future. I believe that there are some reasonable expectations about the future of state boards of higher education that can be projected at this time.

It must be emphasized as strongly as possible that none of this discussion is intended to detract in any way from the vitally important endeavors that are carried on campus by campus in both the public and private sectors of higher education. The vitality of higher education is not to be found in our state governments but on all our varied campuses. I have been fortunate in serving as a faculty member in a leading private university in addition to later service as a state university president and a state government chancellor. I have once again had the opportunity to serve as a faculty member, even if on a part-time basis. I yield to no one in my admiration for the scholarship of faculty members, for the learning eagerness of students, for the devoted service of professional and support staffs, for the earnest efforts of campus managers and executives, and for the concerned attention of governing board members.

If I had my way I would strive to reconcile the interests of campus constituencies as well as the interests of higher education institutions in their relationship to state government. It is a matter of concern to me that tensions and animosities so often characterize both campus relationships and state government relationships rather than mutual understanding, forbearance, and civility.

Defining University Governance and Autonomy

The phrase *university governance* in this study has been employed to designate any institution's concern with its own internal decision-making process having to do with academic and faculty affairs, student affairs, business affairs, and external affairs. In one sense, university governance implies university autonomy. The term *university* here refers to all types of public institutions: the research university, the doctoral-granting university, the comprehensive university, the general baccalaureate institution, the separate professional institution, and the two-year institution. University governance implies the ability and the competence of an institution to make important decisions without external restraint.

A major complication in the campus aspiration for autonomy is the multicampus structure of governing boards that predominates in the public sector. As of 1983, twenty-two states had a statewide governing board for at least all state colleges other than the two-year institutions, and another twenty-seven states (I omit Wyoming) tended to have multicampus governance structures for many if not all of their senior institutions. I count only seven states where all the senior institutions had a separate governing board. (This number would be eight if we were to ignore the Dearborn and Flint campuses of the University of Michigan. Both had fairly sizable enrollments and offered degree programs through the master's level.) Otherwise, there were nineteen states with multicampus systems, many of which were quite extensive in scope, including those in California, Illinois, Indiana, Louisiana, Maryland, Minnesota, Nebraska, New Jersey, New York, Pennsylvania, Tennessee, and Texas.

This study has not been concerned with the multicampus governance structure of state universities other than the statewide governing system. Many of the campus complaints about external controls have to do with the multicampus headquarters and governing board rather than with state government agencies. In my judgment there are many multicampus structures that need to give extensive attention to relaxation of their centralized controls and to delegation of increased management autonomy to campus executives. In spite of the two Carnegie studies of multicampus governance of state universities, this subject requires urgent reconsideration in the interest of campus management efficiency and effective campus governance.

Campus autonomy in an absolute sense is an unreasonable

expectation. Virtually every study has at least agreed upon this proposition. The problem has been how to devise organizational structures in state governments that draw a reasonable distinction between state government concerns on the one hand and campus concerns on the other hand. Up to the present time the problem has defied any simple or universal solution, and it seems likely that it will remain with us for years yet to come. I would insist that some states have made greater progress in the direction of a reasonable solution than have others. I have said for many years that when public campuses aspired to faculty affluence, program expansion (especially at the doctoral degree and first professional degree levels), branch campus expansion, and expanded research and public service activities, they sacrificed their claims to campus autonomy.

Origins, Development, and Sources

This study began with a review of the work of the Academy for Educational Development, which its president, Alvin C. Eurich, prepared in 1980 and shared with officers of the Ford Foundation. It was pointed out that since its inception in 1961 the academy had undertaken thirty-seven studies in twenty-five states dealing with state government concerns about higher education. The grants and contracts for these studies amounted to over 2.6 million dollars. When Ford Foundation officers expressed some interest in this activity, Dr. Eurich asked me to prepare a detailed proposal for a study that would focus on how well prepared state governments might be to cope with the changing circumstances of higher education in the decade of the 1980s. A modest grant from the Ford Foundation followed in April 1981.

Initially it had been my hope to include information about all fifty states in the study. Limited resources prescribed a lesser endeavor, and so it was decided to restrict the inquiry to the twenty-five states where the Academy for Educational Development had undertaken studies between 1962 and 1980. I had personally been involved in studies in eleven states between 1972 and 1980, while two associates had made extensive studies in two other states during these same years.

At first I had expected to be able to rely on the state higher education executive officers in the twenty-five states as resource assistants. Although all these officers expressed their willingness to cooperate, it soon became evident that personal visits and interviews would be necessary. I was fortunate in persuading four friends to share this task with me: Fred F. Harcleroad, Robert B. Mautz, T. Harry McKinney, and Robert C. Wood. As of 1982 Harcleroad was professor of higher education at the University of Arizona, former director of the center for the study of higher education there, former president of the American College Testing Program, and former president of California State University at Hayward. Mautz was Regents Professor Emeritus at the University of Florida, former chancellor of the Florida Board of Regents, former vice-president of the University of Florida, and former dean of the College of Law there. McKinney was professor of higher education at Michigan State University and former director of higher education planning and coordination for the Michigan Board of Education. Wood was professor of political science at the University of Massachusetts at Boston, former president of the University of Massachusetts, and former secretary of the Department of Housing and Urban Development in the federal government. Wood was assisted by Marcy Muringhan, then a graduate assistant in the Graduate School of Education, Harvard University.

Harcleroad prepared reports on his visits to California, Colorado, Montana, Texas, and Washington. Mautz prepared reports on Florida and Georgia. McKinney provided extensive materials on Delaware, Illinois, Kansas, Missouri, New Jersey, Pennsylvania, and South Dakota. Wood and Muringhan visited Connecticut, Maine, Massachusetts, New Hampshire, and New York. In addition to earlier contacts with several of the above-mentioned states, I made visits to Alabama, Indiana, Minnesota, Mississippi, Ohio, and West Virginia. I am grateful to these colleagues for their assistance. They also read the manuscript for this book and made numerous helpful suggestions about findings of fact and about the interpretation of events. I alone, however, have prepared the account of this study and assume full responsibility for its contents. Many statements in this volume are based on facts and impressions obtained by me or my associates in the course of interviews in the twenty-five states we visited. Other statements are based on memoranda and documents that were provided to us and that are not in the public domain. I have made extensive use of these materials but have not cited them as the source of my information because of their confidential or personal nature.

Acknowledgments

As so often in the past ten years, I am indebted to Alvin C. Eurich for his assistance in launching this study and for his continuous encouragement. George B. Weathersby also read this book in manuscript and provided some good advice. My debt to Miami University is very great for the assistance provided by William G. Slover, the secretary of the university. Betty K. Hucke of the secretary's office has been patient and persistent in guiding the manuscript through four versions. Miami University has made a substantial investment in this study.

I am grateful to the Ford Foundation for the grant of the resources with which to undertake the study, even though in the end the commitments of the Academy for Educational Development and of myself substantially exceeded the grant itself.

I would wish for all state university presidents the degree of management autonomy enjoyed by the eight presidents in the statewide governing structure of the Mississippi Board of Trustees of State Institutions of Higher Education. I would wish for all state universities the degree of management autonomy from state administrative controls that exists currently in the State of Indiana and the State of Ohio. I would wish for all higher education, public and private, smoother sailing than I fear will be the case in the decade of the 1980s.

Oxford, Ohio   John D. Millett
December 1983

Contents

The Author

JOHN D. MILLETT is president emeritus of Miami University, chancellor emeritus of the Ohio Board of Regents, professor of educational leadership at Miami University, and a distinguished fellow of the Academy for Educational Development. He received his B.A. degree (1933) from DePauw University in political science, his M.A. degree (1935) from Columbia University in public law and government, and his Ph.D. degree (1938) from Columbia University in public law and government. He holds honorary degrees from twenty-two colleges and universities.

Millett was a postdoctoral fellow of the Social Science Research Council (1938–39), pursuing his research interest at the London School of Economics and Political Science. He served on the staff of the Social Science Research Council's Committee on Public Administration (1939–1941), on the staff of the National Resources Planning Board in the Executive Office of the President (1941–1942), and on the staff of the commanding general of the Army Service Forces (1942–1946) as major, lieutenant colonel, and colonel. He was decorated with the Legion of Merit for wartime service. He was recalled to active duty for six months in 1947 to serve at the headquarters of the European command in Frankfort, Germany.

Millett was associate professor of public administration (1945–1948) and professor of public administration (1948–1953) at Columbia University. While a professor at Columbia he served as executive director (1949–1952) of the Commission on Financing Higher Education sponsored by the Association of American Universities and funded by the Rockefeller Foundation and Carnegie Corporation of New York.

Millett became president of Miami University in 1953 and served in that position until 1964. He served as chancellor for the Ohio Board of Regents from 1964 to 1972, when he retired at sixty years of age. He was a vice-president of the Academy for Educational Development (1972–1980) in charge of management and finance programs. He returned to Oxford, Ohio, in 1980 where he has been an independent consultant and a part-time faculty member at Miami University.

Millett has served as a consultant to the Department of Defense and the U.S. Office of Education. He has served as president of the State Universities Association and of the American Society for Public Administration. He is a member of the National Academy of Public Administration and has served as chairman (1968–1972). He has been a trustee of the College Board, Educational Testing Service, Institute of American Universities, and is currently a trustee of DePauw University. He has received numerous awards.

Millett has traveled extensively in Asia and Europe and has been a consultant in the Philippines and Mexico. He has served on the national board for the United Nations Educational, Scientific, and Cultural Organization (UNESCO).

Millett is the author of nineteen books; the current study is his twentieth volume. He is coauthor of two works in public administration, a contributor to twenty-three other books, and the author of numerous reports and of some fifty journal articles. His writing has been in the fields of public administration and higher education finance, management, and governance.

Conflict
in Higher Education

—⟩┤———————⟩┼⟨———————┤⟨—

State Government
Coordination Versus
Institutional Independence

⊰ 1 ⊱

The States
and Higher Education

IT HAS LONG BEEN EVIDENT that
it is the state governments rather than the federal government that
carry the primary authority and responsibility for higher education
in the United States. The provision for private or independent
institutions of higher education, the organization of publicly
sponsored institutions of higher education, the number and location of public institutions, the mission and program scope of public
institutions, the enrollment size of public institutions, the standards of access and of quality for public institutions, and the
financial support of public institutions — all these matters have
been resolved by action of state governments, not by action of the
federal government. The Carnegie Council on Policy Studies in
Higher Education (1980) may speak of *Three Thousand Futures* for
higher education in America, but it would be more accurate to
speak of fifty futures. The fifty futures are, of course, the futures
determined by fifty different state governments.

It may be appropriate here to acknowledge in passing the
limited role of the federal government in creating and supporting
institutions of higher education. For many years, the Congress of
the United States was in effect the state legislature for the District
of Columbia, and even under so-called home rule for the district
Congress still retains important supervisory and veto authority.

1

In 1867, for example, Congress chartered Howard University in the District of Columbia as an institution of higher education primarily for the instruction of black students; although Howard is usually classified as a "private" institution, it draws its chief financial support from annual appropriations of Congress. Moreover, Congress has formally established the University of the District of Columbia as a "state university" within the district, and has created ten specialized colleges or universities throughout the country for the military services and the merchant marine. Congress has also made possible the establishment of four private universities, six private colleges, and three seminaries within the District of Columbia as of 1982. The federal government has also provided for institutions of higher education in certain territorial jurisdictions of the United States. Yet in spite of this activity by the federal government, only some 20 institutions of higher education operate under federal law, while some 3,230 institutions are sponsored and supported by state governments or operate under the jurisdiction of state law.

Development of State Universities

In the colonial period of America from 1607 to 1776, there were nine colleges established by royal or colonial charter. Two of these colleges became state universities; seven became private or independent institutions that are still in operation today. The first state university was provided for in the state constitution of North Carolina in 1776 and was legally established in 1789. By 1800 the states of Georgia, Tennessee, and Vermont had founded state-sponsored and state-supported institutions of higher education. The Northwest Ordinance of 1787 enacted by Congress under the Articles of Confederation authorized land grants for "seminaries of learning" in the states to be formed from the old Northwest Territory. As a consequence there came into existence Ohio University (1804) and Miami University (1809) in Ohio, the University of Michigan (1817), Indiana University (1820), and the University of Wisconsin (1849). The University of Illinois was not created until 1867, when Illinois took advantage of the Morrill Act of 1862. Most of the states created after 1789 did establish state universities soon after they came into existence. Only the New England and Middle Atlantic states of the original confederation lagged in sponsoring state institutions of higher education. They were disposed to be satisfied with such private institutions as Dartmouth, Harvard, Brown, Yale, Columbia, Princeton, and the University of Pennsylvania.

As the settlement of the United States pushed westward and southward in the years up to the Civil War, an ever-increasing number of private and church-related colleges sprang up in various communities. Many of these colleges were short lived; others survived into the twentieth century; many were still in existence in 1982. Since the early colleges were deemed essential to the perpetuation of the ministry of a church denomination, and equally essential to the formation of an educated lay leadership, the Protestant churches were active in founding colleges. These colleges met much of the need of American society for educated men and women.

The federal government gave a new impetus to state governments to create institutions of higher education by enactment of the Morrill Act of 1862. This law gave land grants to each state for the establishment of colleges of agriculture and mechanical arts. No doubt the Civil War encouraged passage of this legislation; the new land-grant institutions were to include instruction in military science as well as provide programs in engineering and agriculture. In due course, twenty-two states created colleges of agriculture and mechanical arts apart from an existing or from a later established state university. In addition, thirteen southern states between 1875 and 1911 established separate state agricultural and mechanical colleges for black students based upon the doctrine of "separate but equal" educational opportunity, a doctrine not overthrown by the Supreme Court until 1954.

Still another force in the development of the state role in higher education was the expansion of public elementary and secondary schools. As school districts were organized, and especially as the public high school movement gained momentum after 1890, the necessity for teacher education became apparent. By 1910 all but three or four states had authorized normal schools or teacher's colleges, generally under the governing authority of state boards of education. In the southern states and some border states certain teacher's colleges were designated to enroll black students only.

A final force in expanding the scope of state-sponsored higher education was the urbanization of America, especially after 1890. Initially, religious orders of the Roman Catholic church set up colleges and universities in various urban centers because a large proportion of the new urban population was Catholic in religious faith. A few cities — notably New York City — created municipally sponsored colleges and universities. The Young Men's Christian Association (YMCA) also sponsored colleges in urban centers. Then in the twentieth century legislatures in a number of states were persuaded to authorize public junior colleges in urban communities. By 1920 there were some 70 public junior colleges; by 1930 the number was 178; by 1940 it was 258. Then a great era of expansion occurred after World War II. By 1980 there were nearly 1,000 public community or technical colleges in the United States. Although most of these community colleges were locally organized, all received financial support from state governments.

On the eve of World War II many state governments had provided for a four-tiered structure of public institutions of higher education:

1. A state university, with programs from the baccalaureate to the doctoral degree in arts and sciences and various professional fields of study. In a majority of states this university was also the land-grant university under the 1862 federal law.
2. A separate land-grant college of agriculture and the mechanical arts, with programs in engineering, agriculture, general education, and other professional fields.
3. One or more teacher's colleges with programs through the master's degree to prepare teachers for elementary and secondary schools.
4. Junior colleges with two-year programs of college-transfer courses.

Not all states followed this exact pattern; indeed, there were variations in almost every state. Some small states had only one state university to serve all these needs; other small states had developed two or three parts of this structure. One large state, New York, had only teacher's colleges under state government sponsorship and support. Some states had an extensive array of junior colleges, while other states had none. The common factors were that public higher education was relatively modest in cost to the student, relatively modest in cost to state governments, and geographically dispersed throughout the state.

There was another characteristic of major importance. The state universities tended to be located in fairly small communities and not in the principal urban center of the state. The University of Michigan was located in Ann Arbor, not Detroit. The University of Illinois was located in Urbana, not Chicago. The University of Wisconsin was located in Madison, not Milwaukee. Pennsylvania State University was located on a mountaintop, not in Philadelphia or Pittsburgh. The University of Massachusetts was located in Amherst, not in Boston. The University of Georgia was located in Athens, not in Atlanta. Only the University of Minnesota was located in the major urban area of the state.

When state universities were established in the nineteenth century, the conventional political wisdom of the time called for them to be located in small communities away from the evils and temptations of big cities. Higher education was thought to be incompatible with urban life, and in any event the large cities as they emerged between 1890 and 1914 were filled with new immigrants who were not expected to be interested in higher education. It was left, as already suggested, to the Catholic church, the YMCA, and some municipal reformers to undertake to provide opportunities for higher education to the teeming masses of urban America.

State governments, and more particularly the state universities, did not discover urban America until after World War II. The discovery was a matter both of educational need and of political necessity. There was a great influx of veterans seeking higher education, and state universities were simply not prepared to house these enlarged numbers of students on their campuses. These universities were compelled to establish branch campuses in urban areas, and the growth of city populations gave representatives from large urban areas increased political influence in state legislatures. Under Supreme Court edict in the 1950s the over-representation of predominantly rural areas and the underrepresentation of large urban areas came to an end. State governments and state universities had to confront a new political reality.

There were other forces to be reckoned with. For example, World War II changed the employment outlook for the United States and permanently enlarged the proportion of youth interested in higher education. The occupational outlook changed in two directions. First, there was a substantial increase in employment. Second, there was a major shift in the composition of the labor force. In 1940 there were some 47 million persons employed in the civilian labor force and nearly 8 million unemployed. In 1980 there were about 100 million employed persons and 7 million unemployed. In 1940 nearly 9 million out of 47 million employed persons worked in agriculture (19 percent); in 1980 only 2.5 million of some 100 million persons were engaged in agriculture (2.5 percent). In 1940 the composition of the nonagricultural civilian labor force was: (1) blue-collar workers 49 percent, (2) white-collar workers 37 percent, and (3) service workers 14 percent. In 1980 the composition was: (1) blue-collar workers 34 percent, (2) white-collar workers 53 percent, and (3) service workers 13 percent. These two great shifts in employment were strongly assisted by higher education.

The proportion of young people who were motivated, economically able, and intellectually competent to enroll in higher education also increased after World War II. In 1940 about 47 percent of eighteen-year-olds graduated from high school and about 13 percent enrolled in college. In 1980, however, about 75 percent of eighteen-year-olds graduated from high school and some 40 percent enrolled in college. The changing job market, family affluence and the availability of student financial assistance, and various kinds of intellectual encouragement led an increased proportion of young people to seek the advantage of higher education.

Total enrollment in higher education expanded from some 1.5 million students in 1940 to 12 million students by 1980.

Whereas 53 percent of all students were enrolled in public institutions of higher education in 1940, the proportion had increased to 78 percent by 1980. Private institutions of higher education enrolled about 700,000 students in 1940; that number increased to around 2.7 million students in 1980. But whereas 800,000 students were enrolled in public institutions of higher education in 1940, that number had reached some 9.5 million students by 1980. The greatly increased number of students seeking higher education after World War II had to be accommodated in public institutions. Private institutions were unable to obtain the philanthropic support necessary for expansion of their capital plants, and many of them preferred to increase their admission standards rather than their enrollment size.

There was a corresponding increase in the number of institutions of higher education during the postwar years. With data from the U.S. Office of Education, the Commission on Financing Higher Education (1952) as of the academic year 1948–49 counted 1,532 institutions of higher education in the United States, of which 547 were under public control and 985 were under private control (see Table 1).

The Carnegie Council on Policy Studies in Higher Education published a revised classification of institutions of higher education in 1976. Employing the categories adopted by the National

Table 1. Classifications of Higher Education Institutions in U.S., 1948–49.

	Public	Private	Total
Universities	64	57	121
Liberal Arts Colleges			
Complex	22	39	61
Simple	15	377	392
Professional Schools			
Teacher Education	162	8	170
Theology	—	193	193
Other	38	83	121
Junior Colleges	246	228	474
	547	985	1,532

Source: Commission on Financing Higher Education (1952), p. 83.

Center for Education Statistics in 1981 for future statistical reporting, Table 2 shows the number of institutions listed by the Carnegie Council for the year 1976.

These numbers continued to grow: The total was 3,250 as
of 1981–82. Some of the increase from 1948 to 1981 resulted from
the enumeration of branch campuses that had not been listed in
earlier counts. Nonetheless, the number of higher education institutions clearly doubled in the years after World War II. The number of public institutions increased from some 500 to 1,500, while
the number of private institutions increased from around 1,000 to
over 1,600.

The general characteristics of these institutions also changed
during this period, especially in the public sector. Whereas some
64 public institutions were classified as universities in 1948, there
were 119 public doctoral-granting institutions in 1976. Again,
there were 162 public institutions classified as teacher's colleges
and another 22 classified as complex liberal arts colleges in 1948,
but there were 354 comprehensive public institutions in 1976.
The teacher's colleges became doctoral-granting universities or
comprehensive institutions in the postwar years, and new institutions of comprehensive scope were also established. The number
of public two-year institutions increased from around 250 in 1948
to over 900 in 1976.

Table 2. Classifications of Higher Education Institutions in U.S., 1976.

	Public	Private	Total
Doctoral-Granting Institutions	119	65	184
Comprehensive Institutions	354	240	594
General Baccalaureate Institutions	11	572	583
Specialized Institutions			
Medical	32	19	51
Other	38	471	509
Two-Year Institutions	909	238	1,147
	1,463	1,605	3,068

Source: Carnegie Council (1976), p. xii.

It must be repeated that while the number of public and private colleges was about the same in 1976, some 78 percent of all student enrollments were to be found in the public institutions. As a consequence, there were considerable differences between public institutions and private institutions in terms of average size. The average enrollment size of public doctoral-granting institutions in 1976 was 20,000 students, while that of the private institutions was 10,000 students. The average size of public comprehensive institutions in 1976 was 6,700 students, while that of the private comprehensive institutions was 3,300 students. The average size of public two-year institutions was 4,200 students, while the average size of private two-year institutions was 640 students.

In terms of numbers of institutions, all states found themselves with multiple institutions of higher education in the postwar years. The number of institutions by state and by major type as of 1979 is shown in Table 3. These numbers are somewhat less in two categories and larger in one category than the Carnegie Council data because of a reclassification of institutions based on objective criteria of degrees awarded in various fields of study.

In each of the fifty states there was a structure of multiple institutions that offered degree programs as well as rendered other services. This structure evolved in large part because of the desire to distribute higher educational opportunities as widely as possible on a geographical basis. The American political system with its attention to geographical representation has tended to encourage such widespread location of campuses. This political inclination was reinforced by the educational desire to match facilities to the distribution of people in a state.

In any event, state governments did locate various kinds of institutions of higher education throughout each state. The states undertook in the years after 1945 to provide facilities so that any high school graduate with the motivation, the resources, and the ability to undertake higher education had the opportunity to do so in some kind of college or university. This objective was realized in all states.

Table 3. Public Institutions of Higher Education by States and Type, 1979.

	Major Doctoral-Granting	Comprehensive	Baccalaureate	Health Professional	Other Specialized	Two-year	Total
Alabama	3	10	3	0	0	20	36
Alaska	0	2	0	0	1	9	12
Arizona	2	1	0	0	0	14	17
Arkansas	1	4	4	1	0	9	19
California	8	19	0	1	3	106	137
Colorado	3	4	4	1	1	14	27
Connecticut	1	4	0	1	0	16	22
Delaware	1	0	1	0	0	4	6
Florida	3	6	0	0	0	28	37
Georgia	3	10	2	1	1	17	34
Hawaii	1	0	2	0	0	6	9
Idaho	1	2	1	0	0	2	6
Illinois	4	8	0	1	0	50	63
Indiana	3	6	1	0	3	11	24
Iowa	2	1	0	0	0	19	22
Kansas	2	4	1	1	0	21	29
Kentucky	2	4	2	0	0	1	9
Louisiana	1	10	2	1	0	6	20
Maine	1	1	2	0	4	2	10
Maryland	1	6	4	1	1	19	32
Massachusetts	1	8	2	1	3	18	33
Michigan	4	5	6	0	0	30	45
Minnesota	1	6	3	0	0	20	30

Mississippi	3	3	1	1	1	18	27
Missouri	2	7	2	0	2	15	28
Montana	1	1	1	0	3	3	9
Nebraska	1	4	1	1	0	10	17
Nevada	0	2	0	0	0	3	5
New Hampshire	1	2	0	0	0	7	10
New Jersey	1	7	4	1	1	17	31
New Mexico	2	4	0	0	0	10	16
New York	6	18	8	4	3	43	82
North Carolina	3	6	6	0	1	57	73
North Dakota	1	1	2	0	2	5	11
Ohio	8	3	1	2	0	48	62
Oklahoma	2	2	8	2	0	15	29
Oregon	2	2	1	1	2	13	21
Pennsylvania	3	12	5	1	2	38	61
Rhode Island	1	1	0	0	0	1	3
South Carolina	2	2	7	1	0	21	33
South Dakota	1	1	3	0	2	0	7
Tennessee	2	6	2	1	0	13	24
Texas	7	20	1	5	4	57	94
Utah	2	0	2	0	0	5	9
Vermont	1	0	3	0	0	2	6
Virginia	3	6	6	0	0	24	39
Washington	2	3	1	0	0	27	33
West Virginia	1	1	8	1	1	5	17
Wisconsin	2	9	2	0	0	17	30
Wyoming	1	0	0	0	0	7	8
Total	110	244	115	31	41	923	1,464

Source: Education Commission of the States, National Center for Higher Education Management Systems, State Higher Education Executive Officers Association (1981).

Financing Public Higher Education

The growth of enrollment and the increase in the number of public institutions of higher education were paralleled by a corresponding increase in financial support by state governments. Indeed, the increase in financial support outpaced the increase in enrollment. There was also an accompanying expansion in the outputs of higher education, especially in public service activities and in research. Furthermore, the growth of graduate education increased costs and therefore the requirements of income support. Another factor was the presence of an expanding national economy.

At the end of World War II the United States had reason to be grateful to higher education for its contributions to victory in the war. The development of the atomic bomb was the most spectacular of these contributions but by no means the only one. Higher education through its scientists, engineers, and research management had contributed considerably to improvements in weapons, in radar, in communication, and in medical care. The consequence was to give new social importance to higher education.

In July of 1957, several months before the Russians launched *Sputnik*, President Eisenhower's Committee on Education Beyond the High School issued a report declaring that the most critical bottleneck in the expansion and improvement of higher education was the mounting shortage of "excellent" faculty members. The committee asserted that colleges and universities found themselves at a growing competitive disadvantage in the professional manpower market because of low faculty salaries. The committee recommended to "every board of trustees, every legislature, and all others responsible for academic budgets" that the absolute highest priority in the use of available funds should be given to the raising of faculty salaries (President's Committee on Education Beyond the High School, 1957, p. 6). More particularly, the president's committee insisted that the goal should be a doubling of the real level of faculty salaries within the next five to ten years. To a very substantial degree, this objective was realized in the United States by 1968.

As of 1950 public institutions of higher education in the United States had total income, other than income from auxiliary enterprises, of around $930 million. For public institutions this income amounted to about $600 per student, but in terms of 1940 dollars the income per student was only around $340, or about the same as in 1930. Of the nearly $930 million of income for public institutions, some $445 million were provided by state governments. This amount was 48 percent of their total income. In 1950 the federal government provided public institutions with nearly $228 million, or 25 percent of all their income other than that from auxiliary enterprises. Of the total of $228 million, some $123 million came from the Veterans Administration, while about $105 million were for other purposes, especially for research and the support of federally established institutions. Some 16 percent of the income for public institutions was derived from student fees, not including fees paid by the Veterans Administration. About 10 percent of the income of public institutions came from miscellaneous sources including endowment, gifts, farm receipts, play tickets, fees for noncredit courses, and other such sales by educational departments (Millett, 1952).

In 1980 public institutions of higher education had total income of nearly $35 billion, other than income from auxiliary enterprises. This income came from various sources: student charges (14 percent), state governments (52 percent), federal government (14 percent), local governments (4 percent), endowment and private gifts (3 percent), hospital charges (7 percent), and miscellaneous sources (6 percent) (National Center for Education Statistics, 1981b). Thus, state government support of public institutions of higher education increased from $445 million in 1950 to $18 billion in 1980. This increase was one of more than forty times.

Enrollment in public institutions increased from 1.2 million students in 1950 to 9.5 million students in 1980, an increase of just about eight times. Obviously, state support grew much more than enrollment growth alone might explain. There was also the factor of inflation. The consumer price index was 3.4 times higher in 1980 than in 1950. Thus the $18 billion of state government support in 1980 was only some $5.3 billion in terms of 1950 dollars, or an increase of some twelve times rather than of forty times. The increase in state government support was impressive, but an increase of twelve times over a thirty-year span, along with an increase of enrollment by eight times, suggests that there had been an increase of only about 50 percent in support per student enrolled. These figures represent less than a refined or precise analysis of both income and expenditure for publicly sponsored colleges and universities, but they do represent an indication of general trends.

It must be noted that the income of public institutions provided by charges to students increased nearly twenty times between 1950 and 1980. In terms of enrollment expansion the increase would have been only eight times. In terms of inflation plus enrollment, the increase would have been in the neighborhood of twenty-seven times. This relationship suggests that charges to students increased during the years from 1950 to 1980 but that these charges did not keep pace with the ravages of inflation over this same span of time.

In any event, the support given by state governments to public institutions of higher education in the years from 1950 to 1980 was substantial. No doubt from the point of view of the executive leadership and of the faculty within these institutions, the record left something to be desired. Additional support would have been welcomed both for improvement in various outputs and for increases in the level of faculty salaries. Even so, the state governments of the United States as a whole had reason to take some satisfaction in their efforts to provide support for higher education.

There is, however, an additional qualification to this record that must be acknowledged. State government appropriations in support of higher education exceed the amount shown in institutional accounts as income received by state-sponsored institutions. The data given earlier included in the category of public higher education the federal government support of some ten service schools that received a substantial sum of money. Thus, the income reported as the income of public institutions was not entirely the income of state-sponsored institutions. But more importantly, there was a substantial growth in state government support of student financial aid programs in the years after 1950. The exact amount of this support is not reported in the statistics collected by the federal government, but as of 1980 it seems likely that state student financial aid amounted to nearly $1 billion. In addition, some state governments provided financial support to private colleges and universities, often for support of health science programs. There was over $230 million of such support reported by private institutions for the fiscal year 1980. Accordingly, the record of state government must be expanded to include student financial assistance programs and programs of financial support to private higher education, in addition to the support provided state-sponsored colleges and universities.

Variations Among State Governments

An important characteristic of state government financial support of higher education is its variation. Not only do no two states have the same structure of higher education institutions sponsored by the state but no two states provide the same amount of funds. States vary considerably in their commitment to and interest in their public institutions of higher education. To some extent the variation is historical; some states, primarily in New England and the Middle Atlantic areas, developed state universities at a relatively recent time. Some states, especially in the Middle West and Far West, depended in large part upon public higher education from their beginning to provide general and professional education to their citizenry.

Moreover, state governments experience different kinds of economic development over time. A state with substantial resources of mineral and productive wealth tends to provide more generous support than a state with lesser resources and wealth. Some states are willing to tax their citizens more heavily than are other states. Some states spend a larger proportion of their tax income on higher education than do others. Some states have a low-tuition policy for students in order to broaden the economic access of students to higher education, while other states have been willing to pass along a larger part of the costs to students. Such states may depend upon student financial assistance programs to maintain access for students from families of low income. Many factors enter into the variety of financial practices by state governments in support of higher education.

Halstead (1983) has assembled and analyzed a broad spectrum of governmental and institutional statistical data that compare state performance in support of higher education. Table 4 presents four of the seven factors of comparison collected and analyzed by Halstead. These four factors have been selected because they offer informative illustration of the variations that exist in the approaches that different state governments take to higher education. (A more detailed presentation of the Halstead data is offered in Chapter Seven.)

The four factors selected for mention here are (1) the proportion of high school graduates in a particular year to the total state population, (2) the proportion of enrollment in public higher education to the total state population, (3) the proportion of tax revenues allocated by each state government to higher education programs, and (4) the appropriation per student in a particular year.

As for the first factor, an examination of these data reveals that for the United States as a whole there were 13.2 high school graduates in 1981 per 1,000 of population. The fifty states and the District of Columbia varied from a high of 16.5 graduates in Minnesota to a low of 9.7 graduates in Florida. (The Florida figure is explained by the large number of older persons who retire and move to Florida.) States have different proportions of young people who are eligible on the basis of high school graduation to enroll in colleges and universities.

Second, the states vary substantially in the proportion of persons enrolled in public higher education. For the United States as a whole there were 29.4 students enrolled in public higher education in 1981 per 1,000 persons of state population. The highest proportion was that of North Dakota and the lowest proportion (other than that of the District of Columbia) was that of Pennsylvania. This proportion is influenced by tuition policy and by the availability of private higher education in a state.

Third, the states vary in the proportion of their total state and local tax revenues allocated to higher education. For the United States as a whole, 10.4 percent of tax revenues were appropriated for higher education in the academic year 1981–82. This percentage varied from a high of 17.2 in North Carolina to a low of 6.8 in Connecticut; the District of Columbia was still lower. This percentage is affected by numbers of students, the academic programs of students, the costs approved by state governments, and the competition for state and local revenues on the part of other services (such as elementary and secondary education, public welfare, public health, and public safety and corrections).

Finally, there is a variation in the appropriation per student. On the average the appropriation per student was $3,655 in 1981–82. The high was the $12,662 in Alaska and the low was the $1,663 in New Hampshire. This variation again is influenced by tuition policy, programs offered, and approved costs.

Organizational Problems for State Governments

State governments, especially in the postwar years, confronted major organizational problems when they attempted to structure their administrative arrangements for the formulation of public policy on higher education. In the American structure of government, particularly in this era of the administrative state, much of the development of public policy necessarily depends upon the administrative apparatus, that is, upon the bureaucracy. To be sure, it is chief executives and legislators who have the final say in the enactment of the laws that express public policy objectives. But these individuals are not expected to have, nor do they usually claim to have, the same detailed and professional knowledge possessed by administrative experts.

The early state constitutions generally acknowledged some obligation on the part of state governments to support education, including state universities. Today, the constitutions in some twenty-three states make specific mention of a state university. In twelve states where the governing boards of state universities have been established by constitutional mandate, courts have declared that these universities enjoy substantial independence from control or direction by the chief executive and legislature of the state. In another three states the state constitutions have established governing boards for the state universities with broad provisions

Table 4. Characteristics of State Systems of Higher Education.

	1981 High School Graduates per 1,000 Population	1981 Public Higher Education Enrollment per 1,000 Population	Tax Revenues Allocated to Higher Education Percentage 1982–83	Appropriations per Student 1982–83
Alabama	12.5	31.3	14.6	$ 3,229
Alaska	13.4	28.5	5.9	12,662
Arizona	10.1	42.6	13.6	3,097
Arkansas	13.4	22.6	12.3	3,594
California	11.0	40.7	12.5	3,666
Colorado	12.7	37.4	12.5	3,254
Connecticut	15.0	21.0	6.8	3,756
Delaware	14.7	38.6	13.0	3,336
Florida	9.7	22.6	10.9	3,663
Georgia	12.3	21.0	11.8	4,582
Hawaii	14.4	35.1	13.9	5,376
Idaho	13.5	27.2	12.8	3,646
Illinois	13.7	29.7	8.5	3,224
Indiana	14.4	26.8	10.8	3,318
Iowa	16.0	29.3	12.1	4,287
Kansas	13.1	37.8	14.7	3,800
Kentucky	12.6	24.6	13.3	4,041
Louisiana	13.0	27.7	12.1	4,022
Maine	15.4	21.8	6.9	2,906
Maryland	14.3	30.0	10.2	3,681
Massachusetts	15.2	22.1	4.5	2,716
Michigan	15.0	33.9	8.6	2,914
Minnesota	16.5	30.7	9.2	3,350
Mississippi	12.6	32.1	16.4	3,566

Missouri	13.7	25.3	9.3	2,824
Montana	15.2	34.3	11.4	3,580
Nebraska	15.5	34.2	13.9	3,852
Nevada	11.1	26.2	9.5	3,394
New Hampshire	14.6	22.6	5.2	1,663
New Jersey	14.5	22.8	7.1	3,764
New Mexico	14.2	31.5	14.1	4,644
New York	13.1	23.7	6.9	4,578
North Carolina	12.4	31.1	17.2	4,321
North Dakota	16.2	44.3	16.9	3,589
Ohio	14.8	26.5	8.2	2,666
Oklahoma	12.9	33.1	13.1	3,776
Oregon	11.5	36.1	11.2	3,194
Pennsylvania	14.4	19.3	7.5	3,777
Rhode Island	13.5	26.2	8.3	3,416
South Carolina	13.0	27.6	15.4	4,126
South Dakota	16.1	31.8	9.5	2,456
Tennessee	12.2	25.6	11.8	3,246
Texas	12.1	31.0	16.2	4,588
Utah	13.4	32.4	15.0	3,996
Vermont	14.2	27.5	7.0	2,308
Virginia	13.2	33.0	12.7	3,343
Washington	12.6	38.1	11.2	2,764
West Virginia	12.5	27.8	12.1	3,351
Wisconsin	15.8	38.1	11.4	3,364
Wyoming	12.8	31.5	14.3	7,354
District of Columbia	10.2	13.1	5.8	7,348
U.S.	13.2	29.4	10.4	$3,655

Source: Halstead (1983).

for the powers and duties of these boards, but the supreme courts of these states had not as of 1980 had occasion to rule on the administrative independence of the state universities. In one state, however, the state supreme court had specifically denied that the governing board, although specified by the state constitution, had an autonomous status beyond the control and direction of the executive and legislative branches. In the other seven states the state university governing board was provided for by constitutional prescription, but the powers and duties of these boards had not been set forth in any general language; in these states there was a strong presumption that governing boards possessed only such authority and responsibility as might be provided by law.

In the remaining twenty-seven states and the District of Columbia the governing boards of state universities had been established by law and accordingly might be modified or abolished at any time by new laws. This legal status was not likely to be disturbed by light or transient circumstances, and yet the possibility of legally prescribed change was ever present.

Whether a state university was established by constitutional provision or by provision of law, all state universities were dependent upon annual or biennial appropriations. These appropriations were usually recommended by the chief executive and provided for by the legislature, subject to such approval or veto as the state constitution might allow. A state university might have a constitutionally prescribed governing board, but in no instance did such a governing board have the constitutional power to levy taxes for the support of the university. School districts for elementary and secondary education usually had authority to levy a general property tax, often subject to approval of the voting public. Many community college districts in various states also possessed the authority to levy a general property tax, again subject to voter approval. State universities and state colleges have had no such authority. For income other than that appropriated by the state legislature, these institutions must depend on the charges they are authorized to make, including tuition charges to students, as well as on such contracts, grants, gifts, and sales as they may be able to generate.

The considerable array of institutional types supported by state governments has already been noted: some 110 doctoral-granting universities, some 244 comprehensive universities, some 115 general baccalaureate institutions, some 72 specialized professional schools, and over 900 two-year institutions. The number of institutions in a state ranged from 137 in California, 94 in Texas, 82 in New York, and over 60 in three other states (Illinois, Ohio, and Pennsylvania) to 3 in Rhode Island, 5 in Nevada, and 6 in Delaware, Idaho, and Vermont. Rather than a single state university, state governments have found it desirable to create multiple universities, colleges, professional schools, and two-year institutions. There were 28 states with more than one doctoral-granting university. It was this multiplicity of higher education institutions that created a special organizational problem for state governments. In a simpler era, before World War II, it was possible for executive leaders of state universities to negotiate directly with state budget officers and with committee heads of state legislatures about educational programs and appropriation needs. In some states the Depression years from 1929 to 1939 called even this practice into question, with the result that new administrative arrangements were enacted into law or even adopted as constitutional amendments. In the years after 1945 more and more states began to experience the need for some kind of comprehensive and statewide organizational structure for higher education.

From the very beginning of the public school movement in the United States in the 1830s, state constitutions or state law had provided for state boards of education or state superintendents of public instruction. These boards or officials were expected to advise governors and legislatures about the desirable organization, operation, and financing of public schools. In very few states, however, was there a statewide board or officer concerned with all of higher education. The outstanding exception here was the New York Board of Regents, which eventually became a state board of education that supervised public school districts and governed a system of teacher's colleges. Not until 1948 did New York by law establish the State University of New York with a multicampus governing board for these teacher's colleges and for additional units of a state system of higher education.

As state governments came to perceive the need for some kind of administrative organization on a statewide basis in higher education, three primary patterns of structure began to emerge. In a study of statewide coordination of higher education, Berdahl (1971) presented information about coordinating mechanisms in all fifty states. Berdahl listed four states as of 1970 with no legally prescribed coordinating structure: Delaware, Indiana, Nebraska, and Vermont. He then classified the other forty-six states into three organizational categories: state boards of higher education with advisory authority, state boards of higher education with "regulatory" authority, and statewide or consolidated governing boards. Berdahl listed thirteen states with advisory boards, fourteen states with regulatory boards, and nineteen states with consolidated governing boards. One of the advisory boards had been established in 1934, the others between 1956 and 1969. Of the "regulatory" boards the New York Board of Regents went back to 1784; the date of establishment for the others ranged from 1941 to 1969. The consolidated governing board in Nevada went back to 1864, in Montana to 1889, in South Dakota to 1897, in Florida to 1905, and in Hawaii to 1907. Other consolidated governing boards were created in 1909 (Iowa), 1910 (Mississippi), 1912 (Idaho), 1913 (Kansas), 1929 (Oregon), 1931 (Georgia), 1945 (Arizona); six were established in the 1960s.

Millard (1976) classified state boards in three principal categories that he designated as governing boards, coordinating boards, and "nonstatutory boards" with planning functions only. The primary improvement in this classification structure, other than the use of the term *coordinating* instead of *regulatory*, was the extensive array of subclassifications. Millard identified eighteen consolidated governing boards, of which seven involved senior institutions only; thirty coordinating boards with quite different ranges of authority; and three "nonstatutory" agencies.

Some of the categories employed by Millard seem to be somewhat confused, and he omitted one state government agency among the coordinating boards. Millard did note that North Carolina in 1972 and Wisconsin in 1973 had shifted from coordinating boards to consolidated statewide governing boards. He omitted two states with consolidated governing boards and postsecondary

educational planning commissions but then listed eight other
states with planning commissions in addition to statewide governing boards or coordinating boards.

A report of the Education Commission of the States (1980)
presented still another classification scheme, this one divided into
two broad categories: consolidated governing boards (twenty-
two) and coordinating boards (thirty-one). There were six dupli-
cations in the two listings, that is, states with both consolidated
governing boards and planning agencies. In addition, two states
were listed separately where the governor and not the legislature
had authorized a higher education agency. This report appeared
accurate for the most part, and it clearly revealed the differences
among coordinating boards.

This study makes use of the Berdahl classification with one
change. The word *regulatory* is not the descriptive term that should
be applied to many state boards of higher education. The term
coordinating used by Millard and the Education Commission of the
States is preferable. At the same time, three rather than two categories of state agencies must be employed: statewide governing
board, coordinating board, and advisory board. Moreover, there
is a need to draw a clearly defined distinction between coordinating boards and advisory boards. A coordinating board is defined
as one that has three essential kinds of authority: (1) planning,
(2) budget review and recommendation, and (3) approval of new
academic programs. If a state higher education board has only
one or two of these three kinds of authority, that board has been
classified as advisory rather than coordinating.

Table 5 shows this threefold classification for forty-nine
states; Wyoming is omitted because it has a single state university
with only one campus. The Texas Coordinating Board is included
as a coordinating board; while it does not review budget recommendations as such, it does devise the formula upon which all
public institutions must base their appropriation requests.

It is noteworthy that fourteen out of the twenty-two states
with statewide governing boards also have additional higher education planning agencies, sometimes referred to as 1202 commissions because of the provisions of Section 1202 of the Higher Education Act of 1965 as added in 1972. Some of these additional

Table 5. State Government Agencies for Higher Education, 1982.

1. Statewide Governing Boards (22)	2. Coordinating Boards (18)	3. Advisory Boards (9)	4. Additional Planning Boards (14)
Alaska	Alabama	California	Alaska
Arizona	Arkansas	Delaware	Arizona
Florida	Colorado	Michigan	Florida
Georgia	Connecticut	Minnesota	Georgia
Hawaii	Illinois	Nebraska	Iowa
Idaho	Indiana	New York	Maine
Iowa	Kentucky	Pennsylvania	Massachusetts
Kansas	Louisiana	Vermont	Mississippi
Maine	Maryland	Washington	Nevada
Massachusetts	Missouri		New Hampshire
Mississippi	New Jersey		North Dakota
Montana	New Mexico		Oregon
Nevada	Ohio		Rhode Island
New Hampshire	Oklahoma		South Dakota
North Carolina	South Carolina		
North Dakota	Tennessee		
Oregon	Texas		
Rhode Island	Virginia		
South Dakota			
Utah			
West Virginia			
Wisconsin			

agencies were created by law, some by executive order of the governor. In Kansas there is a body known as the Legislative Educational Planning Commission, which is made up of members from the House of Representatives and the Senate; it is not an administrative but rather a legislative agency.

The New York Board of Regents presents a particularly difficult problem of classification. Berdahl classified this board as a "regulatory" board, and Millard placed it in a separate class from other boards. Observers and commentators have been impressed by the board's role in approving the degree programs of both public and private institutions of higher education. Yet the nature of this review has not been carefully assessed. It is evident that the New York Board of Regents is essentially an accrediting agency for the state, primarily concerned with the quality of instructional programs. It exercises the power to "deregister" any program that it finds "inferior" in quality. But this review activity is not concerned with either the need or the cost of programs undertaken by public institutions, which are the primary concerns of state coordinating boards. Moreover, the board does not have authority to review and recommend appropriations for the state university and the city university. The most important higher education role of the board is its legal authority to prepare a periodic master plan. Our inquiries indicated that the program review activity of the board was exercised on an episodic basis; in addition, we found that the state Division of the Budget did make use of the board staff on an informal basis in budget analysis. Under these circumstances it seemed appropriate to classify the New York Board of Regents as an advisory rather than a coordinating agency in higher education.

Pennsylvania presents another difficulty in classifying the State Board of Education and its constituent Council of Higher Education. The Pennsylvania Department of Education is headed by a secretary who sits in the governor's cabinet. Within the Department of Education there is an office of higher education headed by a commissioner. Both the secretary and the commissioner are appointed by the governor, and the staff of the board/council is provided by the commissioner. Nominally the board/council adopts a master plan, approves programs, and recommends a state budget for higher education. Actually, it appears, these powers reside in the secretary, assisted by the commissioner. Although the Education Commission of the States classifies the Department of Education as a coordinating agency, the role of the state board/council appears to be advisory rather than coordinating and has been so classified here. If the commissioner were appointed by and responsible to the state board, and if the supposed powers of the board/council were real rather than nominal, the classification would be "coordinating."

It should be noted here that among the twenty-two statewide governing boards, the boards in eight states had governing authority over senior institutions only, while in the other fourteen states the governing authority extended to two-year institutions as well as senior institutions. The seven states where the governing authority encompassed only senior institutions were Arizona, Florida, Iowa, Kansas, Mississippi, North Carolina, and Oregon. South Dakota had no community colleges.

There are various reasons why state governments have found it necessary to establish some kind of higher education board. One reason has been the desire to have a comprehensive plan for needed higher education services. Another reason has been competition among public institutions for state funds. A third reason has been the proliferation of degree programs, including quite costly graduate, medical, and engineering programs. A fourth reason has been competition in the establishment of branch campuses and in the recruitment of students. Such competition has led to intensive lobbying on the part of university representatives and to bitter political rivalries among institutions and their constituencies.

This study attempts to analyze the problems associated with finding an acceptable administrative arrangement for developing or formulating a state government's interests in higher education. These interests involve a concern with state needs for higher education services, with programs designed to meet those needs, with appropriate geographical and other differentiation of mission among public institutions in serving those needs, and with efficiency and cost effectiveness in performing essential services. Institutional interests are not necessarily identical with those of the state government. An institution often wants to enhance its status, to grow in size, and to ensure itself of constantly expanding financial support, regardless of the activities of other universities and colleges, regardless of desirable patterns of collaboration, and regardless of costs and the economic circumstances of state governments.

It was not possible in this study to undertake an extensive analysis of administrative experience in all fifty states. Rather the study centered on twenty-five states where the author and the Academy for Educational Development had some background of knowledge derived from consulting activity over a twenty-year period. Fortunately, these twenty-five states were widely distributed geographically, as follows:

New England	*Middle Atlantic*
Connecticut	Delaware
Maine	New Jersey
Massachusetts	New York
New Hampshire	Pennsylvania

South	*Middle West*	*West*
Alabama	Illinois	California
Florida	Indiana	Colorado
Georgia	Kansas	Montana
Mississippi	Minnesota	South Dakota
West Virginia	Missouri	Texas
	Ohio	Washington

The twenty-five states were divided by type of higher education board as follows:

Advisory Boards	*Consolidated Governing Boards*	*Coordinating Boards*
California	Florida	Alabama
Delaware	Georgia	Colorado
Minnesota	Kansas	Connecticut
New York	Maine	Illinois
Pennsylvania	Massachusetts	Indiana
Washington	Mississippi	Missouri
	Montana	New Jersey
	New Hampshire	Ohio
	South Dakota	Texas
	West Virginia	

In this study, accordingly, we have looked at six of the nine states with advisory boards, at ten of the twenty-two states with consolidated governing boards, and at nine of the eighteen states with coordinating boards. This sampling should provide an adequate basis for an extensive comparison of performance in the state government search for a reconciliation of the state interest in higher education with the integration or coordination of various kinds of public institutions of higher education.

⇥ 2 ⇤

Studies
of Higher Education
Governance

SINCE THE END OF WORLD WAR II numerous studies and reports have examined the relationship of state governments to public higher education. These inquiries have centered on the degree of autonomy to be vested in the governing boards and the internal governance structures of the individual institutions. On the one hand, state governments have insisted that in the name of administrative efficiency and coordination of effort the individual campuses should be subject to administrative controls and limitations in program and cost expectations. On the other hand, individual institutions have insisted that in the name of educational effectiveness the state government should not exercise "stifling" intrusion into academic affairs.

A report of the Carnegie Foundation for the Advancement of Teaching (1982), to be discussed more fully later, proposed that there are four issues at the core of the academic enterprise: (1) who may teach, (2) what may be taught, (3) how it may be taught, and (4) who may be admitted to study. The Carnegie Foundation report used this concept of an academic core to establish guidelines for the distribution of authority between governments and universities. But it seems important to move beyond this definition of an academic core to mention more specific issues that trouble the relationship between state governments and public institutions of higher education. These issues include the scope and magnitude of public higher education, student access to learning, the learning programs to be undertaken, the kinds of institutions to be established, the geographical location of institutions, the size of institutions, the costs of building and operating public institutions of higher education, the financing of public institutions, and the distribution of state funds among various public institutions of higher education. These issues call for resolution by the joint efforts of state governments and university governance.

Truman Commission Report

In July 1946 President Truman appointed a Commission on Higher Education with George F. Zook, head of the American Council on Education, as chairman. There were twenty-seven other members representing various sectors of higher education, various religious denominations, and the general public. In his charge to the commission, the president proposed that it reexamine the system of higher education in terms of its objectives, methods, facilities, and social role. More particularly, the president mentioned concern about ways and means of expanding educational opportunities for all "able young people," the adequacy of the curriculum in international affairs and social understanding, the desirability of establishing a series of "intermediate technical institutes," and the financial structure of higher education.

The President's Commission on Higher Education issued six reports in December 1947 under the general title of *Higher Education for American Democracy*. The first report set forth some far-ranging recommendations for a greatly expanded higher education endeavor in the United States. The commission asserted that up to 49 percent of all eighteen-year-olds should be enrolled for at least two years of higher education and that 32 percent of all eighteen-year-olds should be enrolled in a four-year curriculum. In terms of numbers, the commission projected by 1960 an enrollment of 2.5 million students in the first two years, 1.5 million in the third and fourth years, and 600,000 in graduate and professional schools (President's Commission on Higher Education, 1947a).

The third report of the president's commission dealt with organizing higher education and the fourth with financing higher education. The commission projected a substantial expansion of public community colleges and of state-sponsored colleges and universities. It proposed careful studies of the need for higher education facilities state by state but suggested "no common pattern" of relationship between public institutions and state governments. In addition, the curricula of the community colleges were to be subject to state approval. The commission then asserted that a "unified educational organization within each state is necessary" (President's Commission on Higher Education, 1947b, p. 25). The commission advocated strengthening state departments of education through the appointment of board members and a full-time professional superintendent or commissioner of education.

The report went on to acknowledge the existence of three types of public control of colleges and universities: (1) a state board of education, (2) a separate state board of regents for all higher education, and (3) separate boards of trustees for each institution. After enumerating various deficiencies in this organizational arrangement, the commission recommended a "stronger, better coordinated statewide program in higher education," preferably under the state department of education or otherwise under a state commission on higher education (p. 30). As for the financing of this enlarged structure of public higher education, the commission projected the need for $2.1 billion as of 1960, with about $1.0 billion to come from state and local governments and about $845 million from the federal government. In addition, the federal government was expected to help finance capital construction for public institutions, and was to establish a student financial aid program of assistance directly to students (President's Commission on Higher Education, 1947c).

The Truman Commission on Higher Education proposed not only a greatly expanded higher education enterprise in America but also a greatly expanded national role in the financing of higher education and a greatly expanded state government role in planning and directing public higher education. The enrollment projections called for the public sector to expand its enrollment from nearly 3 million students in 1952 to 3.7 million students in 1960, while enrollment of the private sector was to remain constant at 900,000 students. The commission had some kind words for the private sector but envisaged the future growth of higher education as restricted to the public sector.

We may note here for the record that as of 1950 there were 2.3 million students enrolled in higher education, of whom 1.2 million were in public institutions and 1.1 million in private institutions. As of 1960, total enrollment had reached 3.6 million students (not the 4.6 million projected by the Commission on Higher Education), of whom 2.1 million were in public instititions (not 3.7 million, as projected) and 1.4 million in private institutions.

Commission on Financing Higher Education

The Truman commission report received a mixed reception from the academic world. The reaction was particularly negative from the private or independent sector and from the leading research universities. The criticisms voiced from several quarters were that the commission had given short shrift to the private colleges and universities, that it had placed numbers of students above quality of students, that it had ignored the importance of university research, that it had proposed an undesirable organizational control upon state universities, and that it had projected a dominant role for the federal government in financing higher education.

The Association of American Universities (AAU), composed equally of the leading private and public research universities, assumed the leadership in responding to the Truman commission. With grants from the Rockefeller Foundation and the Carnegie Corporation of New York, the AAU in 1949 established a Commission on Financing Higher Education. The commission was composed of five university presidents, one college president, the provost of Harvard, and five trustees of leading universities and colleges. The report of the commission, entitled *Nature and Needs of Higher Education*, was issued in the autumn of 1952. It was accompanied by a staff report entitled *Financing Higher Education in*

the United States (Millett, 1952). The commission staff prepared
seventeen research reports. This 1949–1952 study under the auspices of the Association of American Universities (AAU) was the
most extensive study of higher education undertaken in the United
States up to that time, although it was later to be superseded by
the program of the Carnegie Commission on Higher Education
and the Carnegie Council on Policy Studies in Higher Education.

The essential position of the AAU commission was that the
independent sector contributed substantially to the well-being of
all higher education, that variety and diversity of institutional
types and missions were desirable and should be preserved, that
quality in student body composition was preferable to quantity,
that state governments and private philanthropy should continue
to provide important financial support to higher education, that
financial support from the federal government should be focused
primarily on research and financial aid to students, and that state
governments should be cautious about imposing strict controls on
public colleges and universities.

Committee on Government and Higher Education

In 1957, at the behest of several state university presidents,
the Fund for the Advancement of Education of the Ford Foundation sponsored and financed establishment of a new study group
called the Committee on Government and Higher Education. The
committee was chaired by Milton S. Eisenhower, then president
of the Johns Hopkins University and formerly president of Kansas
State University and Pennsylvania State University. The committee was composed of fourteen other individuals, including two
state university presidents, five presidents of private institutions,
and seven prominent lay citizens. The committee's main concern
was that the legal autonomy of governing boards of public colleges
and universities was being eroded by an expansion of administrative supervision on the part of state government officers and agencies. In 1959 the Committee on Government and Higher Education
issued a report entitled *The Efficiency of Freedom*. A staff report was
also published under the title of *The Campus and the State* (Moos
and Rourke, 1959).

The committee sought to define the relationship that should "properly exist" between public officials and state institutions of higher education, to identify the principal areas in which state control appeared to exceed "proper limits," and to suggest remedial lines of action. The committee agreed that responsible management of the academic institution was more likely to result from giving authority to strong, able boards of lay trustees than by scattering managerial responsibility among various agencies of state government. The committee sought to reconcile the goal of efficiency in state government with the freedom required for institutions of higher education.

The committee pointed out that lay governing boards had been created because there was a need for intellectual independence on the part of state universities and because there was a desire to protect faculties, students, and administration from political interference. At the same time, the committee emphasized the responsibility of governing boards to ensure efficient and responsible management of public colleges and universities. It pointed to the imposition of fiscal and management controls by state government as a threat to institutional independence. More particularly, the growth of budget controls, purchasing controls, personnel controls, construction controls, and audit controls were listed as evidence of state government encroachment. The committee noted that it was appropriate for state governments to determine what proportion of state resources should be spent for higher education but that it was the province of governing boards to determine how these available resources should be spent to accomplish the objectives of a state university.

The Eisenhower committee further noted that the issue of state control had come to the fore at a time when the structure of public higher education was undergoing rapid change. A major development in this change was the emergence of state teacher's colleges as comprehensive universities. The committee pointed out that in many states these colleges had grown up under state departments of public education and had been subjected to more strict controls than the state university or the state land-grant institution. The committee expressed the belief that some new governance arrangements were essential for these emerging institutions.

The Eisenhower committee pointed out that there was a movement to achieve "greater coordination of academic activities" among state colleges and universities. It identified eight states in which the pressure for coordination had led to the establishment of coordinating boards for higher education. Apart from noting that the imposition of these boards over the traditional governing boards presented a "delicate problem of balance" in the government of higher education, the committee mentioned only that two problems deserved continuing study. One of these was to determine whether the task of coordination could be performed without intruding upon matters properly within the jurisdiction of governing boards. The second problem was to determine whether a coordinating agency would impose standards of uniformity upon all public institutions.

In approaching the issue of improving relationships between state government and public institutions of higher education, the committee expressed its deep conviction that the essential freedom of higher education was "wholly compatible" with the effective operation of democratic government. The committee presented several recommendations: Trustees and academic officials should make a strenuous effort to explain the case for the independence of higher education to state officials and the general public. State colleges and universities should be candid and communicative in dealing with the state government. They should make every effort to establish and maintain a reputation for efficiency and sound management. State colleges and universities should take the initiative in coordinating their programs through voluntary and cooperative means and should avoid activities not properly within their academic sphere. Finally, governing boards should assert their traditional authority to control the policies and operations of their institutions.

The committee observed that state legislatures deserved a "large share of credit" for their interest in and support of public higher education. At the same time, the committee urged that the legal status of public institutions be clarified. Boards of trustees should be recognized as the responsible supervisors of public institutions of higher learning, and legal autonomy should be given to all public institutions of higher education. In allocating funds to higher education, state legislatures should avoid attempts to legislate specific aspects of educational policy. Legislative committees and agencies should continue to keep legislatures informed about higher education activities but should not act as instruments of control over educational administration. Statutes imposing outmoded fiscal and management controls should be reviewed and revised. Other recommendations had to do with the appointment of trustees, the desirability of lump-sum appropriations, state budget practices, freedom from centralized state purchasing, the need for postauditing but not preauditing of the expenditures of state colleges and universities, autonomy in personnel matters, and a relaxation of state building controls.

The Committee on Government and Higher Education was concerned with the impact of the state government reorganization movement upon public higher education and with the imposition of centralized state government controls on public institutions of higher education. The committee gave only passing acknowledgment to the movement for state government planning and coordination of the programs of state colleges and universities.

The Glenny Study

Under the auspices of the Center for the Study of Higher Education at the University of California at Berkeley and with funds from the Carnegie Corporation of New York, Glenny (1959) prepared a study of state government planning and coordination of higher education. He reported that, as of 1956, some seventeen states had established either a statewide governing board or a state coordinating board for higher education. In several other states there were informal arrangements among state institutions for cooperative planning. Glenny included New York among the states with statewide governing boards, ignoring the existence of both the City University of New York and the New York Board of Regents. Nor did Glenny draw a sharp distinction between a multicampus system of higher education institutions and a statewide multicampus system. He undertook on a sampling basis in eleven states to examine state experience with statewide governing boards, state coordinating boards, and state voluntary planning.

Glenny asserted that there were two major developments that had raised the issue of state coordination. One was the increasing complexity of public institutions of higher education. The other was the increasing size of state government expenditures for various purposes, including higher education. To illustrate the increasing complexity of public institutions, Glenny cited the existence of both a state university and a land-grant university in many states and the emergence of teacher's colleges as state universities. The multiplication of institutions and of instructional programs was bringing about the need for coordination. Competition and rivalry among these institutions for resources and for programs were leading to demands for some kind of restraint. These demands came partly from those institutions that saw their own efforts threatened by the mounting competition. Legislators wanted to economize, to increase efficiency, and to limit program expansion.

Glenny listed four principal functions of central agencies: (1) planning, (2) the allocation of programs among institutions, (3) the determination of budget needs, and (4) the determination of the need for physical facilities. He was generally critical of the information-gathering and planning activities undertaken up to that time in all the states he studied. He found the coordination of functions and programs to be mostly ineffective, although he concluded that the central agencies did "fairly well" in allocating new functions. For the most part Glenny was impressed by the accomplishments in budgeting for current operations. He was less favorably impressed by the methods of budgeting for capital improvements.

In evaluating efforts at coordination up to 1958, Glenny emphasized the importance of an adequate legal or constitutional base, of able administrative leadership, of competent and sufficient staff, and of cooperative relationships with institutional officials. Glenny found relationships between coordinating agencies, on the one hand, and state budget offices and state legislatures, on the other, to be generally unsatisfactory. State officials often considered budget requests to be padded, unrealistic, and wasteful. Part of the problem was the lack of specific information about needs and available resources. Glenny declared that coordinating agencies had difficulty in "defining their role in the scheme of government" (p. 203).

Glenny observed that the first central agencies established for state coordination had been of the governing type. But he found the trend since 1950 to be toward coordinating agencies. Glenny did not state a preference between the two types. He noted, on the one hand, the uncertain and sometimes hostile relationships between individual institutions and a coordinating board. On the other hand, while it enjoyed more authority in relation to individual institutions, the statewide governing board had difficulty in drawing a distinction between its role as a governing board for an individual institution and its role as a coordinating agency for a group of institutions. He declared that both types had been "equally inadequate" in long-range state planning. The coordinating agencies had been unable or unwilling to correct situations of overlap and duplication in program offerings. In budget matters he found differences among agencies, but he was unable to correlate these differences with type of agency. He felt that governing boards were more successful than coordinating boards in obtaining funds from state legislatures. There was more institutional autonomy under coordinating boards than under governing boards. Glenny found that voluntary cooperation resulted in domination by the largest or oldest institutions, maintenance of the status quo, and inadequate representation of the public interest in planning; moreover, it was an ineffective means of coordinating any large number of institutions.

The Glenny study was a landmark work. While it was limited in scope and while the real era of state expansion of higher education still lay ahead, Glenny identified issues of central importance for state governments and for public higher education. He forecast increasing concern on the part of state governments with the organization of higher education. It was an accurate forecast.

The Berdahl Study

In 1966 the American Council on Education sponsored a new study of state government organization for higher education. Berdahl (1971), the author of the study, was a professor of higher

education at the State University of New York at Buffalo and subsequently a professor at the University of Maryland.

Berdahl began his report with a discussion of university
autonomy and the public interest. He insisted that academic freedom and institutional autonomy were not the same thing, that academic freedom was the privilege of faculty members within the
competence of their specialization to espouse any rational idea
they might formulate, while institutional autonomy was the claim of
a university to self-government. Such a claim was unrealistic for a
state university dependent on state government financial support.
Berdahl acknowledged that state control of institutional autonomy might embrace such concerns as the approval of new degree
programs and of new branch campuses.

Apart from voluntary association that still existed in two
states as of 1968, Berdahl identified three primary types of coordinating mechanisms at the state government level: the advisory
board, the regulatory board, and the consolidated governing
board. He enumerated thirteen advisory boards, fourteen regulatory boards, and nineteen consolidated governing boards. The
date of first authorization, the designation, the number of members, and the type of membership for each board were set forth.

Berdahl concluded that there was a "basic and inescapable
need" for the coordinating function to be performed at the state
government level. He pointed out that there was no such thing as
"no coordination"; if there was not a coordinating board, then
coordination would fall upon the governor and the governor's staff
and on the legislature and the legislative staff. Rather than having
coordination undertaken piecemeal by various state offices, it was
preferable from the standpoint of institutional autonomy and the
public interest to have coordination carried out by an agency spe-
cializing in higher education.

Berdahl described at some length the functioning of state
coordinating agencies in thirteen states in terms of their membership, staffing, planning, budget review, and program review. Berdahl also discussed at some length relationships between coordinating boards and state universities, and relationships between
boards and officials of state government. Under the heading of
problems and issues, Berdahl considered the question of the rela-

tionship of state governments to private higher education, and the impact of federal government grants on statewide coordination.

Finally, Berdahl turned to the central issue for state governments: what kind of administrative machinery was appropriate for state needs. He expressed the opinion that at best the relationship of state governments to public higher education was an uneasy partnership. But Berdahl did not express a preference for the advisory board, the regulatory board, or the consolidated governing board. He insisted that each state government must determine for itself the most appropriate mechanism on the basis of its traditions, needs, and resources. He did advocate a strong and independent staff, strong board membership, strong academic advisory committees, strong powers in planning, strong powers in program review, and strong powers in budget review at the state government level. Berdahl did see the possibility of growing friction between higher education and elementary-secondary education because of competition for state funding and disagreement about appropriate standards of student preparation for college. Berdahl enumerated the selection and promotion of faculty and administrative staff, the selection of students, the establishment of degree requirements and curriculum content, the determination of the balance between instruction and research and public service, and the allocation of income among programs as matters that were essential to institutional autonomy.

The Berdahl study was a major endeavor to steer an exact course between university presidents who resented any effort at coordination and state government officials who resented the continuing expectation of university presidents for increased appropriations with no strings attached. Berdahl pleaded for improved relationships between state universities and coordinating boards. For the most part, the plea fell upon deaf ears in the university world.

Carnegie Commission Studies and Reports

In 1967 the Carnegie Corporation of New York and the Carnegie Foundation for the Advancement of Teaching, administered by the corporation, established the Carnegie Commission on Higher Education. Chaired and directed by Clark Kerr, former president of the University of California, the commission was composed of eighteen other members of whom eleven were prominently identified with higher education. The other seven were well-known citizens interested in higher education; one of them had been a state governor and another a cabinet officer.

In the six years of its existence the Carnegie Commission sponsored eighty-three research studies and technical papers written by some 200 authors. The commission also published twenty-two reports setting forth policy positions and recommendations arrived at by the commission members themselves. Altogether the reports and studies constituted the most extensive analysis of American higher education ever undertaken.

Only a limited proportion of this research was devoted to public higher education or to the relation between state governments and higher education. This limited attention is all the more remarkable in the light of the tremendous expansion of public higher education and of state government financial support that was occurring in the years from 1967 to 1973. The work of the Carnegie Commission focused on the characteristics of various institutions of higher education and the federal government's role in higher education.

Two of the studies sponsored by the commission deserve mention. One was a study by Eulau and Quinley (1970) of the opinions and expectations of policy makers in nine states about higher education. The second was a study by Lee and Bowen (1971) of the multicampus university.

Eulau and Quinley interviewed government officials and legislators in California, Illinois, Iowa, Kansas, Kentucky, Louisiana, New York, Pennsylvania, and Texas. Among legislators they found a "great faith" in higher education, an awareness that parents wanted higher education opportunities for their children, some sense of state competitiveness for prestigious colleges and universities, and strong support for the public service activities of colleges and universities. They also found a favorable attitude toward long-range planning and centralized coordination of public institutions, eagerness for federal grants to assist higher education, strong support for community colleges, a cautious attitude toward state support of private institutions, and some understanding of student dissent but a clear belief that such dissent should be firmly handled.

Lee and Bowen studied multicampus public universities in California (two systems), Illinois, Missouri, New York (two systems), North Carolina, Texas, and Wisconsin. None of these systems at the time of the study was a statewide governing system embracing all senior public institutions in the state. All the systems had a chief executive officer. The study noted the necessarily close involvement of state government in the governance of the systems but found that this involvement tended to be concentrated on budget and appropriation issues. Only to a minimum extent had multiple-campus governing boards adapted their functions to multicampus concerns, as contrasted with earlier one-campus concerns. In examining the work of the governing boards, the authors found a good deal of attention given to various operating details but less to the issues of diversity among the campuses, encouragement of cooperation, and enforcement of program specialization. Attention to quality concerns and program review procedures was impressive. The authors declared that a major weakness in the multicampus system was the absence of a clear understanding about the relative roles of state government, state coordinating boards, and the multicampus system in the governance of individual institutions. The authors criticized state governments for inadequate delegation of fiscal authority to colleges and universities, but acknowledged that there seemed to be a lack of confidence on the part of state governments in the budgetary competence of higher education institutions. The authors suggested that multicampus governing boards needed to focus their attention upon systemwide matters and to delegate more authority to campus executives. The authors also expressed some concern about board membership, finding members not to be representative of various groups in society, to be generally distrusted by students and faculty members, and to be insufficiently independent of partisan political currents.

In 1971 the Carnegie Commission on Higher Education issued one of its periodic reports under the title of *The Capitol and the Campus: State Responsibility for Postsecondary Education*. The report acknowledged that among governmental units the states had the primary responsibility for the development of higher education in the United States. It went on to say that this responsibility generally had been "well discharged." The Carnegie Commission asserted that the United States should not move in the direction of a single national system of higher education but that the states should continue to carry the primary governmental responsibility for higher education. The commission then urged the states to broaden their responsibility to include the whole range of post-secondary education and to provide universal access to such education. It expressed concern about "the growing dominance of governors over higher education in several of the states," but it did not identify either the governors or the states (Carnegie Commission on Higher Education, 1971, p. 2).

The commission expressed deep concern "with the development of heavy-handed regulatory councils over higher education" and asserted that there was no need for these councils to duplicate the work already done by administrative staffs, such as departments of finance, and by legislatures and their committees (p. 2). The commission did recognize two functions that should be performed by a state coordinating agency: long-range planning and current consultation. The commission observed that state financial support of higher education varied greatly from state to state, and urged "emergency" efforts to improve such performance in states where fewer than 70 percent of high school students graduated from high school, where less than .6 percent of per-capita income was spent for higher education, where fewer than 30 places were provided by public and private higher education for every 100 persons of college age, and where a state exported more than 15,000 students.

The commission expressed approval of "some" state support for private colleges and universities, primarily through student financial assistance but also through contractual support "for special endeavors" such as medical schools. Finally, the commission said that autonomy of institutions of higher education "neither can be nor should be complete."

In 1973 the Carnegie Commission on Higher Education (1973b) issued a report entitled *Governance of Higher Education.* The commission observed that the independence of the campus from external authority had declined substantially since the end of World War II. It cited the growth of coordinating councils and "superboards" at the state level, the increasing amount of gubernatorial and legislative investigation, and the growth of federal regulations and supervision. While the commission thought that there could not be complete autonomy for an institution of higher education, it argued that higher education should be substantially self-governing in its intellectual conduct, its academic affairs, and its administrative arrangements. The case for independence, the commission asserted, rested on the professional nature of many of the decisions to be made, on the need to elicit the devotion and sense of responsibility of the constituent internal groups, on the usefulness of obtaining advice and support from interested citizens, on the intellectual and other costs of bureaucratic or partisan political intrusion, and on the role of the campus as constructive critic of society.

At the same time, the Carnegie Commission asserted the need for institutions of higher education to earn their independence by maintaining a high level of performance, by demonstrating the capacity for self-government, by making effective use of available resources, by ensuring lawful campus behavior, by maintaining institutional neutrality in partisan politics and in external controversies, by preserving intellectual integrity, and by fully and honestly explaining all matters of broad public concern.

The Carnegie Commission declared the governing board to be an essential element of institutional governance and proposed methods for strengthening board membership. It advocated faculty and student membership on board committees but not on the board itself. The commission also upheld the vital importance of the leadership role of the institutional president. It asserted that faculties should have an appropriate role in institutional governance and urged that faculty collective bargaining should be restricted to economic issues. The commission endorsed the principle of academic tenure and proposed improvements in tenure practices. On the subject of student influence on campus, the commission expressed sympathy for greater student participation in governance issues involving student behavior and activities but noted the need for responsible and orderly student conduct. Finally, the commission urged institutions to plan adequately to meet situations of serious campus disorder.

The major contribution in the Carnegie report on governance was its outline of an acceptable balance between public control and institutional independence, a subject that will be discussed in Chapter Eight.

The Carnegie Commission reports seemed to favor a state advisory board on higher education with no authority to issue any approval of institutional plans, programs, or budgets. The commission seemed to prefer that budget and coordinating issues be handled by governors and legislatures. Yet at the same time it expressed dissatisfaction with the growing dominance of governors and with legislative intrusions into the operations of higher education institutions. In its generally balanced and moderately liberal stance on the many complex problems of higher education, the Carnegie Commission on Higher Education was somewhat ambivalent in its prescription for the exercise of public control.

Carnegie Council on Policy Studies

When the Carnegie Commission on Higher Education completed its work at the end of 1973, its place was taken by the Carnegie Council on Policy Studies in Higher Education. Once more Clark Kerr was both chairman and director of studies. Twenty different persons served on the council in the years from 1974 to 1980, including eleven current or former college and university presidents; all the other members had some connection with higher education, including one who was president of the Carnegie Foundation for the Advancement of Teaching. During its lifetime the Carnegie Council issued fifteen policy reports and sponsored thirty-eight research and technical studies.

The Carnegie Council concentrated its attention on six areas: social justice, the provision of professional skills and new knowledge, the quality and effectiveness of academic programs, the adequacy of governance, the resources available to higher education, and the purposes and performance of institutions of higher education. Most of the policy reports and research studies were generally applicable to both public and private institutions of higher education. Only a few were directed specifically to state government concerns with higher education.

Among the research studies two in particular must be mentioned in the context of state government concerns with higher education. Lee and Bowen (1975) returned to the subject of multicampus systems. The authors sought to bring up to date their analysis of the nine multicampus systems that they had examined for the Carnegie Commission. They noted the complexities created by enrollment shifts among programs and campuses, the increased attention to planning and information systems, the greater concern with program priorities in budgeting, the presence of some flexibility in handling retrenchment through faculty reassignment within the system, and the growing but inadequate attention to admission standards and student enrollment size at particular campuses. The authors declared that important decisions affecting public higher education could be more effectively made within multicampus systems than by arms of state government.

A study by Bowen (1980) on the costs of higher education involved findings and observations that in large part were aggregated to include both public and private institutions. In a chapter on cost differences among institutions, Bowen examined the educational expenditures per student for some 268 "representative" colleges and universities. Of these institutions, 93 were public and 175 were private. For research and doctoral-granting universities Bowen found that the minimum expenditure among 35 private institutions was some $1,500 per student and the maximum expenditure was over $8,000. For 35 public universities the minimum expenditure per student was nearly $1,100 and the maximum was nearly $4,800. For 32 comprehensive public universities the minimum expenditure per student was nearly $1,200 and the maximum expenditure was just over $3,700. For 52 private institutions the corresponding figures were $1,100 and $4,200. For 26 public two-year colleges the minimum expenditure was $1,100, which contrasted with a minimum for 23 private two-year colleges of about $1,600; the maximum for public colleges was nearly $4,800, in contrast to a maximum of $8,000 among the private two-year colleges. All these financial data were for the academic year 1976–77. Bowen presented data for all public institutions on expenditures per student by states. The lowest expenditure was $1,300 in Massachusetts and the highest was $2,900 in Montana. He also set forth differences among public and private institutions in the internal allocation of expenditures.

Bowen concluded that the expenditures of institutions were determined by their revenues. In terms of long-term trends he found that costs per student in constant dollars declined slowly in the period from 1929 to 1950, rose rapidly in the period from 1950 to 1970, and declined slowly after 1970. Bowen noted the imposition of various social costs upon institutions of higher education from governmental regulation. He estimated that to restore costs to the level of 1969–70 would require about a 10-percent increase in expenditures above the level of 1977; to achieve a comparable level of quality in outcomes he thought the increase would have to be about 25 percent. Although Bowen found differences among institutions in support or overhead costs depending upon enrollment size, he did not analyze the differences based upon program offerings or differences based upon selective versus open admission. It was evident that private institutions spent more for student financial assistance than did public institutions.

Among the fifteen policy reports of the Carnegie Council, six had some particular relevance to the concerns of state government in relation to higher education. The first of these was a report entitled *Low or No Tuition* (Carnegie Council on Policy Studies in Higher Education, 1975). The council noted that in 1947 the Truman commission had advocated tuition-free education in all public institutions for the first two years after high school graduation. The council concluded that the adoption of such a policy through state government action was improbable and that federal government action would be difficult to carry out. The council urged that federal action should continue to concentrate on student financial assistance and on research support.

In a report on selective admissions (Carnegie Council on Policy Studies in Higher Education, 1977b), the council emphasized the desirability of a "fairer chance" for all young Americans to offset the consequences of prior educational disadvantage and social discrimination, and urged consideration of the contributions that a student might make to fellow students and his or her fellow-men. The council strongly emphasized the need to find and develop potential talent, to consider individual potential rather than ethnic or other background characteristics, and to allow institutional autonomy in deciding admissions. The Carnegie Council identified three kinds of admission situations: (1) open admission at the undergraduate level, (2) selective admission at the undergraduate level, and (3) selective admission at the graduate and professional school level. It was estimated that at the undergraduate level about half of all admissions were on an open basis and about half on a selective basis. Admission to graduate and professional schools was almost entirely on a selective basis.

The Carnegie Council accepted the proposition that there was a public interest involved in access to higher education and reviewed federal government actions meant to ensure both "affirmative action" and nondiscrimination in selective admission practices. The council outlined the various considerations that should be taken into account in selective admission, with particular attention to students' special abilities, special interests, and special contributions to a campus and to society. But the council made no differentiation between public institutions and private institutions, or between multiple-campus governing boards and single-university governing boards in its presentation of recommended admission procedures. There was an implication for state governments in the emphasis that the council gave to institutional autonomy in admission policies and practices.

Another Carnegie Council report was directed specifically to public institutions and to state legislatures on the subject of faculty collective bargaining (Carnegie Council on Policy Studies in Higher Education, 1977a). The report noted that twenty-four states had laws authorizing "employees" of public institutions of higher education to organize and to bargain collectively and that in three other states individual governing boards had authorized collective bargaining. The practice of faculty collective bargaining was estimated to include about 25 percent of the full-time faculty members and about 30 percent of all campuses in public institutions. The Carnegie Council observed that collective bargaining could have a major consequence for the governance of an institution and that faculty members should be clear as to what kind of governance structure and process they wanted in a particular institution. The council recommended that the election unit should be faculty members on an individual campus; that bargaining should be restricted to issues of wages, hours, and conditions of employment; and that the "employer" should be defined as the governing board of an institution or of a multicampus system. The council was critical of state laws such as that in New York that defined the governor as the employer. The council by implication indicated that a separate state law about higher education collective bargaining was preferable to a general state law applying to all state agencies, including institutions of higher education.

Another report of the Carnegie Council addressed the troublesome question of what state governments should do to ensure the survival and welfare of private colleges and universities (Carnegie Council on Policy Studies in Higher Education, 1977c). Even with the "most conscientious" self-help, the Carnegie Council declared, the long-run position of the private sector was uncertain and insecure, and "more intensive" public support and encouragement were necessary. The council then asserted that financial aid to students should be the "primary vehicle" for the channeling of state funds to private institutions. Need-based tuition grants should be the "mainstay" of state programs of student aid, and such grants should also be provided for students attending public institutions. The council wanted such grants to be available to all students from families in the lower half of income distribution and even to some students in the upper half, and wanted the grants to be of sufficient magnitude to encourage college enrollment and an element of choice in the selection of a private or public institution to attend.

The Carnegie Council included recommendations for such supplemental forms of aid as contracts for educational services, grants for special programs, and awards for capital plant and major equipment. The council warned that grants for direct institutional support should be provided only when there was adequate protection of institutional autonomy. The council endorsed state policies that would enable private institutions to become public institutions, that would encourage mergers of campuses, and that would provide temporary support of "marginal institutions" whose continued existence was in the public interest. The Carnegie Council then declared that tuition levels in public institutions should be determined on "their own merits" and not specifically to aid private institutions and that state aid to private institutions should not be given in amounts that would cause "significant disadvantage" to public institutions. Finally, the council insisted that private colleges and universities should be represented on all state coordinating mechanisms and that coordinating councils, governors, and legislatures should insist that decisions about the expansion of public institutions or their programs should take into account the effect of these decisions upon private institutions.

The most important of the Carnegie Council reports concerning state governments was *The States and Higher Education: A Proud Past and a Vital Future* (Carnegie Foundation for the Advancement of Teaching, 1976) although no explanation was given to account for the change in sponsorship. The preface acknowledged that the subject was "full of controversy" and that there had been many disagreements in the discussions of the Carnegie Foundation board of trustees and among the members of the council. It was asserted that the report represented a consensus from the discussions, although individual members had some disagreements with the report, primarily on the matters of state aid to private institutions and of "preferred mechanisms" for coordination of higher education.

The Carnegie report began with the assertion that the United States had been well served both in quantity and in quality by its public and private system of higher education and by the tripartite method of support from state, federal, and private sources. It noted the expansion of higher education in the 1960s and the emergence of an excess number of schoolteachers and Ph.D. recipients. The report declared that this excess capacity was not the consequence of mismanagement but rather of the decline in economic demand for these professions in the 1970s. The report asserted that there was still much to be accomplished. At the same time, it was admitted that many states were in financial difficulty because of economic recession, the rising costs of welfare, health, and other social benefits, and the impact of "fast-rising" salary and fringe benefits in public employment. The Carnegie report identified five major concerns: the prospect of a decline in the dynamic character of higher education, a tendency on the part of state governments toward parochialism, the need to preserve the private sector, the tendency toward increased centralized control of public higher education, and the erosion of institutional independence.

On the subject of dynamism, the Carnegie report mentioned that there would be little if any expansion of enrollment in higher education in the decades of the 1980s and 1990s. The report feared a loss of the capacity and inclination to bring about innovation and improvement in higher education under the conditions that would be prevailing in these decades. While stating that the preservation of dynamism was mostly up to the institutions themselves, the report asserted that state governments could assist self-renewal by providing funds for innovation, by encouraging institutions to set aside a small proportion of existing funds for new endeavors, by encouraging the introduction of new instructional technology, by avoiding "undue rigidity" in state formulas for financial support, and by relaxing detailed controls that discourage "constructive leadership at the campus level."

As for the tendency toward a new parochialism, the report observed the practice of charging out-of-state students a larger tuition than in-state students, restrictions on the use of state student aid grants in out-of-state institutions, the adoption of quotas limiting the admission of out-of-state students, the pressure to distribute federal research funds geographically rather than on merit alone, and the setting of professional examinations so as to favor locally educated talent. The report expressed opposition to all these practices but admitted that alternative lines of action were not easy to find.

The section of the Carnegie report on preservation of the private sector, anticipated the report that was issued a year later by the Carnegie Council, which has already been mentioned.

The Carnegie report expressed regret about the tendency toward centralization of authority over higher education, a centralization that had proceeded from campus to multicampus systems to state mechanisms of control. The report asserted that this centralization had reduced the influence of faculty members, students, and campus administrators over decision making about campus affairs, had had "no measurable direct impact" upon the improvement of higher education policies and practices, and had caused a deterioration in governance processes. The report acknowledged that public institutions could not be freed from all restraints, but argued that the preferable restraints were those resulting from student choice, competition with the private sector, the state budget, and long-range planning by a state higher education advisory board.

The Carnegie report went on to express a preference for lay boards at the campus level within multicampus systems. It preferred for authority to reside in statewide governing boards or with gubernatorial staffs and legislative staffs rather than in regulatory agencies. Interestingly enough, one argument against the so-called regulatory agency was that its staff tended to come from outside the field of higher education. (But wouldn't that also be true of gubernatorial and legislative staffs?) The Carnegie report declared that the burden of proof should be "on the centralizers and regulators" to demonstrate that they could accomplish something better than what could be realized "under the constraints of an active market and of a well-made budget and of a wisely drawn long-range plan" (Carnegie Foundation for the Advancement of Teaching, 1976, p. 17).

The Carnegie report insisted that institutional independence was a major value long recognized by many state constitutions and state statutory provisions. It went on to declare that the states with the greatest freedom for higher education were also the states that had developed the most outstanding public institutions, but the only evidence cited for this declaration was the state of Michigan. Nothing was said about the leadership of governors and the benefit of state economic resources in the development of outstanding state universities.

We should particularly note the comments in section 3 of the Carnegie report on surpluses and deficits in state higher education. The report suggested that there was excess capacity in teacher education programs in seventeen states, a surplus of Ph.D. programs in sixteen states, a surplus of health science centers in six states, a possible surplus in law schools (four states in particular were mentioned in this connection), a deficiency in open-access institutions in twenty-six states (primarily because of high tuition rather than geographical location), a failure to adopt a state student aid program in eight states, and a deficiency in area health education centers in eleven states. The report singled out four states for outstanding accomplishment in developing places for students in public institutions, twelve states for expansion of their community college system, twelve states for their support of leading research universities that received substantial federal research funds, twelve states for the high rating of their graduate faculties at particular state universities, six states for the high proportion of personal income spent on higher education, four states for increasing substantially their per-student support of public institutions, and seven states for their "especially good start" in the support of private colleges and universities.

In connection with the subject of state centralization, the Carnegie report presented a number of contrasting figures. As of 1940 there were thirty-three states with no coordinating mechanism, while as of 1975 there were none without such a mechanism. In 1940, 70 percent of public four-year campuses (other than teacher's colleges) were governed by their own individual board, while as of 1975 only 30 percent were so governed. In 1940 only one state regulated private colleges and universities, while as of 1975 there were forty-nine such states. As centralization proceeded, three clear-cut choices emerged: Each campus could have its own governing board, each segment (such as the university segment and the state college segment) could have its own governing board, or all campuses could be governed by a single board. The report said that only five states fell into the first category, eight into the second category, and twenty-two into the third category. There were fifteen states described as having a "mixture" of these three arrangements. The Carnegie report then identified four choices in coordination of public institutions: no coordination (nine states), consolidated governing board (thirteen states), advisory councils (nine states), and regulatory agencies (nineteen states). The report also listed five patterns of public policy formulation involving association with the private sector.

The Carnegie report declared that it could not yet be shown that any one coordinating approach was superior to the others. There was no "known quantifiable consequence" to indicate that one mechanism was superior to another in relation to tuition policy, state funds for research, composition of the public sector, and assistance to the private sector. The only correlation to be found, according to the report, was one between money spent per student and the size of the bureaucracy supervising the expenditure.

The final report by the Carnegie Council on Policy Studies in Higher Education was entitled *Three Thousand Futures: The Next Twenty Years for Higher Education* (1980). In the last chapter of this report the council presented advice to state governments for the decades of the 1980s and 1990s. The council observed that the twenty years ahead would be a period of state action for the welfare of higher education, just as the twenty years from 1960 to 1980 had been a period when the federal government took the initiative. The report asserted that the states were in better financial condition to carry out this responsibility than they had been five or ten years earlier—an assessment that events in 1981 and 1982 were to deny except for a handful of oil-producing states. The report expressed two fears: that some state financial planners would overestimate enrollment decline and that such "planners" would seek to seize control of a state system of higher education in the name of rationalization and economy. In commenting on the state planning process, the report observed that in a time of expansion the institutions proposed changes that governors and legislatures then either accepted or rejected. In a time of contraction state governments would tend to make proposals, and the institutions would be under pressure to accept the desired changes.

Once again the Carnegie Council urged that the student market determine the contraction of particular institutions. The report questioned the desirability of state-mandated program review in favor of institutional review and accreditation review. The report recognized that, where contraction of enrollment was sizable, mergers and closings might be necessary and acknowledged that such actions would have to be initiated by state governments.

The final report of the Carnegie Council concluded with a "checklist" of imperatives. There was one set of imperatives for colleges and universities, one for the federal government, and one for states. The checklist of imperatives for the states reads as follows:

1. Maintain at least the current level of per-capita funding of higher education in current dollars.
2. Provide need-based tuition scholarships for all needy students.
3. Support private higher education while maintaining its autonomy.
4. Assist in developing plans for adaption of higher education to changing needs.
5. Avoid excessive regulation of higher education.
6. Use flexible funding formulas.
7. Encourage institutional consortiums and interstate cooperation.
8. Ensure statewide coverage by open-access institutions and by area health education centers.
9. Expend public funds, as far as possible, as though they were private funds (Carnegie Council on Policy Studies in Higher Education, 1980, pp. 131–132).

    With noteworthy candor, the Carnegie Council in a well-prepared summary acknowledged that both the commission and the council had made certain miscalculations (Carnegie Council on Policy Studies in Higher Education, 1981). The council mentioned that both bodies had overestimated the willingness of institutions of higher education and the federal government to entertain and undertake reforms such as widespread adoption of the doctor of arts degree, the utilization of facilities on a year-round basis, the introduction of an urban-grant program, the integration of electronic technology into academic life, the preparation of academic codes of conduct, and drastic revision of federal student loan programs. The commission and the council had expressed too high expectations on several matters such as future enrollment levels, faculty salary levels, and rising real resources per student. Both agencies had underestimated certain forces in American society and in higher education—for example, the unwillingness of the middle class to support adequate financial aid for low-income students without sharing in the available subsidies, the impact of "hedonism" on the willingness of families to support their children in college, the degree of deterioration in the American high school and the qualifications of students entering college, the intensity of the competition between public institutions and private ones, the difficulties for college students in overcoming prior handicaps in family and social circumstances, the willingness of institutions to place survival above the quality of their programs, and the rapidity with which demands for equality of opportunity would be replaced by demands for equality of results.

Sloan Commission Report

In 1977 the Alfred P. Sloan Foundation established the Sloan Commission on Government and Higher Education. The agenda for the commission was set forth in terms of a series of questions:

1. How does the United States strike a balance between institutional freedom and government authority?
2. To what extent is the academic institution to be responsive to what may be perceived as social needs?
3. How shall the public interest be determined in the regulatory process for higher education?

The Sloan Commission consisted of twenty-two members under the chairmanship of Louis W. Cabot, who was, among other things, a trustee of the Brookings Institution, chairman of the Cabot Corporation, and a member of the corporation of M.I.T. The vice-chairman and director of research was Carl Kaysen of the Institute for Advanced Research; Dr. Kaysen had also been a member of the Carnegie Commission. There were two members of the commission who also served on the Carnegie Council. Only five members of the Sloan Commission were administrators involved in higher education institutions and agencies. The report of the Sloan Commission on Government and Higher Education was published under the title of *A Program for Renewed Partnership* (1980).

The Sloan Commission was especially concerned with federal regulation of higher education institutions, a process that affected equally both public and private institutions and one that the institutions found increasingly burdensome and troublesome. A single chapter was devoted to the subject of the role of the states. The report concluded with a chapter that asserted the importance of a strong higher education system in the service of American society.

In the chapter on the role of the states, the Sloan Commission examined several issues. The first had to do with the composition of higher education boards. The commission did not define the kinds of boards it had in mind but recommended that members of such boards should be widely respected individuals of experience and demonstrated abilities who were concerned with the health of the "entire higher education community" within a state. Not more than one third of the membership should be drawn from institutions of higher education, public or private.

Under the heading of retrenchment, the commission urged that each state examine the structure of its entire system to ensure that the mission of each public college and university was clearly defined, that each state periodically review the quality of its public colleges and universities, that funding formulas be revised to reflect the quality reviews, that the "traditional state policy" of supporting flagship research universities be continued, and that all higher education institutions (public and private) be licensed in order to prevent fraudulent or deceptive practices.

The commission pointed out that enrollment-driven funding formulas would be disadvantageous to public institutions in a period of declining enrollments. The commission advocated a "flat basic grant" with a per-student allowance as a supplementary appropriation differentiating lower-division, upper-division, and graduate enrollments. The commission advocated that each state higher education board establish minimum standards of "academic conduct" and enforce these standards through licensure. The purpose apparently was to control the competition for students; the commission referred to "aggressive recruiting techniques" that had included use of "highly questionable practices." Among such practices the commission noted the proliferation of out-of-state branch campuses. The commission commended the model legislation on approval of postsecondary institutions drafted by a task force of the Education Commission of the States.

In connection with faculty collective bargaining, the Sloan Commission recommended that individual governing boards of public colleges and universities be the bargaining representatives of the institution, that state governments reinforce the role of individual institutions, and that states insist on institutional autonomy in personnel matters, academic affairs, and planning decisions.

Under the heading of state oversight and institutional autonomy, the Sloan Commission was critical of the burden imposed upon institutions by reporting and regulatory requirements. The two examples of such burdens that were cited, however, dealt with a multicampus system that was not statewide in scope and with a statewide multicampus system. The commission mentioned that it had studied "the regulatory burden" in ten states but failed to explain that there were very different organizational structures for higher education in these states. As of 1980, in fact, three of the states had advisory state boards, five had coordinating boards, and two had statewide governing boards. The commission was critical of regulations having to do with central purchasing, personnel administration, restriction of out-of-state travel, control of overhead funds and "revolving" funds, and increased financial audits, but here again it failed to make a distinction between actions of state higher education boards and actions of state government administrative agencies.

The Sloan Commission spoke to growing concerns of the leadership of public and private colleges and universities: the burden of federal government regulations, the complexities of federal student aid programs, and the restrictions surrounding federal grants for university research. When the commission turned its attention to state governments, however, the concerns expressed and the recommendations offered added little to the understanding of the subject or to the ongoing discussion of the problems involved.

Selected Studies

In 1971 the Center for Research and Development in Higher Education at the University of California at Berkeley issued a handbook on the activities that should be undertaken by a state coordinating board (Glenny and others, 1971). The report advocated coordinating boards rather than statewide governing boards, citing as the principal advantage of the coordinating board its ability to act as an "umbrella" for a variety of public institutions and agencies of higher education. The report recommended that a coordinating board as a "minimum" should have five kinds of authority: (1) to undertake continuous planning, (2) to acquire information from all postsecondary institutions through a statewide data system, (3) to review and approve "new and existing" degree programs and new campuses or extension centers of public institutions, (4) to review and recommend operating and capital budgets for higher education, and (5) to administer student financial aid programs and federal grant programs to the state. The report presented guidelines on membership selection, board organization, advisory relationships, board staffing, higher education planning, program review, budgeting, information systems, the administration of student aid programs, and interaction with private institutions. It must be said that as of 1983 the center's guidebook was still as useful as a general prescription as it had been in 1971.

Between 1973 and 1976 the Center for Research and Development in Higher Education undertook to study state budgeting and financing of higher education in the fifty states, with information obtained in some detail from seventeen states. Three reports were published, of which one was a general summary addressed primarily to the issue of the role of state higher education boards in budgeting for higher education (Glenny, 1976). After reviewing the research about budget practices, Glenny then discussed the development of state higher education boards, mainly using the classification scheme of Berdahl (1971). He noted that multicampus governing boards tended to have larger staffs than coordinating boards, that statewide governing boards tended to have poorer records in planning and forecasting than coordinating boards, that data systems were generally inadequate for long-range planning needs, and that coordinating boards had a different perspective on budgeting from that of statewide governing boards. Glenny directed attention to both executive and legislative budget offices. He observed that coordinating boards had difficulty in maintaining a balance between executive branches and legislative branches, as well as between state government and higher education institutions. He presented a considerable array of findings and conclusions about budget staffs and their interaction with chief executives, legislators, and coordinating boards. Glenny was critical of what he termed "redundancy" in budget review and recommendation. He appeared to favor executive budget action rather than budget action by coordinating boards. Glenny presented four functions that he thought appropriate to a state coordinating agency: (1) planning and policy studies, (2) information and management systems, (3) program initiatives and control, and (4) budget review of programs in relation to long-range plans and policies. He undertook to allocate particular sets of budget duties among coordinating boards, executive staffs, and legislative staffs.

In his discussion of the autonomy of public institutions of higher education, Dressel (1980) defined autonomy as the ability of a college or university to govern itself without outside controls. Such autonomy, Dressel concluded, would be possible only if an institution were financially independent, and such independence could not be achieved by an institution dependent upon student enrollment, governmental subsidies, and private philanthropy. After an extensive discussion of the nature of institutional autonomy, the case for such autonomy, the reasons for the erosion of autonomy, and the forms of governmental intervention, Dressel presented case studies of state coordination in Ohio, Wisconsin, and Indiana. He concluded that, under a coordinating board or an advisory commission, institutional heads retained their former "status, influence, and authority." The author pleaded for a careful balancing of institutional autonomy, government "regulation," and institutional responsibility. Dressel asserted that the autonomy of any person or institution in a democratic society must be limited and then set forth the essentials of performance by institutions of higher education if they were to preserve an appropriate degree of independence.

Education Commission of the States Reports

Two reports from the Education Commission of the States should be mentioned here. Established by interstate compact in 1965, this commission was formed with a dual objective: to bring state governments together as a counterweight to the increasing role of the federal government in educational affairs, and to give governors and state legislatures a common meeting ground to exchange information about their educational interests. The commission was made up of seven commissioners from each state: the governor, two legislators, and four persons usually appointed by the governor.

In 1973 the commission published the report of its Task Force on Coordination, Governance, and Structure of Postsecondary Education. The task force was chaired by Governor Robert W. Scott of North Carolina and consisted of sixteen regular members and three consultant members. The members included one state senator, one state representative, one state budget officer, two state coordinating officers, one head of a statewide multicampus system, one officer of a state board for community colleges, one state university president, one private university president, two professors of higher education, and three representatives of higher education associations. The title of the report indicated the thrust of its argument: *Coordination or Chaos?* The task force declared that there was no one "best formula" for planning, program review, and budget review at the state level. It asserted that state planning should include a clear definition of the objectives, as well as the role and scope, of the various institutions of postsecondary education. It endorsed the concept of institutional "leeway" in institutional operations, and said that the "appropriate state agency" should include the "full range of postsecondary education" in its planning process. The task force then commented on the desirability of broadening access to postsecondary education and voiced concern about articulation with elementary-secondary and occupational education. The task force insisted that planning and "its effective implementation" were the keys to effective coordination and governance, and urged careful attention to the changing needs of society. The task force then declared that the "public responsibility" for postsecondary education rested with the legislative and executive branches of state government.

In 1980 the Education Commission of the States issued a report prepared by the staff of the commission with the assistance of three review panels. Entitled *Challenge: Coordination and Governance in the 1980s*, the report noted again that "no single model" had emerged for state higher education agencies, although it observed that smaller states tended to have statewide governing boards and that larger states with more complex systems of higher education institutions were more likely to have coordinating boards. The report identified the major issues confronting state governments in the 1980s as educational quality, accountability, social justice, inflation and limited resources, and the need for institutional cooperation. The report then set forth the essentials of a state planning process, insisting that it should be flexible, comprehensive, and continuous. The report asserted that the setting of priorities and the reallocation of funds in the light of these priorities should be an "essential part" of the planning process. The report also set forth the essentials of institutional evaluation and appraisal. A third set of recommendations had to do with program review. Other basic concerns were considered under the headings of state management and financing and budgeting. The report declared that the states could help improve internal institutional management by eliminating detailed state-level management controls, which the report said seldom promoted institutional effectiveness.

The two reports issued by the Education Commission of the States carefully avoided any attempt to evaluate state government agencies responsible for higher education planning and coordination, although the second report encouraged periodic evaluation within each state of the performance of the state agency. The reports advocated that management authority be vested in governing boards and implicitly criticized state government administrative controls. The reports said nothing about the extent to which public institutions of higher education were governed as parts of multicampus systems. They emphasized the importance of state planning and coordination without detailing the institutional and political opposition to such planning and coordination.

Carnegie Foundation Report

In 1982 the Carnegie Foundation for the Advancement of Teaching under the new leadership of Ernest L. Boyer published a report entitled *The Control of the Campus*. The report asserted that on balance higher education's partnership with governments both at the state and at the national level had been productive and had generated more benefits than it had administrative burdens. At the same time the report insisted that the "powerful impact" of external influences was not to be discounted and that current trends ran in the direction of more rather than fewer controls. The principal thrust of the report was that governance initiatives should be returned to the institutions of higher education and that in turn the institutions should more effectively regulate themselves.

The Carnegie Foundation report noted with approval a concurring opinion of two Supreme Court justices in a 1957 case. The justices stated that there were four essential freedoms of a university: to determine on academic grounds who may teach, what may be taught, how it shall be taught, and who may be admitted to study. The report declared that these particular freedoms were rooted in a long tradition. Moreover, if the integrity of higher education was to be maintained, institutions must continue to have "full authority" over the essential functions relating to instruction and research. These essential functions were enumerated as selection of the faculty, selection of the content of courses, determination of the processes of instruction, establishment of academic standards, and assessment of student performance. In addition, institutions must have control over the conduct of campus-based research and dissemination of research results. These functions, the report insisted, were the "essential core" of academic life that must be "uncompromisingly defended."

The Carnegie Foundation report devoted a brief section to

the importance of boards of trustees as the governing authority of institutions of higher education. But nothing was said about the prevalence in public higher education of multicampus systems under a single governing board or about the complex relationships of institutions to multicampus governing boards.

The second part of the Carnegie Foundation report was concerned with campus governance, with accrediting and other voluntary associations formed to assist self-regulation, and with the divisive effect of accreditation by professional bodies. The report noted the linkage between professional accreditation and professional licensure by state governments. It brought out that departments and schools within a university were not above using professional accreditation as a lever to acquire advantages over other departments and schools.

The third part of the Carnegie Foundation report was devoted to the subject of the service that higher education had rendered to the nation. It noted that, in the period of expansion after World War II, state governments had created multicampus systems, statewide governing boards, and coordinating boards. Then in the 1970s retrenchment became a primary concern, a concern further evident during the economic recession of the early 1980s. The report argued that the creation of coordinating boards was "a reasonable approach" during the period of expansion but questioned the utility of such agencies in a time of fiscal stringency. The report saw dangers ahead in budget decisions that would affect campus operations, in program review at the state level, and in enrollment-driven formulas. The report warned that to "impose suffocating requirements on colleges at a time when flexibility is required is the wrong prescription" (Carnegie Foundation for the Advancement of Teaching, 1982, p. 44). There was the additional assertion that "to cut back in both money and flexibility is to make a difficult situation almost hopeless" (p. 44).

Although several warnings in general terms were directed at state governments, the Carnegie Foundation report gave far greater attention to the federal government's incursion into academic matters, as well as to the role of the courts in undertaking to resolve conflicts about racial or other discrimination by institutions of higher education, about health and safety requirements, and about personnel actions. The report deplored the suspicion and lack of trust evident in the relationships between higher education institutions and federal agencies.

In undertaking to establish desirable limits to governmental controls, the Carnegie Foundation report criticized efforts to administer campuses by "remote control" and declared that decentralization rather than centralization was the avenue to "good management" and efficiency. The burden of reports and paper work imposed by centralization was cited. The report asserted that there were limits to the capacity of government to regulate higher education. The alternative to government regulation was more effective ways of self-regulation by higher education institutions.

The fourth and final part of the Carnegie Foundation report was thus devoted to the theme of institutional self-regulation through an appropriate framework of governance and effective leadership. A number of recommendations were set forth for the functioning of governing boards, for governance of faculty concerns, for regional and specialized accreditation, and for federal regulation. The report provided six recommendations for improving relations between state governments and higher education:

1. State governments working primarily through coordinating boards should plan and provide basic support for a comprehensive system of higher education.
2. State governments should encourage good management by permitting administrative decisions to be made as close as possible to the point of action.
3. In budget matters state governments should create broad categories of expenditure rather than line item budgets.
4. In academic matters state officials should protect the integrity of the campus. They should not directly review academic programs.
5. State coordinating agencies should work closely with regional accrediting associations.
6. Diversity should be a primary goal of statewide coordination (Carnegie Foundation for the Advancement of Teaching, 1982, p. 81).

If one were to quarrel with the Carnegie Foundation report, it would be on the grounds of its generalizations and its optimistic expectations. The report was balanced in its point of view but lacking in many necessary qualifications. For example, there is a difference between a coordinating board's approving a new degree program and its ordering discontinuance of an existing program. And discontinuance might be ordered either because of duplication or because of lack of state need. In addition, while it may be hoped that in a period of retrenchment institutions of higher education will display greater self-control and restraint than they did in a period of expansion, the evidence of this self-control is still to be provided.

In the years since the end of World War II, there has been extensive concern over the role of the federal government and state governments in university governance, as well as concern over the autonomy of institutions in making decisions about academic affairs, faculty affairs, student affairs, and financial and administrative affairs. Part of this concern was directed toward the federal government. We have not sought to review that development here; we may note in passing, however, that as federal financing of research and student assistance has expanded, so has federal control over university governance. Insofar as state governments have been involved, two concerns have appeared.

The first concern of governing boards and presidents of public institutions centered on state government administrative controls, controls that reflected in large part the governmental administrative reform movement in the United States. This question surfaced in the 1950s, and reappeared in the work of the Carnegie Commission and Carnegie Council, as well as in the report of the Sloan Commission. The second concern centered on the development of state government boards for higher education — statewide governing boards, state coordinating boards, and state advisory boards. Beginning with Glenny's study in 1959, this concern has tended to eclipse the earlier one. The issue has been the articulation of the state government interest in higher education and the coordination of multiple institutions of higher education in the pursuit of that interest. Necessarily such articulation and coordination have infringed upon the right of universities to make autonomous decisions about mission, program, and financial need.

It seems likely that as the decade of the 1980s unfolds the tension between state governments and public institutions of higher education will increase. And private institutions of higher education will have a growing stake in the decisions of state government. The new battleground will not be state government action to approve new degree programs — an action relevant to the circumstances of the 1960s and 1970s — but state action to approve existing degree programs. At the heart of the conflict will always be the issue of funding: How much should the programs of higher education cost and how should they be financed?

⇥ 3 ⇤

Higher Education Concerns
of State Governments

FOR A NUMBER OF YEARS the Education Commission of the States, on behalf of the State Higher Education Executive Officers, has published annual reports of major state developments in higher education. These annual reports provide a periodic review of the problems of state government relationships to higher education. The commission also sponsored a special report dealing with state higher education policy issues and with the major concerns of higher education agencies in state governments (Berve, 1981).

In addition, in the autumn of 1981 the Education Commission of the States conducted a survey of emerging issues in postsecondary education. It was expected that this survey would become an annual undertaking. Some 323 policy leaders, including governors, the education and appropriations committee chairmen of state legislatures, state budget officers, and state higher education agency heads were asked to respond to a questionnaire. A further questionnaire was enclosed for response by a staff aide. Altogether some 680 survey instruments were distributed, and 214 usable survey instruments, or 31 percent, were returned. Forty-eight responses were received from governors and their staff aides, 81 from legislators and their staff aides, and 52 from state agency heads and their associates; 33 miscellaneous responses were also received (Van de Water, 1982).

This survey identified five leading issues: the quality of instructional programs in state colleges and universities, basic skills and remedial development programs, physical plant replacement and improvement, tuition levels at public institutions, and the impact of changing federal government appropriations on student grants and loans. About three fourths of all respondents said that they expected state government appropriations in support of higher education to lag behind the rate of inflation. As a consequence, both increases in tuition to students and reductions in expenditures would be necessary. Insofar as the family burden of higher education expense was concerned, state leaders saw a greater family contribution or a state loan program as the desirable response. Increases in student grant programs were regarded as unlikely. In general, issues relating to changes in funding formulas, changes in governance structure, aid to private institutions, and faculty collective bargaining received low priority ratings.

In a five-year period from 1975 to 1980 the Management Division of the Academy for Educational Development conducted studies in six states as directed by state legislatures or in one instance as instigated by a governor. Four of these studies involved extensive inquiry. As a result of these studies, the academy acquired its own sense of the perspectives of state government leaders, and especially of state legislators, on the problems of higher education. The problems noted here are somewhat different from the concerns expressed in the survey made by the Education Commission of the States. Yet the differences tend to be more ones of classification and discussion than of substance.

The principal problems confronting state government leaders as they looked at higher education in the decade of the 1980s appeared to be:

1. Planning for enrollment decline.
2. Program quality and coordination.
3. Relations to private institutions.
4. Financing higher education, including student aid.
5. Vocational-technical education in relation to postsecondary education.
6. State government administrative organization for higher education policy formulation and accountability.

The problem of administrative organization for policy formulation and accountability will be considered by governors and legislative leaders in the context of how the other problems are approached and resolved. If there is general satisfaction among state government officials with the approach of state higher education to the other five of the issues outlined above, then there will be little disposition within a state government to alter the existing state administrative machinery, whatever its current arrangement. But if there is general dissatisfaction with the approach of the existing state higher education establishment to these critical substantive issues, then there will be a disposition to believe that tinkering with the administrative organization will improve the handling of these troublesome concerns.

Unfortunately, there is also another disposition to alter administrative arrangements that operates in the American political system. When one governor succeeds another, and especially when the new governor is of a different party, there is a likelihood that the new governor will want organizational change. In recent years, in several states, successful business executives have been elected governor because of their claim that they would introduce "business methods" into the conduct of state government. Such "business" governors may be particularly disposed to want organizational change in higher education because they are likely to look upon institutional autonomy as the enemy of an orderly, coordinated, and accountable operation.

An extensive and often bitter controversy about the organization of higher education in Alabama during the period of Forrest James' governorship (1979 to 1983) illustrated this concern. Governor James pushed the Alabama Commission on Higher Education toward a more vigorous role in coordination of programs and off-campus instruction. When he encountered opposition from the state universities to these efforts, he advocated first a statewide governing board for all of higher education in the state and then a greatly strengthened coordinating board. Neither recommendation was adopted by the state legislature, but the conflict scarcely advanced the cause of higher education in the state. Disagreements between governors and/or state legislatures and the higher education establishment bring about proposals for organizational change. Such change may or may not be desirable, but proposals for change are bound to emerge when the higher education establishment fails to be responsive to various substantive concerns.

Planning for Enrollment Decline

State government officials as of 1982 were not persuaded that higher education officials had planned adequately for the enrollment decline widely predicted to occur in the 1980s and 1990s. A recent and much-quoted forecast of trouble ahead was that prepared by Breneman (1982). Breneman pointed out that the number of eighteen-year-olds in the population doubled between 1950 and 1980, with a 45-percent increase occurring in the 1960s and a 13-percent increase occurring in the 1970s. The number of these eighteen-year-olds would decline 18 percent between 1979 and 1986, 26 percent between 1979 and 1991, and would still be 22 percent below the 1979 level as of 1995. The percentage decline varied substantially by region. The decline in the number of eighteen-year-olds would be 40 percent by 1994 in the Northeast region of the United States, 32 percent by 1994 in the North Central region, 13 percent by 1991 in the Southeast and South Central, and 16 percent by 1991 in the Western region. Breneman also provided data on the number of eighteen-year-olds state by state as projected by the Western Interstate Commission for Higher Education.

To be sure, higher education enrollments may not parallel the decline in the number of eighteen-year-olds in the population. The proportion of eighteen-year-olds who graduate from high school may increase, and the proportion of high school graduates who enroll in higher education may go up. Both proportions increased dramatically during the 1960s, thus adding to higher education enrollments. (But both proportions also tended to stabilize in the 1970s.) Student aid programs might encourage more students from low-income and middle-income families to continue their schooling. Once enrolled in college, more students might actually obtain a bachelor's degree. More older persons might enroll; such enrollment increased notably in the 1970s. At the same time, higher standards of access to higher education and reduced student financial aid might lower enrollment. If governors and legislators were confused about enrollment prospects and desirable enrollment policies, they had much company in the higher education establishment.

As of the autumn of 1982 public higher education enroll-ments were still greater than in 1981; in fact, they were at the peak level in the history of higher education. Yet even so, there were individual state universities that had experienced enrollment loss in the 1970s. Residential state universities in several states of this study experienced enrollment loss in that decade. In contrast, community colleges, technical colleges, and urban universities tended generally to grow in enrollment. For the nation as a whole, enrollment declines in public institutions had not occurred as of 1982.

Institutional officials were reluctant to develop, and espe-cially to announce, contingency plans for enrollment decline. This reluctance had many sources. State college and university officials were likely to believe that enrollment loss might occur elsewhere but not at their particular institutions. Planning for en-rollment decline was feared as a disruptive influence for current activities. Such planning was likely to undermine faculty morale and to discourage both current and prospective students, and it might also encourage faculty collective bargaining. Such planning might become a self-fulfilling prophecy, and it might overstate or understate actual experience. Finally, some institutional officials preferred to cope with disaster when it happened.

State boards of higher education were reluctant to push contingency planning for enrollment decline because such plan-ning tended to alienate institutional executives. Having as they did a reluctance to undertake contingency planning at the institu-tional level, these executives were not appreciative of such plan-ning at the state government level. Ohio provided an instructive illustration. Making use of an extensive historical data base county by county and employing a sophisticated enrollment model, the Ohio Board of Regents projected prospective enrollment trends for twelve state universities and sixty-two two-year campuses institu-tion by institution in preparing its 1982 master plan. Not surpris-ingly, the individual projections were almost uniformly rejected by institutional executives. As a result, the published master plan

simply called attention to the prospective decline in the number of
eighteen-year-olds and then suggested the possible demographic
impact on undergraduate enrollments at three types of institutions: the urban university, the residential university, and the
residential-commuter university. For the two-year campuses, the
board contented itself with simply publishing the service patterns
as they existed in 1980.

      State government officials had heard so much about enroll-
ment decline that they came to expect such a decline to occur.
They observed that decline had occurred in some institutions, and
they noted in other instances that the total enrollment growth projected in the 1960s did not actually take place. There were situations in several states where institutional capacity was built for
enrollments that did not materialize. Since increases in appropriations had often been provided on the basis of enrollment increases,
the expectation was created that enrollment losses would then
bring about decreases in appropriations.

      Apart from the possibility of appropriation reductions, the
prospect of enrollment decline in public institutions of higher education raised certain related issues. Should some public institutions be closed or merged? How small should a college or university become before it should be considered ready for merger or
closing? Should maximum enrollment limits be placed on some
state universities in order to distribute enrollments more evenly
among other state universities? Was it desirable to limit the
enrollment of urban and commuter universities in the interest of
residential universities that were more costly for students to attend?
None of these questions was easy to answer, especially when there
was considerable competition and rivalry among state universities
for enrollment and funding and when local communities opposed
both mergers and closings. All these issues had been vigorously
debated in several states of this study.

      The final report of the Carnegie Commission on Higher
Education in 1973 dared to fix maximum and minimum enrollment sizes for various types of institutions. The report stated: "We
have been concerned that some campuses are too small to have a
well-rounded academic program for their students and that others
are too large to have a sense of cohesion and an effective gover-

nance, particularly at the departmental level, with faculty and student concerns too fractionated" (1973c, p. 30). The minimum desirable full-time equivalent enrollment for a university that granted doctoral degrees was set at 5,000 students and the maximum at 20,000. The minimum desirable size for a comprehensive university was set at 5,000 students and the maximum at 10,000. The minimum enrollment size for a community college was set at 2,000 students and the maximum at 5,000.

In its various reports between 1973 and 1980, the Carnegie Council did not return to the subject of appropriate enrollment size. Rather, it advocated that the student market should determine enrollment, although the possibility of mergers and closings was mentioned as one consequence of reduced student interest in enrollment on a particular campus. The point at which enrollment should be considered as too small for effective operation was not specified.

The experience of the 1970s in several states clearly indicated that mergers and closings of public institutions would not be simple to bring about. Among the twenty-five states reviewed in this study, at least seven had considered proposals for closing or merging public institutions. One notable accomplishment was in Minnesota, where five community colleges were merged insofar as their administration and support programs were concerned. Legislators were reluctant to approve closings or mergers because of local opposition to the loss of a college or university. The black community in some states insisted that predominantly black institutions should be retained regardless of enrollment size. Three states in this study had attempted to restrict the enrollment size of certain universities, but the effort had not been notably successful. The approach to the problem in Colorado will be noted later in this discussion.

In the 1981 survey sponsored by the Education Commission of the States, seven out of ten policy leaders thought enrollment levels would be an issue in their states. State colleges and some comprehensive universities were expected to decline in enrollment, while the major state universities or flagship universities were expected to remain fairly stable in enrollment. The enrollment of all independent institutions was expected to fall.

The respondents expecting enrollment declines were located primarily in the Northeast and Midwest. Seventy percent of the respondents also expected mergers and closings to become an important issue as a possible response to enrollment decline. Some 75 percent of those responding expressed a preference for cooperation among institutions over mergers or closings. Efforts at merging two state universities in Montana were defeated in the legislature. One merger did occur in Massachusetts, and merger efforts were pending in two other states at the end of 1982.

While there appeared to be general concern about planning for enrollment decline at the state government level, there was also a general reluctance on the part of state boards and of state government leaders to push the matter unless a crisis actually developed. There was a disposition to let student preferences determine enrollment size and to worry about small size only when the continued operation of the institution required special appropriations above the enrollment entitlement, as was occurring in at least five states of this study. It seemed likely that before the end of the 1980s even larger appropriation support per student would be needed in several states in order to sustain the operation of some two-year colleges, some state colleges, and some state universities.

Program Quality and Coordination

Probably no set of issues was expected to be more complicated than that having to do with program quality and program coordination. From the point of view of state political leaders, there were in reality two somewhat different concerns here. One had to do with access to higher education and the quality of degree programs, the other with program duplication and competition over programs among state universities. The caution with which state boards of higher education approached these matters tended to arouse skepticism about their credibility. In fact, the caution seemed easily justified in terms of the conflicting interests and pressures involved.

Access. An early objective of state higher education planning in the late 1950s and throughout the 1960s was to provide an opportunity for every high school graduate to enroll in a college or university. There were three characteristics of this planning. The first characteristic was to locate community colleges or other two-year institutions within commuting distance of most of the population of a state and, at the same time, to locate state universities in the major urban areas of a state. By means of geographical proximity and low-cost tuition, the access of high school graduates to higher education was to be greatly expanded. This kind of planning was evident in all the larger states of this study.

The second characteristic of state planning was to provide access to public higher education on the basis of "open admissions." Access was to be available to every high school graduate, regardless of high school grades and regardless of scores on any tests of academic aptitude or achievement. Moreover, older individuals who had not obtained a high school diploma before entering the labor market could take an equivalency examination and thus obtain admission to higher education. In other words, there were to be no academic barriers to access to public higher education.

A third characteristic of state planning was the inauguration of state programs of student financial assistance to help eliminate the economic barriers to a higher education. The federal government had begun a vast student assistance program with the so-called GI Bill of 1944. A student loan program was authorized by the National Defense Education Act of 1958, and a student grant program was authorized by the Higher Education Act of 1965 — a program that was greatly extended by the Education Amendments of 1972. Public institutions, especially the residential institutions, had always provided part-time employment to students as a means of financial assistance. Under the influence of the 1958 federal law, states began to administer student loan programs with federal guarantees. In the 1960s, several states began to organize student grant programs for low-income students. This movement was recognized and encouraged by the Education Amendments of 1972, which authorized, among other programs, federal grants to state governments for student financial assistance. The most extensive student aid programs among the states in this study were the programs in New York and Illinois, but by 1980 there were student aid programs of some kind authorized in all but two of the twenty-five states of this study.

State planning and action to reduce the geographical, academic, and financial obstacles to higher education enrollment were generally successful. Facilities were provided in the 1960s and early 1970s that made it possible for every high school graduate who wanted to enroll in higher education to do so. In almost every state it was possible to say that no high school graduate had been prevented from enrolling somewhere in the state system because there was no place for him or her. This expansion of access led to a substantial increase in the proportion of college-age youth who enrolled in higher education. This was a major accomplishment of state planning for higher education.

To a large extent the so-called open-door policy in higher education was realized through community colleges, other two-year campuses, and urban universities. Some of the state teacher's colleges that became comprehensive state colleges or universities in the 1950s and 1960s also became open-door institutions. Some of the 1862 land-grant state universities practiced open admission, and in a few instances so did the flagship state universities. California in 1960 became the only state to establish by statute a tiered system of access to higher education. In general, high school graduates in the top 12.5 percent of their class had access to one of the eight campuses of the University of California that admitted students to the first year of study. The California State University System, which was eventually to have nineteen campuses, was required to admit high school graduates in the upper third of their high school class. The community college system was the open-door institution. No other state enacted so definitive a scheme of access, although a somewhat similar arrangement emerged in Texas.

The whole matter of access became a subject of increasing state government concern during the 1970s. There were many reasons for this concern. One reason was the accusation that open access had lowered the standards of expected student performance and had even led to grade inflation. Concern was voiced about the loss of quality standards in student performance. A second reason was the discovery that high school standards of student performance left many students inadequately prepared for higher education. State governments were suddenly confronted with requests for appropriation support for remedial or developmental services to students. A third reason had a racial aspect. Large numbers of black students, it was discovered, were enrolled in the open-door public institutions, and particularly in community colleges. The state universities that practiced selective admission were charged with racial discrimination, especially if they used test scores as a major factor in admission decisions.

State boards of higher education and public institutions found themselves in a difficult situation, and state government leaders expected them to resolve the controversy. In some states new attention was given to the standards of high school preparation for higher education. In 1981 the state higher education executive officers met with the chief state school officers to discuss their mutual concern with standards of secondary schooling. This joint meeting was the first of its kind. State universities began to demand that a prescribed set of high school courses should be expected of any high school graduate seeking admission.

Access to graduate education and to professional schools (such as those in law, medicine, dentistry, optometry, and veterinary medicine) was almost entirely on a selective basis. But here again state universities and state boards of higher education had to worry about access for blacks and certain other minority groups. The Bakke case involved access to the medical school of the University of California at Davis. The Supreme Court in its divided decision appeared to reject quotas for racial or ethnic groups but to approve special consideration of racial and ethnic background in admission to graduate and professional programs.

Higher education in general, and state higher education in particular, were caught in a complicated dilemma in the 1980s. Open access to higher education was perceived as having reduced standards of quality in student performance and so to have reduced the quality of service to the public rendered by college graduates. Selective admission was seen as having reduced access to higher education for blacks, Hispanics, American Indians, and other groups. Open admission was recognized as requiring increased funds to provide remedial service to students. Special access to instructional programs for racial or ethnic groups also was seen as requiring increased expenditures. Governors and legislators were reluctant about having to meet these costs.

Moreover, as state government revenues declined and federal government student assistance programs were cut back, public institutions of higher education had to begin raising tuition fees. Economic barriers to higher education would continue to rise unless state governments or state institutions of higher education somehow could find the money for increased student financial assistance. State higher education planning was supposed to find solutions to the problems of access in the decade of the 1980s.

Institutional Mission. The large number of public institutions of higher education in each state raised the inevitable question of duplication in their programs. This question had become particularly troublesome in the years since the end of World War II for two primary reasons: (1) the transformation of limited purpose institutions into multiple-purpose institutions and (2) the insistence of faculty members and even of institutional executives on the expansion of graduate education and research activity. These two factors led to the belief in almost all states that there was widespread duplication of programs among the public institutions of higher education.

We have noted earlier the general outlines of the transformations that took place in public higher education after 1945. The junior college that was originally conceived as a lower-division general education institution became a community college in which the college-transfer program was but one of several endeavors. The community college expanded into technical education and into public service. In some states such as Indiana, Ohio, and Pennsylvania university branches were established to provide the college-transfer program. Then area vocational schools expanded into postsecondary education; from many of these schools emerged two-year technical colleges. Other vocational schools continued to offer postsecondary education.

Another transformation was that of state teacher's colleges into state colleges or state universities. This transformation involved the expansion of undergraduate programs to include majors in the arts and sciences, business administration, and fine and applied arts (music, art, drama), and in other fields such as agribusiness, industrial technology, computer science, nursing, and health sciences. The transformation from state college to state university also meant an expansion into graduate education and research.

Yet another transformation was that of the separate colleges of agriculture and mechanical arts (in twenty states) into full-fledged state universities to rival (or compete with) the so-called original or flagship state university. In some states such as Indiana this transformation was well under way before 1950; in all states it was fully achieved during the 1950s and 1960s.

Still another transformation was that of municipal universities into state universities, and even the transformation of some private universities (New York, Pennsylvania, Ohio, Kansas, Missouri, and Texas) into state universities. One change of this kind occurred when the City University of New York became a state university in 1980. City governments found themselves unable to finance universities, and some private universities with an urban orientation found themselves without the endowment of other support to function in an educational climate of rising costs. In other instances, as in Florida and Ohio, private colleges were merged into public universities.

Apart from these transformations and at the same time inherent in the changes was the expansion of graduate education and research. As a consequence of World War II, university research took on a new importance to the national welfare and to economic advancement. Achievements in research meant the likelihood that individual scholars would receive federal research grants that would be advantageous to the faculty member and a matter of prestige for the university. Moreover, achievement in research resulted in publication, which in turn advanced recognition of a scholar in his or her discipline and brought academic advancement as well as salary increases. Research endeavor was encouraged by programs for the doctoral degree that tended to emphasize research activity. In turn, the recognized research scholar and the would-be research scholar wanted to participate in graduate education at the doctoral level since such graduate education tended to assist their own research expectations.

Federal research grants encouraged state universities to expand graduate education.

Graduate education was further encouraged by the rapid expansion of higher education faculties in the late 1950s and throughout the 1960s. It became apparent by the mid-1950s that there was a shortage of persons with the Ph.D. degree to staff the expanding and new colleges and universities in the United States. One choice in this circumstance was to increase the number of graduate students in the universities with long-established records in graduate education at the doctoral level. Another choice was to increase the number of state universities awarding the Ph.D. degree. This second choice was made in many states because of pressure from faculty members seeking the recognition associated with graduate education at the doctoral level and because expansion of graduate education in only a few universities seemed unlikely to meet the need for new faculty members. With public institutions accommodating 80 percent of the enrollment growth between 1955 and 1975, the need for educated scholar-researchers and scholar-teachers was especially evident to state higher education planners and to public institutional executives.

Another pressure for expanded graduate education was geographical in nature. States without a major or leading research university felt that they were put at a disadvantage in their economic development. Research was widely perceived as instrumental in the development of new industries and new production processes, and all states desired to participate in such research. The National Science Foundation announced a science development program in 1965 to provide institutional grants to those universities not then ranked in the top tier of leading research universities. Of thirty-one recipients of these grants, nineteen were state universities in sixteen different and widely dispersed states. In addition, governmental research laboratories and high-technology industries urged universities in their vicinity to offer graduate education on a part-time basis to their professional staff in order to upgrade their research competence. The availability of doctoral education in a community was important to the recruitment and rentention of staff, and it was also a crucial factor in many location decisions made by the top executives of industry.

These geographical considerations helped stimulate an expansion of graduate education and research by state universities.

By the early 1970s it was evident that the supply of doctoral degree recipients would soon exceed the demand except in a very few fields. This oversupply was readily apparent by the end of the 1970s. A question then arose about the need for all the existing doctoral programs. Since these programs were the most expensive of all instructional programs, with the exception of medical education, and since they were used to justify enlarged appropriations to state universities, state government officials and state legislatures began to ask why doctoral programs should not be eliminated at many public universities.

All these circumstances led to a criticism of state universities on the grounds that their programs tended to be duplicative of one another, that all state universities wanted to be major research universities, that the social need for many programs no longer existed, and that the costs of institutional aspirations exceeded the reasonable resources a state government should be expected to devote to the support of public higher education.

The first step in a planned effort to rationalize the program scope of various public institutions of higher education was to define differential missions or prescribed purposes for the various state-supported institutions. In some instances this effort was referred to as fixing a particular role and scope for each public university. This subject of institutional mission is so important that we shall address it further in a subsequent chapter.

Here it is essential to underline the concern of state government officials with what they saw at the end of the 1970s as widespread duplication of programs, primarily at the graduate level and in particular at the Ph.D. level. The mass communication media were likely to recount stories of doctoral degree recipients who were taxicab drivers, or bricklayers, or factory workers, or even unemployed. National professional associations, particularly in the humanities and social sciences, drew attention to the plight of young scholars unable to obtain appropriate faculty employment. Given these conditions, state government officials began to call upon state boards of higher education to reduce graduate programs and to redefine institutional missions. And, at the same time, these boards were called upon to reduce the appropriation expectations of state universities. The state boards were thus caught in another squeeze between institutional aspirations and state government expectations.

Off-Campus Programs. Striking evidence of program duplication was provided in instances where two or more state universities had undertaken off-campus instruction in the same city. On occasion there might be justification for this circumstance; for example, the universities might offer quite different programs. Off-campus instruction was offered under various conditions. In some instances a community college might invite a state university to use the college's facilities to offer upper-division courses. In other instances a state university might rent facilities in office buildings in order to provide courses. Sometimes high school facilities or even business facilities were used for off-campus instruction.

More recently a new concern arose when out-of-state institutions, both public and private, undertook to offer courses in various cities or at military installations. This kind of activity appeared as an affront to in-state colleges and universities competent to offer the same courses. Some state universities were much more aggressive than others in seeking to extend their off-campus outreach.

Much off-campus instruction resulted from requests from employers. Public school administrators were often eager to have courses offered for the benefit of their teachers. Employers in business and industry were likewise eager to have courses offered to their employees in order to upgrade their competencies in various lines of work, from computer science to marketing management to electrical or mechanical engineering. Sometimes the request for local instruction came from groups of schoolteachers or employees who were seeking increased salaries or better positions. Unless there was a state university or private college or university in every middle-sized city in a state, there was no way for universities to respond to these pressures except by offering off-campus instruction.

State governments came to have two somewhat different concerns about off-campus programs. One concern was with the quality of these programs, the other with their cost to state governments. Most off-campus instruction made use of facilities that were not always suitable for classroom purposes. Often no special library facility and instructional equipment were available. The faculty employed for off-campus instruction was usually made up of part-time professional individuals who taught as an avocation or as a means for additional income. Such faculty members might or might not be competent and interested instructors. Support services such as student counseling were often not available to part-time students enrolled in off-campus instruction. All these aspects of off-campus programs added up to questionable quality in the provision of courses for the award of a degree.

At the same time, off-campus instruction was often less expensive than on-campus instruction. The faculty was often not paid at the same rate as on-campus faculty. The facilities might be less expensive, and, as noted, support services might be lacking. Some state universities were in fact known to undertake off-campus instruction as a means of obtaining additional income to meet on-campus costs. Some state universities engaged in off-campus instruction in order to provide additional salary to their on-campus faculty members.

Because of the cost situation, some state governments took the position that they would not appropriate any funds in support of off-campus instruction. These state governments declared that off-campus courses must be self-supporting; that is, student charges must meet all direct costs, including any cost of facility rentals. There were at least four states in this study that had taken such a position. Other state governments such as those in Alabama and Mississippi were willing to make appropriations for off-campus instruction but at a lesser cost per student credit hour than for on-campus instruction. In these circumstances the state government necessarily had to take some interest in the way in which off-campus instruction was organized and conducted. Because of the proliferation of off-campus courses, several state legislatures — for example, in Alabama, California, Colorado, Ohio, Texas, and Washington — had broadened the authority of their state boards of higher education to approve off-campus courses. In Alabama by the summer of 1982 a 50-percent reduction had been achieved in off-campus course offerings on the grounds of their low quality and duplication.

The competition among some state universities for off-campus enrollment might show itself in several ways: in price competition per credit hour charged to the student, in credit hours awarded for particular courses, in modification of course or other requirements for award of a degree, and in the recognition of experience as an equivalent for some course requirements. This kind of competition did little to enhance the reputation of a state university for integrity or quality. Such competition was reduced in states such as Florida, Mississippi, and Ohio by a geographical restriction on areas to be served. In some states the boards of higher education had also been given authority to license out-of-state institutions to offer off-campus courses. Such authority existed in Colorado, Ohio, and Texas.

The conduct of off-campus instruction by state universities sometimes led to "horror" stories that reached the ears of state legislators. Complaints were made about instructors who failed to meet some classes, who were poorly prepared, and who took little or no interest in student performance. Other complaints were voiced about instructional facilities and course credits. Some students felt that they were charged for more than they received. These criticisms led legislators to question the conduct of off-campus courses and to insist that state boards of higher education assert some kind of quality control over such courses.

Program Review. A major aspect of program coordination emerged in the late 1970s in terms of both institutional and state-level review of instructional programs. At the state government level some controversy developed over both the desirability and the criteria for program review. It is important, however, to distinguish between state-level review by a statewide governing board and state-level review by a state coordinating board. In the case of a statewide governing board, review and evaluation of the program offerings of various campuses are surely appropriate functions. In the case of such review and evaluation by a state coordinating board, some understanding of the criteria employed in the review process is needed.

It has not been a simple matter for either kind of board to

develop and articulate specific criteria for the review of instructional programs. There has been a good deal of controversy about the use of the criterion of quality. The New York Board of Regents, which is a state advisory board for the State University of New York and the City University of New York, tended to make the quality of graduate programs at the Ph.D. level its principal criterion in the evaluation of such programs. Quality was assessed by peer-review panels drawn from the leading research universities, public and private. Inevitably such quality review leaned toward emphasis on competence in scholarly research and gave scant attention to criteria of geographical service and local employment needs. The State University of New York insisted that the quality of Ph.D. programs should be judged by the governing board, rather than the coordinating board, on the basis of regional accreditation and its own internal review procedures. Eventually, however, the authority of the New York Board of Regents to order the deregistration of instructional programs was upheld by the highest court of the state.

A report to the Ohio Board of Regents by a private consulting firm in 1979 proposed criteria for the review of instructional programs by individual institutions different from those appropriate to the review of instructional programs by the state coordinating board. The report recommended that institutional assessment of instructional programs be based upon program objectives, student enrollment, instructional priorities, the quality of learning accomplished, the placement of degree recipients, and program efficiency in terms of costs per student and costs per degree awarded. At the state level the report recommended that program assessment employ the criteria of statewide needs in relation to professional requirements, statewide and local employment needs, geographical access to needed programs, program costs, and institutional mission.

In 1982 the Ohio Board of Regents was uncertain about its competence to review and evaluate existing instructional programs, although the original statute establishing the board in 1963 had specified its right to review such programs and had given it authority to recommend discontinuance of a program to an institutional governing board. The board did have full power to approve new degree programs. The board decided not to approve any new degree programs unless the requesting institution demonstrated that it had in place an effective program review process and had established program priorities. Such a position was deemed necessary in light of the appropriation recessions that had occurred in the fiscal years 1982 and 1983.

In Texas, the coordinating board found it essential to approve individual courses added by individual campuses because the board was receiving requests for the approval of new degree programs with the statement that all the courses needed to award the proposed degree had been created. The institutions had discovered that the way to circumvent the authority of the coordinating board was to put in place all the necessary courses and then to dare the board to deny approval of the program. There was considerable complaint in Texas that the board had invaded the governance role of various multicampus systems and institutions. However, the board felt that if its authority to approve new degree programs was to be meaningful, it had to exercise some approval of the courses that would lead to creation of such programs.

In the state of Washington, the Council on Postsecondary Education had authority to review academic programs and to advise that "low-producing" graduate programs be terminated. Low-producing programs were defined as master's degree programs where there were fewer than three degrees awarded each year and as doctoral degree programs where there were fewer than two degrees awarded each year. In 1973 the council voted to recommend termination of forty-eight graduate programs and to approve the continuation of thirty-five others on a two-year basis. Further reviews were conducted after 1973, and by 1977 still other programs were recommended for closing. The actions of the council became recommendations to the governor and the legislature. Since 1977 the biennial appropriation bills have provided that no state university may operate a graduate program that has not been approved by the council.

The board of regents in both Florida and Kansas is a statewide governing board for all senior public institutions, but the record of the two boards has been quite different in the field of program review. In Kansas the board established some very definite standards of low productivity on the basis of which master's degree and doctoral degree programs would be terminated. In Florida the board undertook program review without first establishing definite criteria for identifying unsatisfactory graduate programs, with the result that the effort generated considerable controversy but almost no action. It should be emphasized again that the authority and responsibility of a statewide governing board for program review are quite different from those of a coordinating or advisory board.

By 1982 there appeared to be general agreement that the state government interest in program review was essentially twofold: an interest in professional employment needs and an interest in costs. It was inevitable that high-cost programs such as medical education, other health science instructional programs, and graduate education at the doctoral level should come under particular scrutiny. Not only were these instructional programs expensive to operate, but there was some evidence that more professionals were being educated than were needed. Of course, institutions and the geographical areas they served were bound to resist the curtailment of instructional programs useful to individual career aspirations and to local employers.

Program review had become a statewide concern of substantial proportions by 1982. But the criteria to be employed in program assessment, as well as the process of evaluation to be used, were matters by no means easy to resolve. Program review will remain troublesome in higher education throughout the 1980s and into the 1990s.

Program Articulation. Since state systems of higher education included two-year (associate degree) institutions and four-year (baccalaureate) institutions, it was inevitable that the problem of transfer, or articulation, should arise. In the two-year institution, apart from one-year certificate programs, the curriculum usually consisted of a college-transfer program and of one or more technical education programs. The college-transfer program presupposed that upon completion of two years of study the student would want to transfer course credits to a four-year institution and pursue a bachelor's degree program. The student who completed a two-year technical education program might also wish, sooner or later, to undertake a bachelor's degree program.

The complication in this arrangement was that faculties tended to set their own course requirements for award of the bachelor's degree. The courses completed by the transfer student in a two-year institution might or might not meet the four-year institution's requirements. It was not uncommon for the student who completed a two-year transfer program to find that he or she had to take three years in a senior institution in order to fulfill the requirements for a bachelor's degree. This circumstance led to criticism of both two- and four-year institutions within a state. In turn, this criticism led to demands for better articulation between the two kinds of institutions.

One solution in some states, such as Florida and Texas, was to create so-called upper-division universities that automatically gave a transfer student third-year class standing upon admission. In addition, in Florida limits were placed on freshman enrollments by the older universities. The upper-division universities, however, were not entirely successful in achieving their purpose. In Florida the four upper-division universities in 1980 proposed to add lower divisions; although this change was not approved by the state legislature except for one institution, there remained some pressure for the different arrangement. In Texas the coordinating board was given authority to establish a "core curriculum" in the junior colleges that would be freely transferable to senior public institutions.

Most states found it necessary to work out articulation plans or agreements between their two-year institutions and their four-year institutions. Furthermore, such plans or agreements required a certain amount of policing to make sure that they were honored in practice. Four-year institutions complained that transfer students were not taught as much or as well as their own freshman and sophomore students. They complained that transfer students were not prepared to meet upper-division course standards. Articulation plans then endeavored to fix standards for transfer student instruction in the two-year institutions, tried to facilitate the movement of students between institutions, and provided certain student support services to the transfer student.

Articulation became a program coordination need at the level of state government in almost all the states in this study.

Vocational-Technical Education. Governors and legislators are necessarily interested in jobs. Apart from the impact of economic circumstances upon political fortunes, the condition of the economy in a state determines in large part whether or not the state treasury has a surplus. Unemployment is often attributed not simply to a decline in productive activity but also to a lack of necessary skills on the part of job seekers. And higher education is looked upon as essential to the most highly skilled occupations, that is, the professions. Education and jobs have long had a symbiotic relationship in the American economy and the American polity.

Governors and legislators encountered a complicated organizational issue in attempting to assist and support vocational-technical education in their respective states. The issue had been made complicated by the competitive struggles of educators, who in turn were aided and abetted by the federal government. As early as 1917, at the time of American entry into World War I, Congress passed the Smith-Hughes Act, which gave federal grants to the states to aid in the training of teachers for vocational education below the college level. Federal support of vocational education was extended by a series of laws that culminated in the Vocational Education Act of 1963. By this time, however, the law had come to refer to vocational-technical education without even trying to define the term. This legislation was enacted just as the community college movement was beginning its great forward surge in the United States.

Federal law required that vocational-technical education be administered in a state by a single agency. Amendments to the law in 1968 and 1976 required each state to establish a state planning body that would include representatives from community colleges and other institutions of higher education. By federal law at least 15 percent of federal grants for vocational-technical education had to be allocated to institutions of postsecondary education. Of the twenty-five states examined in this study, there were many different means employed in order to accommodate both the secondary and the postsecondary programs of vocational and technical education.

In twenty-one of the states, the state board of education was designated or in fact served as the state board of vocational education. In Colorado a State Board for Community Colleges and Occupational Education was the state board for vocational education. In Indiana there was a separate State Board of Vocational and Technical Education made up of ex officio members, members representing vocational secondary schools, and members representing Indiana Vocational-Technical College, a unique delivery system with one board of trustees and thirteen campuses that provided both secondary and postsecondary programs. In South Dakota there was a separate board of vocational education. In Washington the Commission for Vocational Education was the state board for vocational education. This commission prepared the required plan and distributed the federal funds among the twenty-seven community colleges and vocational-technical institutes supervised by the state board of education.

In the states where the state board of education was the board for vocational education, different methods were devised to bring about some coordination of activities and some fairness in the distribution of funds. In California a joint Committee on Vocational Education, equally representative of the board of education and Board of Governors of the California Community Colleges, advised the board of education on vocational-technical education matters. In Florida the state board of education was made up of seven elected officials, with the governor as chairman and the commissioner of education (also elected) as secretary. The Department of Education, which reported to the commissioner and through him to the board, had four divisions, one each for elementary-secondary, vocational-technical, community college, and higher education. Some of the community colleges had also been designated as area vocational-technical schools. In Illinois the board of education and the board of higher education had a joint committee for their common interests in vocational-technical education. In Kansas the state board of education had responsibility for community colleges as well as for area vocational-technical schools. In New Hampshire the state board of education was the governing agency for technical institutes. In Montana the 1973 constitution established a board of education of fourteen members that was divided into two parts, namely, a board of regents for higher education and a board of public education for the public school system. The board of education also had three ex officio members: the governor, the superintendent of public instruction, and the commissioner of higher education. The governor voted only in case of a tie when the two boards met as a joint board. The joint board in turn has undertaken to prepare the vocational plan for the state. In Ohio a legal definition had been provided by law to differentiate vocational education (a secondary program) from technical education (a higher education program), but some conflict remained in the distribution of federal funds between the board of education and the board of regents. In Pennsylvania the board of education was divided into two councils, one for basic education and one for higher education. Presumably the state board was in a position to adjust common concerns between the two councils about vocational-technical education.

The linkage of vocational and technical education in federal law created some twenty years of organizational difficulty for state governments. In order to comply with federal laws and regulations, state governments had to find ways to undertake both vocational and technical education under some kind of joint planning and fiscal coordination. The search for the appropriate mechanism eluded most governors and state legislators because of the intense opposition of vocational educators to any arrangement that would restrict their opportunity to be part of both secondary and higher education. State governments as of late 1982 were still trying to achieve some position on vocational-technical education that would satisfy federal bureaucrats, the competing claims of secondary and higher education, and the need for a closer relationship between employer expectations and educational preparation. In our study, this concern appeared to have been addressed with some success in California, Colorado, and Washington. But such "success" required a fairly strong administrative arrangement at the state government level. Interestingly enough, an extensive federal study of vocational education published in 1981 failed to address this basic problem.

Collective Bargaining. Our study found that state governments tended to have an ambivalent attitude toward collective bargaining by state employees. Liberal governors and legislators were inclined to favor unionization and collective bargaining by state employees, although this inclination waned as state government officials, particularly in the Northeast and Midwest, began to wrestle with economic recession and reduced state revenues. More conservative state government leaders were opposed to collective bargaining. Whatever the attitude of state governments, however, state laws on collective bargaining have necessarily applied also to state universities, state colleges, and two-year institutions. No state legislation on collective bargaining has exempted public higher education, and few laws recognize any special status for state universities in collective bargaining.

A major problem in public collective bargaining was the issue of whom to recognize as "management" in the collective bargaining process. The so-called Taylor Law in New York recognized the governor as the "management" of state government, and some other states followed this precedent. When state governments centralized the authority to conduct collective bargaining negotiations with faculties and other groups in higher education, this action necessarily compromised the authority of governing boards. Moreover, as was evident in New York and New Jersey, collective bargaining agreements tended to increase the proportion of the state appropriation devoted to faculty salaries and to decrease institutional expenditures for various support operations, including plant maintenance. It was notable that the Montana Board of Regents of Higher Education was recognized as "management" for faculty collective bargaining, and the Board of Personnel Appeals ruled that faculty collective bargaining should be conducted institution by institution rather than on a system-wide basis.

It is possible that faculty collective bargaining in states with coordinating boards or advisory boards may encourage the establishment of statewide governing boards. Where statewide governing boards already exist, faculty collective bargaining may then be utilized as a mechanism in state government to control faculty work loads, faculty salaries, and faculty personnel practices.

Relations to Private Institutions

As the 1970s came to an end, the future of private or independent colleges and universities looked increasingly uncertain. For well-endowed and prestigious private colleges and universities, of course, the prospects were not too unfavorable, provided that federal research grants were not drastically curtailed and that federal student assistance programs, including federally guaranteed and subsidized student loans, were not seriously cut back. But for other private colleges and universities the prospects were problematical.

State government planning and action during the 1960s had two principal consequences for private higher education. One consequence was the introduction of state universities into many urban areas where private institutions, often under church or YMCA sponsorship, had largely provided the available higher education opportunity. The YMCA institutions had in large part disappeared by the end of the 1970s; some of them became nuclei for new state universities, and others were absorbed into existing state universities or state university systems. In contrast, the church-related universities in urban areas tried to survive in the face of direct geographical competition from state universities. The second consequence of state government policies was that the tuition gap between public and private institutions continued to expand in terms of the dollar amounts involved. This gap tended to encourage students and their families to choose public over private institutions.

State government planning and action during the 1960s intended to create difficulties for private higher education. The objectives of such planning were to expand the opportunity for higher education as widely as possible and to meet the challenges of economic growth. The expansion of geographical access and the continuation of the low-tuition commitment of public higher education were critical means to the realization of these objectives.

As it became evident that the expansion of public higher education, especially in urban areas, was leading to competition with private higher education, some state governments came to the assistance of private colleges and universities. New York State began a program of assistance to private institutions in the 1960s by providing them with subsidies based on the number of degrees they granted. Illinois and Minnesota developed programs of assistance on a contract basis with private institutions. Several states undertook student aid programs that provided greater assistance to students in private institutions than to those in public institutions. Florida authorized a flat grant of $1,000 to every Florida student enrolled in a private Florida institution as a full-time undergraduate; this grant, which was not fully funded by the state legislature, was intended to help bridge the gap between public tuition and private tuition. In some states a subsidy was provided to each private institution for each recipient of student financial assistance enrolled at that institution.

By 1980 only four states out of fifty had still not enacted some program of assistance to private higher education (O'Hara, 1983). Forty-four states had scholarship or grant programs that provided financial assistance to students in both private and public institutions. Sixteen states provided funds for the operating expenses of private institutions, mostly in the field of medical education. Thirteen states provided assistance to private institutions for the construction of facilities, usually through the sale of self-liquidating tax-exempt bonds.

Section 1202 of the Education Amendments of 1972 required state governments to establish planning commissions that would include representatives from the private sector. These commissions were to receive federal grants to assist their planning activity. In most states the existing state board of higher education was designated as the 1202 commission, usually with one or more advisory committees of institutional representatives attached to it. The future of these commissions was made uncertain by the termination of federal support in 1982.

The federal government through its student financial aid programs did much to encourage students to enroll in state-supported institutions. By limiting the amount of aid available to the individual student under veterans' benefits, social security, and basic educational opportunity grants, it encouraged the recipients to enroll in public institutions with their lower tuition. While supplementary grants and state grants did help to give students some choice in deciding where to enroll, these grants often did not equalize the tuition gap between public and private institutions.

Whereas public institutions on the average obtained about 65 percent of their instructional income from state appropriations, private institutions depended upon charges to students for from 75 to 80 percent of their instructional income. With educational costs rising about equally for the public and private institutions, the dollar difference in tuition became greater each year. Only the perception that many private institutions provided a better education than did the public institutions enabled the former to maintain and even increase their enrollment. Federally subsidized student loans helped this enrollment. A decline in the freshman enrollment at private institutions in the autumn of 1982 was blamed upon the curtailment of subsidized loans as well as upon the current economic recession.

Private colleges and universities frequently hurt their own cause because of uncertainties and confusion in their approach to state governments. Some institutional leaders were fearful that governmental financial assistance would impair their efforts to obtain philanthropic support. Some institutional leaders identified their institutional interests only marginally with the states where they were located. Some of them had little if any experience in political action efforts. In the states making up this study, it was evident that private institutions were only gradually perceiving that they had a stake in the way that public higher education was organized and that they were only slowly acquiring some competence in making their political voice heard.

The problem of state government assistance to private higher education arose at a time when most state governments were hard pressed financially to maintain their public institutions. Even though state political leaders might be sympathetically disposed toward the private colleges and universities, they were likely to see their primary responsibility as the support of public colleges and universities. Some leaders might appreciate the argument that private institutions achieved levels of quality and of academic freedom that could serve as standards for public institutions. Other leaders might appreciate the argument that the loss of private institutions would increase public enrollment and the

costs of public higher education. But these arguments were not
sufficient to override the concerns of voters with current tax levels
and current economic circumstances. Somehow state boards of
higher education were expected to assist private colleges and universities without increasing state costs and without depriving
public higher education of essential income.

Funding Worries

Without trying to consider the financing problems of public
higher education in detail, we may nonetheless note the various
monetary concerns of state governments that came out in the
course of our study. First, there was the concern about appropriations for current operations and for renovating and adding to
capital plants. Second, there was the concern about the distribution of funds for current operations among major program categories such as student instruction, research, public service
(including teaching hospitals), and student financial assistance. In
the third place, there was the concern about the equitable distribution of both capital and operating appropriations among the
multiple state-supported institutions. Fourth, there was the concern about how much higher education programs ought to cost in
order to meet state government objectives in higher education and
to fulfill the assigned missions of individual institutions. There was
also the corollary concern about how to contain the cost increases
sought by public institutions of higher education and by the agencies handling student financial assistance. Finally, there was the
concern about how to divide student instructional costs between
charges to the student and subsidy by the state government.

These concerns were matters of great importance, calling
for careful analysis as well as thoughtful judgment. They were not
matters for hasty or ill-considered political judgment. These were
all matters in which state boards of higher education were heavily
involved.

It is a basic proposition of this study that higher education
issues are so vital and so complex that specialized and expert
advice from those who understand the nature and needs of higher

education is indispensable to the chief executive and legislature of a state. It has been suggested by some studies that such specialized and expert assistance is not required except for planning. In large and affluent states, the chief executive and legislature may be blessed with numerous staff assistants, some of whom specialize in higher education affairs. Even where this situation prevails, however, some question may arise as to whether the fiscal experts and policy analysts can in fact resolve the complex set of concerns set forth herein.

Almost all states have decided they need some kind of specialized and expert administrative organization that will give its exclusive attention to the problems of higher education. This organizational arrangement in most states is more than advisory. The preferred kind of organization is one that can seek to resolve some, if not all, the issues presented here. Chief executives and legislators are busy persons. They have concerns other than higher education: public welfare, mental and public health, criminal justice and law enforcement, prison administration, economic development, taxation, and elementary-secondary education, just to mention the more troublesome areas. If some of the issues of higher education can be resolved by administrative action rather than executive and legislative action, the better satisfied will be chief executives and legislators.

➤❙ 4 ❙◀

Types of Administrative

Organization

WHEN A STATE GOVERNMENT
decides to give special or particular administrative attention to
higher education, then the appropriate organizational arrangement for such special attention must be worked out. There is no
need to review the history of various organizational arrangements.
Such a history has been provided by Glenny (1959), Berdahl
(1971), and Millard (1976), among others. It is necessary, however, to emphasize that organizational arrangements are never
static. In recent years, Maine (1968), Utah (1969), North
Carolina (1972), Wisconsin (1973), and Massachusetts (1980)
have drastically altered the state administrative arrangement by
abolishing their coordinating boards and by establishing statewide governing boards. In other states such as Connecticut, the
authority of the coordinating board has been substantially increased.
A reorganization of the Pennsylvania higher education structure
was provided by law in 1982. Recommendations of the governor
for reorganization of the higher education structure were presented to the state legislature in Alabama in both 1981 and 1982
but were not enacted into law. At any rate, no current organizational structure can be considered fixed and immutable.

As of late 1982 all but one of the fifty state governments
had created some kind of administrative agency to provide a focus
for state government concerns with higher education. Only in

Wyoming, which had one state university with a board of trustees and seven community colleges under the supervision of a community college commission, was there no central state administrative agency for higher education. A higher education council established by law in 1965 had not been funded since 1978. All the other state governments had found it necessary or desirable to create some kind of organizational arrangement for supervising higher education and state governmental policy toward it.

It is possible to classify organizational arrangements in different ways. One classification is based upon legal status; that is, whether the organization was created by constitutional, legislative, or executive order. Among the twenty-five states in this study, state constitutions provided the basic framework in four states, statutory enactment established the organizational arrangement in twenty states, and executive order of the governor created the organization in one state. Classification by legal status, however, is not very informative. A more meaningful classification is one based on the type of authority exercised by the organization.

As indicated in Chapter One, in this study we make use of a threefold classification of higher education organizations in terms of the authority vested in them. The three types are: (1) statewide governing board, (2) state coordinating board, and (3) state government advisory board. There are at least three variations upon these types of organization to be found in some states, such as executive departments with vague supervisory roles in relation to the higher education boards, advisory boards in addition to statewide governing boards, and coordinating boards that function as executive departments. Our attention in this study, however, has been concentrated on the three primary types of boards.

Statewide governing boards are multicampus governing boards with statewide authority and responsibility for the governance of all public higher education within the state. But when we use the phrase "all public higher education," an immediate qualification is necessary. Some statewide governing boards have jurisdiction over junior or community colleges as well as over senior colleges. Of the ten statewide governing boards in this study, five of them had authority over all public institutions. In South

Dakota there were no community colleges, and in the other four states the statewide governing board was the governing board for senior institutions only. These states were Florida (nine state universities), Kansas (six state universities and one state technical institute), Mississippi (eight universities and a health science center), and New Hampshire (one university, two state colleges, and a two-year college). These four states had provided for local governing boards for community colleges and the one municipal university (in Topeka, Kansas); in three of these states community college boards were supervised by a state department of education, while in Florida there was a community college coordinating board located in the state department of education.

Statewide governing boards have different designations. Of the ten statewide governing boards in this study, seven were designated as boards of regents and three as boards of trustees. In Georgia the board was referred to as the Board of Regents of the University System of Georgia, in Mississippi as the Board of Trustees of State Institutions of Higher Learning. In Montana the board was the board of regents of higher education; this board, along with the members of the board of public education, comprised the state board of education. Apparently the joint board seldom met except to fulfill certain required functions.

It is not a simple matter to distinguish a coordinating board from an advisory board. As we shall observe later, there are state advisory boards that have begun to have a kind of influence not too different from that of a coordinating board. We have made a distinction between them in this study because such a distinction was made by Berdahl (1971) and because the Carnegie Commission and the Carnegie Council were critical of coordinating boards and sympathetic to advisory boards. For these reasons it is important to observe the actual differences that characterize the two kinds of boards.

Rather than use the term *coordinating board* to refer to all three kinds of state higher education boards, we have defined a coordinating board as one having a particular kind of authority. The coordinating board has no authority of governance over public institutions. It has only the authority to prepare a master plan, to approve degree programs, and to review and recommend the appropriation needs of institutions of higher education. In contrast, the advisory board may prepare a master plan and may review program offerings and budget requests but does not have the authority to approve degree programs or to recommend operating and capital appropriations. If a board has two of these three powers but lacks any role in the appropriation process, it has been classified here as an advisory board.

Both coordinating boards and advisory boards may have some authority over branch campuses, off-campus instruction, and the administration of student financial aid programs. The coordinating board usually has authority to approve the establishment of branch campuses and the initiation of off-campus instruction; the advisory board usually has authority only to review such activities.

The essential difference between a coordinating board and an advisory board is a matter of authority. The coordinating board has authority to take action on degree programs, branch campuses, off-campus instruction, and appropriation requests. The advisory board has authority to review such matters, but its recommendations must be implemented by legislative action. The Carnegie studies disliked the coordinating board because of its authority to act on various matters and favored instead the advisory board because its recommendations required approval by the legislative process. The Carnegie Commission and Carnegie Council were fearful of administrative politics but not of legislative politics.

In terms of their influence with governors and legislative leaders, it is not always an easy matter to distinguish between coordinating boards and advisory boards. In the past four or five years, some of the six advisory boards examined in this study have become quite influential in providing advice about policies and financing—advice that eventually finds its way into provisions of law. In addition, some statewide governing boards act very much like coordinating boards. The two kinds of boards often engage in much the same kind of activity: long-range planning, the approval of new degree programs, and the preparation of appropriation recommendations for consideration by the chief executive and/or the state legislature.

The principal difference between the statewide governing board and the state coordinating board is a matter of legal authority in relation to individual campuses. The statewide governing board has at least three kinds of authority not vested in the state coordinating board. First, the governing board is the governance agency for each campus and as such appoints and evaluates the chief administrative officer of each campus. Second, the governing board can intervene whenever necessary in the internal affairs of any campus; thus, it can approve personnel policies and actions, establish admission standards, approve internal organization, and discontinue any programs. Third, the governing board is concerned with governmental appropriations, as well as with the total operating and capital budgets of each individual campus. These kinds of authority are not conferred upon coordinating boards. Nor is it suggested here that these kinds of authority should be exercised by a coordinating board.

Even though there are similarities of activity, statewide governing boards, coordinating boards, and advisory boards are substantially different from one another. The differences are very important and must not be ignored. Each kind of board has its advantages and disadvantages.

Advantages of Statewide Governing Boards

The ten statewide governing boards examined in this study were founded at various times: 1889 (Montana), 1897 (South Dakota), 1905 (Florida), 1910 (Mississippi), 1913 (Kansas), 1931 (Georgia), 1963 (New Hampshire), 1968 (Maine), 1969 (West Virginia), and 1980 (Massachusetts). There were various motivations involved: small population size of the state, the desire to check gubernatorial political interference, a concern with the need for statewide planning, and economic depression. Four of the ten governing boards were created between 1960 and 1980 in an era when priority was given to state coordination of public institutions of higher education. In New Hampshire two teacher's colleges were merged with the state university to form a consolidated University of New Hampshire; the result was to facilitate program development and expansion at the undergraduate level, particularly at the two former teacher's colleges. In Maine a consolidated university was also established in order to achieve coordination among the principal state university, a comprehensive university, two state teacher's colleges, and two university branches. As of 1982 the university had seven campuses. In West Virginia, in a last-minute political move, plans for a state coordinating board were suddenly changed into legislation for a statewide governing board. In Massachusetts, after sixteen years of unhappy experience with a state coordinating board, the governor and the legislature joined hands to establish a statewide governing board with authority over the state university (three campuses), two comprehensive universities, ten state colleges, and fifteen community colleges.

At different times between 1962 and 1980 the Academy for Educational Development was called upon in all ten states with governing boards to provide advice about various aspects of their higher education operations. In Kansas in 1962 the academy called attention to the need for greater variety in instructional programs and improvements in program quality, for increased emphasis on research at the University of Kansas and at Kansas State University, for incorporation of the University of Wichita into the state system, for expansion of the community college system, and for increased financial support for higher education. In 1966 the academy recommended the creation of a statewide system of higher education and the development of a master plan for public higher education. These recommendations were adopted by the state. In Montana the academy was involved in a study that helped lead to the adoption of the 1973 state constitution. This constitution provided for a board of regents and a board of public education, which together were to comprise a state board of education. In South Dakota in 1974 the academy urged development of a community college system under the jurisdiction of either the board of regents or a separate state governing board. The academy also noted that six state college and university campuses were too many in a state with less than 700,000 population; two or three consolidations were recommended. But neither the legislature nor the board of regents was disposed to carry out these recommendations.

In 1973 the academy made an extensive study of higher education in Massachusetts, but the issue of governing structure was omitted at the direction of the secretary of educational affairs. In Georgia and New Hampshire the academy was asked to assist in the preparation of parts of a master plan; again issues of governance were not involved. In three other studies late in the 1970s, the academy was asked specifically to evaluate the performance of governing boards in Florida, Mississippi, and West Virginia.

Since the new board of regents in Massachusetts became operational only in 1981, it was too early to make any judgment about its eventual success or failure in achieving unity and cohesion in a public system of higher education that encompassed some twenty-seven different campuses. Whether mergers, the retrenchment of program offerings, and the differentiation of missions could be achieved in the state remained to be demonstrated. What had been demonstrated in Massachusetts was the inability of a state coordinating board and a secretary of education to bring about substantial change. The coordinating board and the secretary of education were dependent on legislative action to accomplish the changes desired by the governor and some legislative leaders. The statewide governing board was established with the idea of removing controversial political issues from the legislative arena and putting them into the hands of a governing board. As of the end of 1982 it was uncertain whether or not the legislature would in fact permit the governing board to make decisions that would have an impact upon local loyalties and aspirations.

The primary advantage of the statewide governing board is its authority to govern individual campuses in a state system of higher education that embraces all senior institutions or all senior institutions and all two-year institutions. Such authority is not unlimited, however. The legal powers of a governing board may be altered as they were in Florida in 1979. The legal status of the governing board's chief executive officer may be altered, as it was in South Dakota in 1981. The threat of legislative action may lead to a change in the leadership of the chief executive officer as in Maine and West Virginia. And always there is the threat of change in appropriation procedures and amounts as happened in Florida and South Dakota. As a consequence, the authority of a statewide governing board is not so impressive in fact as it may appear in law.

Presumably a statewide governing board may exercise its governance authority in various ways. It may define the mission, or the role and scope, of each campus within the system with some degree of precision. It may enforce the assigned mission by the discontinuance of some programs and the initiation of new programs where needed. It may fix admission standards for each campus. It may determine charges to students at each campus and allocate state appropriations to each campus in accordance with assigned mission and assigned programs. It may establish the internal organizational structure of each campus. These kinds of authority are extensive indeed. Our study indicates that they are exercised with considerable restraint, and with a cautious eye on the possible political reactions to given decisions.

A second advantage of the statewide governing board is its authority to select and appoint the chief administrative officer of each campus. The power to select and appoint is also the power to evaluate and remove. If a chief administrative officer does not loyally accept and implement the policies and programs of the governing board, there is always the possibility of removing him or her. In addition, the governing board may approve the appointment of the chief administrative officer's principal colleagues in the leadership and management of the campus. The governing board is expected to fix the salary for the chief administrative officer and for his or her principal associates. This authority to appoint, to remove, and to compensate is important for the development of unity and cohesion in a state system of higher education. Yet here again our study found that this authority is exercised infrequently and with some reluctance.

A third advantage of the statewide governing board is its authority to establish the operating budget and the capital improvement budget for each campus. The state appropriation for a residential campus usually amounts to only about 40 percent of its total income. Student fees and charges for room and board, gift and grant income, and other income are substantial additional sources of current operating receipts. The advantage to central approval of campus budgets is that it helps to prevent undesirable

competition among campuses in charges or in the allocation of
expenditures. Moreover, central approval of budgets may bring
about intercampus cooperation in the costs of support programs
and even in the costs of student instruction. A coordinating board
can exhort institutions to cooperate; a central governing board
can direct campuses to cooperate. Yet we have found that
statewide governing boards generally tend to make very limited
use of their authority to approve the operating budgets of individual campuses as a policy-making tool.

There is one other advantage in the statewide governing
board. This kind of organizational arrangement may encourage a
state legislature to appropriate a single lump-sum amount for all
public institutions or for all public senior institutions. In some
instances a statewide governing board may receive lump-sum
appropriations for a small number of line items of expenditure,
such as personal services, plant operation, supplies and equipment, and contract services. Among the ten statewide governing
boards, we found eight that received lump-sum appropriations,
usually in four or five line items. There were usually some additional appropriations for agricultural research, agricultural extension services, and hospital costs of health science centers. Two
statewide governing boards — those in Florida and South Dakota —
found the legislature unwilling to continue making lump-sum
appropriations. In South Dakota in 1981 the legislature specified
the appropriations for each campus by major program categories
and by major objects of expenditure. Obviously, these actions
expressed legislative discontent with previous allocations of
income and an attempt to specify what each campus should spend
from each source of income.

In Georgia, a state with fifty years of experience with a statewide governing board and with a constitutionally prescribed
board of regents, we found substantial maturity and stability in
operation. The public higher education system in Georgia consisted of thirty-three institutions: four institutions that granted
doctoral degrees (including the Medical College of Georgia), ten
comprehensive institutions, two baccalaureate institutions, and
seventeen junior colleges. The state constitution even mandated a
lump-sum appropriation, although some additional specialized

appropriations have developed from law and custom. Because of gubernatorial interference in the early 1930s, the state undertook to "remove higher education from politics," and the commitment to a politically insulated system of public higher education has continued to the present time. Moreover, the quality of individuals who have served on the board of regents has been of a high order. In addition, the board and its executive staff have understood the necessity to work closely with governors and the legislative leadership, responding to their concerns about substantive matters of major importance and resisting any suggestion of political favoritism. Some recently proposed constitutional changes that would have altered the composition and authority of the board of regents were strongly resisted by the state legislature. The budget formula submitted by the board to the governor and legislature consisted of about fifteen lines; the only arguments likely to arise concerned average faculty salaries and the inflation factor for nonpersonal services.

A long history of interinstitutional rivalry in Montana culminated in the ratification of a new state constitution in 1972, which provided for a powerful board of regents and for a commissioner of higher education. In succeeding years the board of regents had to resist several legislative attempts to weaken its powers; a state supreme court decision in 1975 affirmed the constitutional authority and autonomy of the board. Further attempts at legislative intervention in higher education have also been resisted. The board of regents developed a plan for continuing program review of all instructional programs, introduced a comprehensive information system and a uniform accounting procedure, and undertook various master plan studies (on such subjects as institutional missions, access to higher education, continuing education activities, and the desirability of a common calendar). In 1976 the board of regents directed that a cooperative instructional arrangement between the University of Montana and Western Montana College be adopted. In 1979 the board drafted a far-reaching statement on the role and scope of each campus in the university system. Duplication of programs was largely ended at that time. An outsider can only conclude that the 1972 promise of the Montana Board of Regents had been largely realized by 1982.

With the advent of a new executive director in 1982, the Kansas Board of Regents indicated that reductions in state funds for higher education would not thereafter be made on an across-the-board basis but on the basis of program priorities. In addition, the board adopted a procedure for periodic evaluation of presidential performance and established a process of systematic review of all institutional programs on a five-year cycle.

We cite these particular examples because they appear to give concrete evidence of what can be accomplished by a state-wide governing board. We would mention also the remarkable improvements in the university system of Maine under the second chancellor, who was appointed in 1975, and the promise of note-worthy improvement in the West Virginia system under the third chancellor, appointed in 1980.

Disadvantages of Statewide Governing Boards

Our review of the experience of ten statewide governing boards and the earlier studies of the Academy for Educational Development in three states have indicated several disadvantages in the organizational arrangement for such a board from the point of view of state government. The disadvantages are apparent in four general areas of operation.

First, the expectations of state chief executives and legis-latures have not always been fulfilled by the establishment of a statewide governing board. If the expectations had to do with the removal of higher education from blatant political interference, they seem to have been satisfied in Georgia and Mississippi. If the objective was to introduce a new element of central authority into the operation of individual campuses, as seems to have been the expectation in the other eight states, there have been disappoint-ments from the point of view of state officials. Governors and legis-lators have complained that the central board became a spokes-man, and even a "cheerleader," for the institutions rather than for the state government. These state officials further asserted that the central board tended to impose only limited restrictions upon presidents and faculties in their drive for new instructional pro-grams, higher salaries, and reduced instructional work loads. In two or three states we encountered complaints that the central board had protected the flagship status of the older, better established state university and had not given proper encouragement to the development of new state universities located in major urban areas. In other instances, especially in two states with small populations, we found criticism that the central board had not moved to merge or close small and inefficient campuses. In other words, we found that a statewide governing board was no magic solution for handling the complicated problems of state policy and practice in the field of higher education.

The second disadvantage of the statewide governing board was closely related to this first criticism; that is, the board remained ed vulnerable to political influence and pressures. Just as legislatures have found it difficult to make firm decisions about the issues confronting institutions of higher education — issues involving size and geographical location, selective versus open access, response to community aspirations, and costs — so do statewide governing boards find such decisions difficult. Boards find these choices difficult because they must still depend upon state legislatures for appropriations and for goodwill. Statewide governing boards cannot separate themselves from the interests and concerns of state legislatures. When these boards undertake to make difficult choices, they run the risk of alienating influential legislators, and that loss of support can and does translate itself into legislative intervention. We encountered such action in at least half of our ten states.

We found the university system in Georgia to exemplify the necessity for a close working relationship between state government officials and the statewide governing board. When state officials complained about the inadequacy of the appropriation and allocation formula, the board of regents cooperated with the governor's office and the legislature in developing a more sophisticated and useful formula. In West Virginia a new chancellor made it a first order of business to develop closer cooperation with the governor's office and several key legislators. The attack on the Florida Board of Regents in the 1979 session of the legislature expressed an accumulation of legislative grievances that an expanded board and a new chancellor had to address in 1981. The legislature in

South Dakota substantially reduced the appropriation authority of the board of regents in 1981 as a means of expressing legislative displeasure.

The statewide governing board cannot consider itself as isolated from the political process of state government. The statewide governing board has a very difficult role to perform: It must convince state officials that it is endeavoring to meet state needs for higher education services both effectively and efficiently, while it simultaneously avoids political controversy and the alienation of legislators. The only solution is to consult continuously with political leaders but at the same time to maintain some semblance of political independence. When governing boards make decisions perceived to be political, they invite legislative intervention and legislative decision making.

We found that a third disadvantage of the statewide governing board was its tendency to remove lay influence from the governance of an individual campus. The theory of higher education governance in the United States emphasizes the importance of the governing board of lay citizens as a link between institution and society and as a check upon institutional leaders and faculty members. In the case of statewide governing boards, as well as in that of the multicampus governing boards that dominate most public insitutions of higher education in this country, the lay governing board's influence has been diluted. The statewide governing board in practice has found it almost impossible to think and act as the governing board of an individual campus. The board is expected to fulfill a dual role: to serve as a state government agency for higher education and to serve as the governing board of each individual institution in the system. In fact, the board is likely to find itself preoccupied with state government concerns and unable to give very much attention to the concerns of individual campuses. puses. Moreover, the lay governing board is typically composed of persons who are able to contribute only one or two days a month to the higher education enterprise and who are not experts in higher education.

We found only two statewide systems out of ten that had tried to make use of local advisory boards of lay persons at the institutional level to assist the governing board. In one state the arrangement was too new to allow any assessment of its utility. In the other state institutional presidents said that the advisory boards were helpful to them but acknowledged that such service simply did not have the prestige or status of membership on the governing board. Moreover, presidents learned that local advisory boards worked better on an ad hoc basis, when there was a specific problem to consider, than on a continuing basis.

One criticism we encountered was that the statewide governing board tended to treat all campuses alike when considering various policies. The president of a campus tended to think of his or her campus as having unique concerns, and wanted these concerns to be considered in the decision-making process. Yet at the same time the president didn't want his or her campus to be considered so unique as to be put at a disadvantage in relation to any other campus. Presidents of flagship state universities within state systems seemed to believe that their institutions had been treated unfairly by governing boards and had been "leveled down" while newer institutions were "leveled up." In fairness, we must acknowledge that this complaint was widespread in all states regardless of organizational structure; there was some indication that this concern was being addressed in various ways in the different states as the 1980s unfolded.

One response of the statewide governing board to the problem of the operation of the individual campus was to delegate substantial management authority to the president. In no state had this management policy been more fully articulated or more carefully observed than in Mississippi.

A fourth disadvantage of the statewide governing board was its inadequacy as a state planning and advisory agency in higher education. As a governing board the statewide board had a definite obligation to be concerned with the welfare of the particular public institutions that comprised the state system. This obligation was indeed the primary responsibility of the governing board. The result necessarily was that the governing board became a partisan for certain sectors of higher education. As we have already noted, only five of the ten statewide governing boards in this study included the community college sector of the state. None of the boards included the vocational-technical sector. And of course none included the private sector. A governing board was thus in a poor position to become a statewide planning agency for higher education.

It is noteworthy that among the ten states with statewide governing boards, eight had seen fit to establish a postsecondary education planning commission apart from the governing board. This action was taken because of the realization that the governing board was not impartial in its relationship to public institutions and was thus not the appropriate agency to prepare a master plan concerned with the welfare of all sectors of postsecondary education. Undoubtedly this postsecondary planning had been encouraged by the provisions of Section 1202 of the Higher Education Act of 1965, as added in 1972. With the elimination of federal funds to support 1202 commissions, this planning activity was likely to decline or cease altogether. Indeed, in one of the eight states the 1202 commission was said to have become completely inactive by the autumn of 1982. Only in Florida did the postsecondary planning commission appear to have strong state government support.

Advantages of State Coordinating Boards

All nine of the state coordinating boards included in this study were created between 1957 and 1971: 1957 (Illinois), 1963 (Ohio and Missouri), 1965 (Colorado, Connecticut, Texas), 1967 (New Jersey), 1969 (Alabama), and 1971 (Indiana). Two boards have had a change in title since their establishment (Connecticut and Missouri), and all have had additional duties conferred upon them by law since they were created. Two of the states (Indiana and Ohio) had established strong voluntary arrangements for interinstitutional planning and budgeting, but these arrangements collapsed under the impact of institutional rivalries and state government concerns. Only one state in our study had abandoned a state coordinating board in favor of a statewide governing board, but governors in two other states had advocated such action.

We found that the major advantage of the coordinating board in contrast with the statewide governing board was the comprehensive scope of its coordinating authority. In every one of the nine states of this study that had coordinating boards, that board had been designated as the 1202 commission for the state. The coordinating boards had coordinating authority in relation to the state universities, the state colleges, the community colleges, the technical institutes or colleges, and, to some uncertain extent, the vocational-technical schools. In addition, the coordinating boards endeavored to give some attention to the interests of the private sector, although this interest had gone farther in some states than in others. The coordinating board was concerned with postsecondary or higher education in all types of institutions, private as well as public.

A second advantage of the state coordinating board was the limitations placed upon its powers to bring about a coordinated structure of higher education in a state. As noted earlier, these powers were three in scope: the power to prepare a master plan and/or to engage in continuous planning, the power to approve or veto new degree programs, and the power to recommend state appropriations for both current operations and capital improvements. In the case of two of these powers—those to prepare a master plan and to recommend appropriations—the authority of the coordinating board was advisory rather than final. The master plan set forth the state's need for higher education services. Decisions about mission, programs, access, and geographical location, however, were to be settled by the legislative process. The authority of the coordinating board to recommend appropriations was advisory to the legislative process; the decision was that of governors and legislatures. Only in the instances of new degree programs, location of branches, and off-campus instruction was the authority of a coordinating board final. Still, the master plan was a guide for approving new degree programs, and the authority to recommend appropriations was a means of implementing master plan provisions.

A third advantage of the state coordinating board was its identification with the interests of state government. The role of a state coordinating board was one of advocating the state's interest in higher education, not that of institutions. Institutional leaders and faculty members tended to believe that institutional interests and state government interests were identical. State government leaders, on the contrary, tended to see, not an identity of interests with public institutions of higher education, but a divergence of interests. As a consequence, state government leaders welcomed the existence of a higher education administrative agency that identified itself with the perspectives of state government rather than with the interests, and rivalries, of individual state universities and colleges.

A fourth advantage of the state coordinating board was its lack of management authority over individual campuses. The coordinating board was not responsible for the selection of presidents, the preparation and approval of institutional budgets, the conduct of student affairs, the determination of faculty personnel policies and practices, the development of an internal organizational structure and governance process, and so forth. The coordinating board was able to concentrate its attention on the essential ingredients of state coordination: a master plan, approval of programs (including off-campus location of programs), and appropriation recommendations. Attention to these vital procedures of state government was not complicated by the necessity to give attention to campus management concerns.

There have been some commentators, such as T. R. McConnell (1981), who insist that a coordinating board should serve as a spokesman for public institutions of higher education. McConnell sees the board's coordinating role as one of helping to protect public institutions from "ill-advised" incursions by state legislatures and the executive branch of state government and of "leading" the state system of higher education to meet demonstrated public needs, with the board nevertheless retaining the confidence of both state government and public institutions. This prescription is at best a counsel of perfection; at worst it is an unrealistic expectation. Coordinating boards should advise against undesirable forms of state government intervention in the affairs of public institutions, but they can do no more than advise. Intervention would be less likely to occur if the institutions of higher education would exercise some caution in their own actions. And as far as "leading" public institutions is concerned, most presidents and governing boards perceive no need for such leadership on the part of a coordinating board. They much prefer to do their own leading. These circumstances were illustrated several times in different states during the course of this study.

We found some evidence of an inclination on the part of state governments to broaden the authority of their coordinating boards in the 1970s and early 1980s. In Connecticut and Missouri the coordinating agencies were restructured and their authority expanded in the 1970s. After a period of legislative disenchantment, the authority of the coordinating agency in Colorado was strengthened in the 1970s. The most far-reaching action was taken in Connecticut in 1982 when the newly designated board of governors was given authority to order the discontinuance of existing degree programs at any state institution and to direct the closing or merger of state institutions, subject to legislative veto.

Disadvantages of State Coordinating Boards

The first disadvantage of the state coordinating board that we found was its lack of authority to implement a master plan, to eliminate existing programs (except in Connecticut as of 1983), and to control institutional budgets. Coordinating boards had to depend on governors and legislatures to implement master plans, to merge or abolish existing campuses, and to eliminate current degree programs. The board's appropriation recommendations might be directed to these ends, but the appropriation process then had to determine state government action. As a consequence, governors and legislators were invited to make decisions that in many instances reflected parochial rather than statewide interests.

A common criticism by governors was that coordinating boards could not control the actions of the presidents of individual campuses—for example, their lobbying efforts. This criticism led Governor James of Alabama to try to change the structure of higher education in Alabama in 1981 and again in 1982. This criticism was the basis for Governor King's insistence that the coordinating board be abolished in favor of a statewide governing board in Massachusetts in 1980. And this criticism was also voiced by Governor Grasso and then by Governor O'Neill in Connecticut. Governors in particular, but some legislative leaders as well, are likely to prefer statewide governance to statewide coordination as a means of bringing a central authority to bear upon higher education. They hope thereby to bring some order into what they see as the chaos of higher education and to achieve this with as little involvement on their part as possible. It is a hope not always realized, as we have noted earlier.

We found that a second disadvantage of the state coordinating board was the independence evidenced toward it by institutional governing boards and campus presidents. And, in fact, there is no reason why institutional governing boards and campus presidents should have any particular loyalty to a coordinating board or its chief administrative officer. Campus presidents may continue to lobby legislators as they please, and they generally tend to do so. Campus presidents and governing boards are not obligated to accept a master plan unless some provision for one is enacted into law. Campus presidents are free to criticize and to object to the appropriation recommendations of the coordinating board, and sometimes they are successful in obtaining additional appropriations for current operations or capital improvements. Campus presidents can mobilize their various constituencies— faculty, students, staff, alumni, and community friends—to assist in arguing the special needs of a particular campus. Even the authority of the coordinating board to approve new degree programs is no particular threat to presidents at a time when new degree programs are not currently needed. And in several instances in the 1970s certain state universities in Ohio persuaded the General Assembly to provide for new degree programs by law when their approval had been denied by the Ohio Board of Regents. Since campus presidents are not appointed by a coordinating board, these presidents cannot be disciplined when they undertake to attack the board. It must be said, however, that governing boards have also been overruled by legislatures.

A third disadvantage of the state coordinating board is its lack of a political constituency. There is no political power base for a coordinating board other than the governor and the legislature. In the case of a multicampus governing board, there is the power base composed of the various campuses, although these constituencies tend to identify themselves with their own campuses rather than with a system. In the case of a coordinating board, however, there is no faculty, student body, alumni, or local community with a particular interest in the influence of the board. The coordinating board has influence only to the extent that the governor and the legislative leaders have confidence in the board and its administrative officer. If the governor and the legislative leaders understand and support the actions and recommendations of the coordinating board, that board becomes an influential participant in the state government political process. If the reverse is true, then the coordinating board is left with little influence and is likely to be ignored by institutional governing boards and campus presidents.

We have observed the truth of this in each of the nine states with coordinating boards. There have been times when governors and legislative leaders have been supportive of the coordinating boards, and there have been times when coordinating boards have been given little attention in the state political process. The most influential board over a sustained period of time appears to have been the coordinating board in Texas. The Ohio Board of Regents was quite influential at one time, lost much of that influence for a time, and recovered it between 1978 and 1982. The Commission for Higher Education in Indiana had very little influence in the first years of its existence, gained stature later, and has had considerable influence in recent years. Similar records of ups and downs have occurred in the other states.

We found that in several instances the coordinating board decided to work very closely with the leadership of one or two universities in an effort to come up with recommendations that would be supported by those universities. In these instances campus leaders came to see that the coordinating board served as a protection for their institutions and so were inclined to give the board political support. In one or two other instances governors and legislative leaders understood fully the usefulness of the coordinating board as an antidote to interinstitutional rivalries and so supported its role. Without one or the other arrangement, coordinating boards were likely to be without real influence.

The fourth disadvantage of the coordinating board was its uncertain relationship to the executive and legislative branches of state government. Traditionally, most, if not all, the members of coordinating boards were appointed by the governor, confirmed by the state senate, and served terms of several years' duration. In Ohio the term of members of the board of regents was nine years; three members were appointed by the governor every three years. In Alabama the members also served nine-year terms. Coordinating board members in five states served six-year terms and in two states four-year terms. All terms overlapped so that the entire membership did not turn over at the same time. Governors tended to find this board membership arrangement disconcerting, especially when a newly elected governor was of a different political party or faction from that of his or her predecessor.

The consequence, we found, was that the coordinating board was insulated from the immediate political influence of a newly elected governor but at the same time was largely dependent upon that governor for its influence in the political process. In Illinois some effort was made to bridge this problem of political relationship by providing by law for the governor to designate the chairman of the coordinating board. In other states as a matter of practice rather than of legal requirement, board members elected a chairman who had just been appointed by the governor or who was known to be acceptable to the governor. But this arrangement did not necessarily resolve the issue of the proper relationship of the chief administrative officer of the board to the governor.

Other arrangements have been instituted in three of the nine states with coordinating boards. In Colorado the executive director of the Commission on Higher Education, although appointed by the commission, served as head of the Department of Higher Education and sat in the governor's cabinet. In Missouri the commissioner of higher education, although appointed by the Coordinating Board for Higher Education, served as head of the executive Department of Higher Education. In New Jersey the chancellor was appointed by the Board of Higher Education for a five-year term of office with the approval of the governor; the chancellor was the head of the Department of Higher Education. There was some evidence that these arrangements facilitated communication between governor and coordinating board, but they had by no means solved all the difficulties inherent in this relationship.

Advantages of Advisory Boards

In our study there were six states that we classified as having state advisory boards for higher education. The original dates of establishment and the current designations for these boards are as follows: 1784 (New York Board of Regents), 1960 (California Postsecondary Education Commission), 1963 (Pennsylvania State Board of Education Council on Higher Education), 1965 (Minnesota Higher Education Coordinating Board), 1969 (Washington Council for Postsecondary Education), and 1974 (Delaware Postsecondary Education Commission). The size of these boards varied from eight members together with a chairman in the case of the Council on Higher Education in Pennsylvania to twenty-three members in the case of the California Postsecondary Education Commission. The terms of office varied from four years to seven years.

The board of regents of the University of the State of New York was a unique governmental agency provided for in the 1784 constitution of the state. In fact, the University of the State of New York was a paper fiction; it did grant external degrees but otherwise was not an instructional or research entity. The board of regents headed the state department of education and appointed the commissioner of education. In the field of higher education the board had authority by law to prepare a master plan, but this plan was simply advisory to the governor, the General Assembly, and the public and private institutions of the state. The board had the authority to register degree programs of public and private institutions, to review such registrations, and to order the deregistration of any program deemed deficient in quality. This authority over instructional programs was a major power of the board and led to its general reputation as one of the most powerful state boards of higher education in the country. Yet the board of regents had no budget authority in relation to either the State University of New York or the City University of New York, and it had no authority to coordinate the programs of the two multicampus public systems. The board on occasion enjoyed considerable influence with governors and legislative leaders and on other occasions was ignored by the political leadership. The board's power over public school districts and over professional licensure in the state was quite real. In the higher educational field, the board of regents appeared to have greater advisory than coordinating authority.

Pennsylvania likewise had a unique structure of education as set up in 1963. The State Board of Education consisted of a chairman appointed by the governor and eight members of each of two councils, a Council on Basic Education and a Council on Higher Education. The two councils meeting together on stated occasions made up the Board of Education. Meeting separately under the chairman for both councils, the Council on Higher Education was an advisory body in the field of higher education. There were also a secretary of education and a commissioner of higher education, both appointed by the governor. At times the secretary of education also served as chairman of the board of education. The commissioner of higher education was an administrative officer for the Council on Higher Education and until 1983 was also administrative officer for the Board of State College and University Directors. A new statute in 1982 created a new board of trustees for a system of state universities; the trustees in turn were to appoint a chancellor as chief executive officer of the system. The commissioner of higher education was presumably subordinate to the secretary of education. The Council on Higher Education prepared the master plan and might comment on the budget needs of higher education, as might the secretary of education. The primary budget authority, however, belonged to the governor's office.

Pennsylvania was unique also in its classification of institutions. The new system of state universities as established in 1982 comprised 14 "state-owned" institutions. There were also 4 "state-related" institutions that were in effect state universities: Pennsylvania State University, the University of Pittsburgh, Temple University, and Lincoln University. Each of these institutions had its own board of trustees, some of whom were appointed by the governor. In addition, there were 12 "state-aided" institutions, that is, private colleges and universities receiving state financial assistance for their current operating expenditures. Finally, there were 14 community college districts that also received state financial assistance and some 102 private institutions whose students were eligible to participate in the state student financial assistance programs.

The Delaware Postsecondary Education Commission was created in 1974 by executive order of the governor. As of 1982 the commission consisted of fourteen members, eight of whom were appointed by the governor for three-year terms and six of whom were ex officio and advisory members. The chairman of the commission was named by the governor; as of July 1, 1982, the commission was designated as an "independent" unit of the state budget office. The postsecondary commission had undertaken preparation of a master plan, including a definition of mission for the three public institutions in the state, had reviewed new degree programs, and had studied the financial needs of the institutions. The commission also administered a student financial aid program. Proposals to establish a coordinating board in Delaware on a statutory basis were put forward several times but were defeated in the legislature because of opposition from the three public institutions.

The commission, board, and council in California, Minnesota, and Washington well illustrated the degree of influence that an advisory board might achieve over a period of time. Indeed, the governor of Minnesota in 1981 recommended that the Higher Education Coordinating Board be abolished and that most of its functions be transferred to the Department of Administration; the state legislature, however, ignored the recommendation. All three agencies received instructions at almost every legislative session to make various studies of higher education operations. The scope of activity of the California Postsecondary Education Commission indicated the kinds of problems on which legislators in particular have sought assistance. The commission was directed by law to prepare a master plan every five years and to update that plan annually. It was asked to develop a comprehensive information system about higher education, to review and comment on institutional budget requests in terms of the master plan, to develop a comprehensive master plan for vocational and continuing education, to study regional needs and approaches to higher education services, to include proprietary institutions in the master plan, and to prepare plans for increasing the access of women and minorities to higher education.

In Minnesota the Higher Education Coordinating Board was required by law to present recommendations concerning higher education to the governor and legislature every two years. The 1981 report was a printed document of some 125 pages that included discussions and recommendations about the current condition of higher education in the state, enrollment projections, appropriation support, financial needs, proposed goals, and activity in reviewing instructional programs (the board could not disapprove any programs). Also included were results of studies of nursing education, teacher education, articulation between two-year and four-year institutions, faculty compensation, community college enrollments and costs, vocational-technical education, and part-time enrollments. There was also a report on the programs administered by the board: student financial aid, state scholarships, student loans, interstate tuition reciprocity, private college contracts, a private institution registration program, and an interlibrary exchange program. Action on these and other studies could only be implemented by action of the legislature or by action of one of the system governing boards in Minnesota. But governing boards and system executives increasingly found it undesirable to ignore the recommendations of the coordinating board.

In Washington State the Council for Postsecondary Education prepared general plans for higher education services, reviewed and recommended degree programs, analyzed tuition and fee charges of the public institutions, reviewed (but did not recommend) operating and capital budgets, studied admission and transfer policies, and prepared study papers that set forth standards of quality in instructional programs. It also developed reciprocity agreements with British Columbia and Oregon, assisted in the development of interstate agreements on medical education and graduate education, developed plans for a joint center for graduate education at the Hanford atomic energy facility, studied some 300 graduate programs to determine if they cost too much or duplicated one another, studied the needs of the Indian population for higher education, analyzed the financial needs of public higher education, and examined other special problems of concern to state legislators. The council also administered several programs, including one to determine the eligibility of institutions for the education of veterans and another to determine residency requirements for in-state students, and it directed an educational services registration program and a program for displaced home-makers. The council was regarded by most governmental officials and even by institutional leaders as having been "fair and reasonable" in its study and recommendations on the elimination of graduate programs.

This record indicated the particular advantages of the state advisory board to higher education. First, the influence of the board depended upon its objectivity and persuasive reasoning, not upon its authority to act. Second, the advisory board was non-threatening to institutional governing boards and institutional executives. Third, governing boards and institutional executives discovered that they were well advised to pay attention to the work and recommendations of the advisory board. Finally, the advisory board was available as a state government agency to administer certain general higher education programs not appro-priate for administration by a particular institution or system of public higher education.

Disadvantages of Advisory Boards

The first disadvantage of the state advisory board that we found was its lack of authority to require institutional collabora-tion. To the extent that a governor or legislative leaders respected an advisory board and were inclined to implement board recom-mendations, to that extent an advisory board had some influence with, and obtained cooperation from, public institutions.

The second disadvantage arose from the board's depen-dence upon gubernatorial or legislative instruction in undertaking plans and studies. Permanent legislation might direct the advisory board to prepare a master plan, but there was no way in which the board could act to give effect to that plan. The studies that an advisory board pursued depended upon directives received from the governor or the legislature, usually in connection with the appropriation process. These studies were carried out in the hope that some legal action might follow. But the initiative of the advisory board depended upon the political process and so did any implementation of its advice.

The third disadvantage of the state advisory board was that such an agency tended to increase rather than decrease the legislative burden in regard to higher education. There could be no transfer of higher education issues from the legislative to the administrative arena under an advisory board arrangement. Indeed, an advisory board was well advised not to overload the agenda that it presented to the legislature. If the advisory board's recommendations fared badly in the legislature, the utility of the board was necessarily called into question.

Like the state coordinating board, the state advisory board had to be concerned about its relationship to the governor's office and the legislature. In Delaware, after several years of existence, the advisory board came to be lodged in the budget office and its function regarded as primarily one of budget analysis. This arrangement advanced the interests of the postsecondary education commission in that state.

No Easy Answers

It is apparent that none of the twenty-five states of this study had found a satisfactory and successful solution to the problem of administrative organization for the provision and support of higher education services. Some kind of centralized administrative agency is desirable, indeed essential, for such important activities as management of state financial assistance programs, the licensing of postsecondary proprietary schools, and the handling of contracts with or grants to private nonprofit higher education institutions. There are also such duties to be performed as statewide planning, specification of institutional missions, review and approval of instructional programs, encouragement of interinstitutional articulation and cooperation, promotion of satisfactory interrelationships with elementary-secondary education and vocational education, and determination of appropriation recommendations. No state government can escape the necessity of giving careful and professional attention to these concerns. Statewide governing boards, state coordinating boards, and state advisory boards have all proved to have both advantages and disadvantages in coping with these concerns. None has been such an outstanding success as to warrant general acceptance or general emulation.

The statewide governing board has the major defect of not being sufficiently broad and objective in the scope of its authority and responsibility to handle the range of state government concerns. The statewide governing board is not an appropriate administrative instrument for student financial assistance programs and the conduct of relations with independent institutions. The state coordinating board and the state advisory board are more appropriate arrangements in this respect, as is being realized in more and more states. Before the end of the 1980s, most states with statewide governing boards will also have postsecondary advisory boards. Developments in eight of the tend states with governing boards pointed in that direction.

As between the coordinating board and the advisory board, the coordinating board is preferable if some way can be found properly to relate the coordinating board to the governor and the legislature of the state. In several ways the advisory boards included in this study seemed to have been more successful than the coordinating boards in achieving a working relationship with governors and legislatures. In Minnesota, when one governor seemed to have little interest in the advisory board, legislative leaders did. In Delaware, when the legislature seemed little interested in the advisory board, the governor placed the board in his own office.

The coordinating board is superior to the advisory board as a means of transferring a certain amount of political conflict from the state legislature to an administrative agency. The coordinating board and the coordinating staff are more likely to evidence the understanding necessary for a careful resolution of higher education conflicts than is the trading pit known as the state legislature.

Whatever kind of board is chosen in a state, two troublesome issues remain: its relationship to the governor and its relationship to elementary-secondary education, including vocational-technical education in most states and community college education in many states. We have found no satisfactory answers to these two issues in this study. In three of our twenty-five states there was an executive department of education or higher education; in two of these instances the chief administrative officer of the coordinating board was thereby the head of the executive department of higher education. In Florida there was a unique constitutional arrangement whereby the statewide governing board was subordinate to the state board of education, which was composed of seven elected state officials, including the governor as chairman. In Massachusetts the position of secretary of education was abolished when the statewide governing board was established in 1980. In three states—Montana, New York, and Pennsylvania—the state higher education board was organically linked to a state board for elementary-secondary education. In all the other states voluntary cooperation had to be sought between higher education and elementary-secondary education.

The board principle of organization is deeply imbedded in the tradition of both elementary-secondary education and higher education. Although it is unrealistic to think that a board can remove higher education from politics, a board can be a means of insulating higher education from direct political manipulation. The utility of an executive department of education similar to an executive department of health or welfare or highways is open to doubt because of past experiences, tradition, and the sensitive nature of the educational endeavor.

At one time several states included in this study provided for institutional representatives on state coordinating and advisory boards, often in dominating numbers. By 1981, these representatives had either been eliminated or, in two instances, been made a minority of board membership. The importance of "public" rather than institutional representatives as members of state higher education boards had been clearly recognized.

There remains the problem of how to relate the organizational structure of the board to the policy leadership role of the state governor. Two devices tried in some states were to have the board chairmanship subject to designation by the governor or to have an executive department of education that was related in some way to the higher education board. Still a third arrangement was to have the appointment of the executive officer of a state higher education board subject to formal approval by the governor. This latter practice tended to encourage a fixed term for the executive officer in order to give succeeding governors an opportunity to approve selection of the officer. None of these three different kinds of arrangements, however, seemed to be notably successful in achieving its objective.

Yet a further organizational problem is that of how to ensure a proper degree of integration between elementary-secondary education and higher education. If voluntary cooperation is ineffective, then some more formal arrangement may be appropriate. The device used in Montana and Pennsylvania may be worth further consideration. In each of those states there is a state board of education composed of two constituent boards, namely, a board of basic education and a board of higher education. Under such an arrangement it is essential to prescribe with care the authority of the state board of education as distinct from the authority of the two constituent boards.

There was no evidence uncovered in this study to suggest that a single state agency for all education from kindergarten through the doctoral degree had been more successful in achieving cooperation and articulation between elementary-secondary education and higher education than had voluntary efforts. Higher education is different from elementary-secondary education, and any effort to suggest otherwise is to belittle elementary-secondary education and to insult the role and achievements of higher education.

It may be concluded that no state government organizational structure for higher education as of 1982 was clearly and unquestionably satisfactory. Perhaps none can be. But there will be further experimentation in the 1980s and into the 1990s.

⊰⊱ 5 ⊰⊱

State Higher Education
Executives

BOARDS OF HIGHER education, regardless of type, have members who serve on a part-time basis as a civic duty. These boards meet periodically, usually monthly, for a day or two days at the most. They are in reality dependent on a full-time executive or administrative officer with some professional and/or administrative competence related to the field of higher education. These executive or administrative officers in turn are responsible for such staff as state governments may authorize for performance of the duties entrusted to the boards.

The size of staffs for the states in this study varied from a total of 4 persons serving the advisory board in Delaware (two professionals and two support persons) to 166 serving the Texas Coordinating Board (some 60 professionals and 100 support personnel). The coordinating board in Indiana had a staff of 12 persons (8 professionals and 4 support persons), aided by a computerized information and analytical system. The size of a staff depended on the scope of the administrative duties assigned to the board, especially in the areas of student financial assistance, institutional licensing, and public information about programs available to students and adults. The largest administrative staff in the United States was that of the New York Board of Regents, but it was not easy to separate the personnel exclusively concerned with higher education from those concerned with various other duties, such as professional licensure. A similar situation existed in Pennsylvania.

Higher education boards were served by two kinds of full-time staff officers. In general terms, the two types of staff officers may be designated as executive officers and administrative officers. The difference between the two types lies in the nature of the board and in the role of the staff officer in relation to the board. The executive officer tends to have a dominant influence in the work of the board; such dominant influence is partly a matter of personality. The administrative officer serves the board in the capacity of an executive secretary who organizes issues for consideration by the board but does not tend to dominate its decision making.

It is easiest to see this distinction between an executive officer and an administrative officer in the case of the statewide governing board. When a governing board designates a staff officer as chancellor, the board is in effect appointing an executive officer; indeed, the board is in effect naming a president for each institution—a president who is responsible not only for institutional governance but also for statewide planning and coordination. As for state coordinating boards, some are served by an executive officer to whom substantial authority has been delegated to perform the work of the agency and to maintain relationships with state government officials. But coordinating board executive officers have no governance authority in relation to any individual campus.

There are two major decisions that confront state higher education boards when naming a chief staff officer. The first decision involves the kind of role to be performed: the role of executive officer or that of administrative officer. The second decision concerns the kind of qualifications in terms of education, experience, and personality that the board considers desirable and even necessary to the performance of the assigned role. Again in general terms we may describe the choice as one between a scholarly/administrative set of qualifications and an administrative/political set of qualifications. We shall have more to say about this distinction later.

Governing Board Officers

Of the ten states in this study with statewide governing boards, seven had established the position of chief executive officer and three that of administrative officer. The difference turned on the relationship between the governing board and the individual campuses. Under the chief executive officer arrangement, the president of each campus reported to the chief executive officer, and only that officer reported to the governing board. Under the administrative officer arrangement, the president of each campus reported directly to the governing board, and the administrative officer also reported to the governing board. The administrative officer supervised the central staff, prepared the agenda for board members, and transmitted directives in the name of the board (not in his or her own name).

Of the seven states with a chief executive officer for the governing board, six designated the chief executive as chancellor while the seventh (Montana) employed the title of commissioner. Interestingly enough, none of these states had a flagship state university that rated membership in the Association of American Universities (AAU), although there were two states not included in this study with statewide governing boards that did have a component institution with status in the AAU. The title of chancellor seemed to be the appropriate one by which to designate a system executive. The other three states with an administrative officer instead of a chief executive officer utilized two different titles: executive director and executive secretary and director.

Of the seven states with a chancellor (or commissioner) as chief executive officer, circumstances in 1982 were such as to preclude any meaningful assessment of performance in four of them. The statewide system in Massachusetts was barely two years old as of the summer of 1982. Considerable upheaval had occurred in the Florida system between 1979 and 1981, and a new chancellor had been appointed early in 1981. In West Virginia a new chancellor had been appointed in 1980 and as of the autumn of 1982 appeared to be having a positive and favorable impact upon the system. In New Hampshire the first chancellor had been succeeded by a new incumbent in 1981; he was still striving to develop a definite role in a system comprising one doctoral-granting university, two comprehensive institutions, and one two-year institution.

In the other three states with a chancellor or commissioner, some clear patterns had already emerged. Thus, the chancellor's office appeared to be well established in Georgia; and although a new incumbent and recently been named, the position remained one of strong executive leadership in the system. In Maine the chancellor since 1975 had developed close working relationships with both higher education institutions and the state government. He had been quite successful in changing the climate that had existed under his predecessor.

In Montana, where there had been a single statewide governing board since the state was established in 1889, several different organizational arrangements had followed one another. By 1900 four different state colleges had been created, and thereafter various demands to abolish or consolidate these institutions began to be heard. In the 1920s two additional institutions were created; in the 1930s the position of chancellor was created at the state university in Missoula, but this arrangement had collapsed by 1945. Thereafter the governing board was served by a succession of administrative officers. When a new state constitution was established in 1973, a strong board of regents with ten members was provided for, along with a commissioner of higher education. In 1976 the board adopted a set of duties for the commissioner and declared that the commissioner outranked the presidents and that the presidents should report to the board only through the commissioner. A relatively small state of under 800,000 population in 1980, Montana continued to struggle to support a system of nine public institutions scattered throughout a state that geographically was the fourth largest in the United States.

The position of chancellor in a statewide governing system had special requirements insofar as his or her role was concerned. Six of the seven chancellors as of 1982 held doctoral degrees, and all had had previous experience in the administration of higher education. Two had been presidents of a college or university, four had been vice-presidents, and one had been administrative officer of a state coordinating board. Five of the seven were listed in the 1982–83 edition of *Who's Who in America*. The challenge for a chancellor was a double one: to provide leadership but not suffocation for each individual campus in the system and, at the same time, to provide effective working relationships with state government officials. This dual role had to be accomplished within the framework of institutional or campus aspirations for maximum possible managerial autonomy and of state government expectations for systemwide quality, planning, coordination, and efficiency in the use of available resources. Campus executives and faculty members expected chancellors to obtain increased state government financial support without increased state government controls. Chancellors had to represent institutional aspirations in the context of beneficial service to the people of a state, while responding in some way to state government charges that academic institutions had been guilty of inadequate planning, program duplication, mismanagement of resources, and failure to come to grips with economic recession.

On the one hand, chancellors were expected to be academically oriented, that is, to understand and appreciate the interests and concerns of the campus community. On the other hand, they were expected to understand and appreciate the political process and to guide both institutions and governing board past the political whirlpools of state government. In an instance involving a multicampus system, the Academy for Educational Development recommended that the governing board draw a distinction between the scholarly/administrative qualifications expected of a campus executive and the administrative/political qualifications expected of a system executive. The recommendation was as applicable to a statewide governing board as it was to a multicampus governing board.

Chancellors found that in large part their role was one of responding to state government expectations. While they tried to defend the values and soothe the anxieties of the academic community, they had to reassure state government officials that the university system was alert to the needs, the economic circumstances, and the political concerns of state government. In the long run, a multicampus system had to learn how to deal effectively with state government leaders. The chancellor who could not achieve cordial and respected relationships with campuses, with the governing board, and with state government officials was not fulfilling the expectations of his or her position.

The board of regents in Florida illustrated well the pitfalls of a statewide governing board. Apart from the unusual and complex relationship of the board of regents to the state board of education and to the commissioner of education, the board found its state planning role and its relationship to the legislature particularly difficult to handle. Much of the criticism was directed at the chancellor who served from 1975 to 1980. This chancellor became entangled in controversy about certain constitutional amendments that were submitted to the voters of the state in 1978 and were then defeated. The 1979 state legislature substantially altered the relationship of the board to the individual campuses and restricted the governing authority of the board. Legislation to clarify the situation and to direct certain changes in the system was vetoed by the governor in 1980. In 1981 and 1982 the board of regents, with a new chancellor, sought to reassert both its governing role in relation to the individual campuses and its governmental role in relation to state government. The success or failure of this effort will depend upon the leadership qualities of the chancellor and upon the support given to her by state government officials.

About the three states having statewide governing boards with administrative officers, certain other observations must be made. The administrative officer served as the chief staff officer of the governing board but not as the administrative superior of the campus presidents. In other words, the administrative officer served the governing board but did not directly supervise the individual institutions. The principle involved in this organizational arrangement was that the president in each of these systems reported directly to the governing board. The governing boards in effect tried to draw a distinction between their role in relation to each campus and their role in relation to state government. This turned out to be a difficult distinction to make and to observe in practice.

Two of the three administrative officers included in this

study had doctoral degrees. All three had had faculty as well as administrative experience in higher education, although none had been a university president or vice-president. One had been the chief staff officer for a coordinating board in another state. Only one of the three was listed in *Who's Who in America* for 1982–83.

From 1968 to 1981 legislation in South Dakota provided for the position of commissioner as the full-time professional head of the staff for the state board of regents. The commissioner was given status superior to that of the presidents of the seven institutions of higher education in the state, and the presidents were directed to report to the board through the commissioner rather than directly. During these years the state system moved from one of seven separate institutions to a more closely knit system with a unified budget, common accounting procedures, a systemwide academic program review, and a systemwide approach to priorities in capital construction. Then in 1981 the state legislature enacted a law changing the title of the staff head from commissioner to executive director and providing for the presidents to report only to the full board.

The reasons given for this legislation were several. It was said that the legislators desired to reduce the authority of the commissioner and to reassert the authority of the board of regents in relation to that of the presidents. The legislature was also said to be dissatisfied with the large number and high salaries of the staff members in the commissioner's office. In addition, the legislature wished to reestablish direct communication between the presidents on the one hand and the governor and the legislature on the other. The law seemed to express dissatisfaction with the performance of the commissioner from the point of view of the presidents. Yet the board of regents still had to deal with the academic affairs, student affairs, budget affairs, and external affairs of each campus. The executive officer became a separate source of advice and counsel on these issues instead of the primary source as in the years from 1968 to 1981. At the same time, the legislature asserted much more detailed control over each campus through the appropriation process.

The most direct and clear-cut definition of institutional autonomy was the policy statement of the statewide governing board in Mississippi. The board of trustees declared that it had delegated management authority for each campus to the respective presidents and that it expected each president to establish such organizational and governance arrangements as seemed appropriate to his or her campus. The presidents had to seek formal approval from the board for some arrangements and for the appointment of key personnel, but these actions were seldom questioned by the board. The presidents in Mississippi had formed a council for joint consideration of their common concerns, and the council had a session with the board of trustees at each monthly meeting. The presidents appeared to believe that individually they each enjoyed the full support of the governing board and that internal governance and management problems were being satisfactorily handled. Each president had individual access both to the Commission on Budget and Accounting and to the legislature. The administrative officer for the board of trustees was expected to handle the problems of systemwide planning, systemwide standards of access and operation, systemwide information, and systemwide budgeting and allocation of available resources on behalf of the board; however, final approval of all statewide policies and practices was left to the governing board.

Whether an executive officer or an administrative officer, the professional head found his work complicated by governance, as well as political, issues. There was always the problem of maintaining some kind of balance between the individual concerns of each institution and the collective concerns of state government. But both executive officers and administrative officers of statewide governing boards learned that state legislatures seldom had statewide points of view. Legislators reflected the interests of the institution that happened to be located in their legislative district. Some legislators were more influential than others in asserting this special interest and in achieving legislative recognition of it. Executive officers and administrative officers had to worry constantly about legislative reactions to the decisions of their boards. When legislative dissatisfaction became general, organizational upheaval followed, as in Florida in 1979 and in South Dakota in 1981. Sometimes legislative dissatisfaction resulted in external studies being conducted by outside consultants, as in West Virginia in

1979. There was no simple answer to the problems caused by conflicts between planning and costs and local concerns with preserving or advancing the status of an individual institution.

Officially, a statewide governing board had the authority to discipline institutional presidents who were not properly cooperative. Over a ten-year span in the ten states with governing boards, we encountered nine instances in three different states where the statewide governing board had put pressure on a campus president to resign. In a few other instances presidents resigned because of internal campus friction or disagreement with central board policies. Although we did not make a formal analysis, we had the impression that the longevity of presidents in office in statewide governing systems was about the same as that of presidents in multicampus systems or in individual governing board structures.

We also found that, among the seven other states with governing boards, three boards in the past ten years had put pressure on a chancellor to resign, and that in two states both the board and the chancellor parted on a fairly amicable basis but with some relief on the part of the chancellor that his tenure was over. The pressures on a chancellor were considerable, and the prospects of "success" were not especially bright in the years after 1973.

There was a disposition on the part of statewide governing boards in most states to favor chancellors over administrative officers. With a chancellor, the reporting burden placed upon the board was reduced. Moreover, the board could hold the chancellor responsible for the actions of individual campus presidents and could expect the chancellor to recommend dismissal of a president who was not properly loyal to the system. We found that campus presidents in a statewide governing system almost never failed to build their own local political support.

We found that good communication between governing board and chancellors, or between governing board and administrative officers and presidents, was an absolute necessity. For the most part, communication was extensive and informative, although we found one instance where a statewide governing board lost confidence in the reliability of the communication of a chancellor and forced him to resign. In two other instances where the governing board came into open conflict with the state government, the governing board expressed complete confidence in the chancellor's performance. Communication could not prevent conflict between a governing board and the state government, but it could prevent conflict between a governing board and its chief executive officer or its administrative officer.

Boards tend at best to be difficult agencies to operate, and we found that statewide governing boards were no exception to this rule. Board members might individually be prominent and influential citizens, but the amount of time and energy that each member could devote to the work of the board was limited. Moreover, board members might know something about public affairs without necessarily being well informed about higher education. In addition, boards are supposed to make collective decisions; no individual board member necessarily speaks for other board members, and no individual board member is supposed to make decisions for the whole board. In the highly charged process of state government decision making, governing boards (and other boards) had to be cautious, judicious, and concerned about political reactions. The statewide governing board had to depend upon its professional staff head for both academic and political guidance. It was no wonder that chancellors and administrative officers had only a limited life expectancy in their positions.

Staff Heads of Coordinating Boards

The complaint was voiced in two of the Carnegie reports that the administrative officer of coordinating boards tended to be a bureaucrat rather than an experienced academic officer. Of the nine coordinating boards in our study, we found that, as of 1982, each one had a professional staff head with experience in the administration of higher education. Each of these staff heads held the doctoral degree. One had been a state university president, three had been vice-presidents, three had been deans before joining the staff of a central higher education agency, and two had been faculty members who had specialized in the study of higher education. Of the nine staff heads, six were listed in *Who's Who in America* for 1982–83. Not a single officer as of 1982 could be described as lacking academic experience.

Of the nine coordinating boards, two designated their staff head as chancellor, three as executive director, and four as commissioner. While their duties tended to be similar, there was some evidence that the boards had tended to delegate considerable decision-making authority to the two chancellors. Moreover, the intent seemed to be to give the chancellors executive status comparable to that of campus presidents. The title of commissioner was employed to give the head of the professional staff a certain degree of status in state government, while the title of executive director had the virtue of being nonthreatening to institutional presidents and state government officials.

The basic difference between the professional head of a coordinating board and the chancellor of a statewide governing board turned on their relationships to campus presidents. The professional head of a coordinating board had only a persuasive role, not a supervisory role, in relation to presidents. The presidents of individual institutions were responsible to multicampus governing boards, as in two of the four senior systems in Illinois, to the heads of multicampus systems, as in two systems in Indiana, or to their individual governing boards, as in Ohio. The staff heads of coordinating boards endeavored to build cooperative relationships with presidents, but they lacked any authority to enforce the desired cooperation. Some statutes establishing coordinating boards directed public institutions of higher education to provide the board with all desired information. In addition, the budget review and recommendation function of coordinating boards and the new-program review and approval function of coordinating boards gave the boards some leverage of cooperation. But the possibility of institutional hostility and political opposition remained quite real, and staff heads always had to be prepared to cope with this possibility.

The role of the staff head of a coordinating board was a relatively simple one compared to that of a chancellor for a statewide governing board. The staff head served the state government, not higher education institutions, and endeavored to build close working relationships with state governors and state legislative leaders. Among the nine staff heads of coordinating boards, we concluded that most had been fairly successful in developing such relationships, even though two of the eight had been in office only about two years. The ninth staff head was appointed only in 1982.

The staff head did not have to be subservient to governors and their staffs or to legislative leaders and their staffs in order to be effective. An effective staff head was one who had gained the confidence of state officials. No staff head could ever expect to achieve all that he or she might desire in the way of financial support for higher education. This situation was particularly evident after 1973, when economic recession became endemic, inflation remained high, and state government revenues came under pressure from unemployment and welfare demands. The staff head could only offer governmental officials alternatives of financial support and of higher education services based upon such support. Some were more effective than others in developing and providing choices of public policy.

From the point of view of campus presidents, the performance of the staff head of a coordinating board was often a disappointment. In general, presidents expected the staff head to be a full-time lobbyist for their institutions. The effectiveness of the staff head was thus measured by the extent to which he or she persuaded the governor and the legislature to provide the resources desired by each institution. Any sizable gap between what was desired and what was obtained was considered to be an indication of the failure of the staff head to serve higher education in the way he or she was supposed to do. Presidents reflected the interests of their faculty members, who wanted new programs and higher salaries, and of their students, who wanted tuition to be kept low.

For their part, state government officials expected more than information and advice from the staff head. They wanted small campuses merged or closed, but not of course in the home district of any influential legislator. They wanted duplication of programs among institutions eliminated. They wanted off-campus course offerings to be more closely controlled. They wanted the quality of higher education programs to be improved, but they also wanted open access in admissions. They wanted remedial or developmental education curtailed. Finally, they wanted greater harmony and cooperation between elementary-secondary education and higher education, between vocational-technical education and two-year institutions, and between community colleges and senior colleges. State officials did not like to hear that these problems were complicated and intractable or that coordinating boards lacked the authority to order public institutions to take corrective actions.

In his or her relationships to state government, the staff head of a coordinating board had a role different from that of a chancellor of a statewide governing board. The staff head was an advocate of the state needs for higher education services. The staff head was not an apologist for all higher education institutions but rather an advocate of the public interest in higher education. Moreover, the staff head of a coordinating board was a spokesman for all of higher education, that is, for private as well as public higher education, for technical as well as general education, for under-graduate as well as graduate education, for "commuter" as well as residential education, for selective as well as open-door education. It was not easy to define the public interest in higher education, but no staff head of a coordinating board doubted that advancement of the public interest was his or her primary assignment.

It was disconcerting to discover in this study that presidents in 1981 and 1982 continued to be as hostile to the idea of state government coordination as they had been in 1961 and 1962. The development of a common front by coordinating boards and institutional governing boards, or by staff heads of coordinating boards and campus presidents, was still a long way from realization in 1982. Maybe such a common front, even in the face of the adversities of the 1980s, was too much to expect.

Advisory Board Executives

Of the six boards having essentially advisory authority, one was headed by a commissioner of education, one by a commissioner of higher education, one by an executive coordinator, one by a director, and two by an executive director. The commissioner of education in New York did not hold a doctoral degree, but he had a deputy commissioner who served as the staff specialist in the field of higher education who did hold the doctorate. Five of the six staff heads as of 1982 held the doctoral degree; and, if we include the deputy commissioner of higher education, we may count all six as having the doctoral degree.

When a board has responsibility for both elementary-secondary and higher education, then the staff head will almost always be an individual with teaching and administrative experience in elementary-secondary rather than higher education. Such was the case with the commissioner of education in New York. Since the authority of the board of regents in New York was so much more extensive in relation to elementary-secondary education than it was in relation to higher education, this arrangement was necessary. The commissioner of education in New York was the only one of the six heads of advisory boards who was listed in *Who's Who in America* for 1982–83.

The staff heads of the advisory boards had more bureaucratic backgrounds than did the staff heads of coordinating boards. All had had administrative experience in higher education institutions or in government agencies prior to their selection as staff head of the advisory board. In higher education institutions the role had been primarily in the support services rather than as faculty members or managers of academic programs. Two had had staff experience in higher education boards in other states before becoming staff heads in the states that they served as of 1982.

The role of the staff head of an advisory board was more closely oriented toward state government than was the role of staff head for statewide governing boards or for state coordinating boards. There was no doubt about whom staff heads of advisory boards were expected to advise. The staff head was expected to advise the governor and the legislature, through such intermediation as the board itself might require. Indeed, the role of the advisory board tended to be primarily advisory to the staff head, and the staff head in turn provided advice to the governor and to legislative leaders. None of the staff heads would approve this interpretation of the role of the board that he or she served, but objective assessment of the circumstances of operation clearly suggested that this was the relationship between the staff head and the advisory board.

In two states as of 1982 relations of the advisory board

and its staff head with the governor were something less than cordial. In both instances, however, the relationship of the staff head to legislative leaders was quite close. Through provisions in appropriation measures or in reports accompanying appropriation measures, the legislative leaders indicated the particular subjects that they wished to have studied and on which they wished to receive expert advice. This kind of directive was common in at least three of the six states with advisory boards and kept the staffs continually at work for the legislatures. In another two states the staff head was quite close to the governor, and much of the impact of the board's work was reflected in the governor's decisions, particularly decisions about budget recommendations.

In the case of the staff heads of advisory boards, administrative discretion dictated consultation with the staffs of system executives and institutional executives. In two states it was fairly common practice for the staff head to show drafts of advisory reports to institutional representatives. This clearance served two purposes. It presented an opportunity to correct any factual data or general impressions that were faulty or misleading. It also gave the institution some advance notice about the kind of advice that the board was disposed to present to the governor or the legislature. There was some danger in giving advance notice, however, since it alerted institutional representatives to the need to mobilize opposition to reports that were unacceptable to the institution. At the same time, however, it was important to the advisory board and its staff head to be able to say that a particular report had been seen by the higher education institutions, and the practice tended to assist data collection by the staff of the advisory board.

Much of the work of the advisory board staffs was to supply the legislature with general information about educational issues. These general studies were not intended to bring about legislative action so much as they were intended to forestall inadvisable legislative action. One of the concerns of statewide governing boards, coordinating boards, and advisory boards was to prevent legislative action that would reduce the effectiveness or efficiency of higher education institutions. Indeed, the need for preventive action of this kind often exceeded the need for supportive action. As an illustration, we may cite two papers prepared by the staff of one state advisory board. Both papers dealt with the subject of quality in the performance of higher education institutions. The papers briefly reviewed writings on the various definitions of quality and on the difficulties of measuring quality. The papers were helpful in explaining to legislators and others that there were no simple ways to achieve quality performance and that the quest for it was better left to institutional endeavor than to legislative directive.

It was not possible in this study to determine the effectiveness of the advice rendered to state government officials by the staff heads and their advisory boards. All staff heads were involved in preparing information about the operations of the state's higher education institutions and in incorporating this information into a master plan. The master plan might be comprehensive in scope, or it might consist of a series of papers and policy statements. The extent to which these master plans influenced legislative action was uncertain; in the late 1970s and at the beginning of the 1980s state government officials were little disposed to undertake any new initiatives in higher education. State governments were more concerned with the possibilities of retrenchment than of expansion.

That state governments had some interest in receiving advice from advisory boards was shown by the number of study requests given to these boards. In three of the six states with advisory boards, the volume of such requests in the bienniums 1979–1981 and 1981–1983 was quite impressive. In two of the states the advisory arrangement was institutionalized to a considerable extent; in one case it was highly formalized, and in another it was highly informal and political. In the sixth state the advisory board had too small a staff to do more than assist the governor's office on a few selective matters, primarily involving appropriation issues.

In every instance the effectiveness of advisory boards or councils depended on the quality of both the staff leadership and the staff in general. Our subjective judgment was that staff quality was high in four of the states and, with due allowance for particular circumstances, was good in the other two states as of 1982.

Boards are necessarily dependent on their staff heads for the work they undertake and for the effectiveness of their performance. The prevailing pattern among statewide governing boards was to designate a "superpresident" as chief executive and to have campus presidents work under his or her general supervision. In these situations much depended on the personality of the chancellor (or commissioner) and on his or her special competencies in an administrative/political role. In three of the ten states with state-wide governing boards, the boards preferred an administrative officer to an executive officer and relied upon direct communication between board and president to varying degrees. All statewide governing boards found it essential to instruct their staff heads to encourage the exercise of a considerable degree of management autonomy on the part of campus executives. Governing board executive officers and administrative officers necessarily found a major part of their time devoted to state government concerns.

Coordinating boards had staff heads who tended to have academic backgrounds and who at the same time offered some promise of developing effective working relationships with state government officials. A considerable measure of discretion in the conduct of these relationships was usually delegated to the staff heads. In some instances these relationships were advanced by the status of title and salary, in other instances by the particular competencies of the staff head. This latter circumstance was particularly noteworthy in one state where the staff head had made a comprehensive and computerized data information system the basis for meeting state government questions about higher education performance and resource use. In contrast, we found that relations between coordinating boards and institutions were without exception somewhat strained. There appeared to be an inherent antipathy between presidents of public institutions and coordinating board executive or administrative officers. These strained relationships could not be anything but unfortunate for the future of higher education, both public and private.

The staff heads of advisory boards depended for their effectiveness on the extent to which their advice resulted in legislative action helpful to the state government interest in higher education. In at least three and possibly five of the six states with advisory boards, the staff heads appeared to have cordial and useful working relationships with the current governors and/or legislative leaders. In general, we must conclude that state boards of higher education—governing, coordinating, and advisory—were well served by their staff heads and their staffs as of 1982.

➤❙ 6 ❘◀

Definition of
Institutional Mission

A MAJOR COMPONENT OF A
statewide master plan is a definition of institutional mission. The
handbooks on state postsecondary education issued by the Education Commission of the States provide some indication of the current status of master plans by states. These data reveal that as of
1980 master plans had been prepared in twenty-eight states;
another five states reported that they had a continuing planning
process that resulted in the essentials of a master plan; and seventeen states reported that they did not have master plans. Of the
seventeen states without master plans, nine were states with statewide governing boards. Of eighteen states with coordinating
boards, seventeen had prepared master plans. In the other states,
the task of preparing a master plan had been assigned to a postsecondary education commission, but only six of these agencies had
completed a master plan.

Master plans tended to be similar in nature and scope. State
needs were defined in terms of access goals and program requirements vis-à-vis state patterns of employment. Access goals usually
involved open admission to certain institutions in the system, selective admission to other institutions and programs (especially graduate and first professional), the geographical availability of programs,
and the reduction of economic barriers. State patterns of employ-

145

ment were analyzed, and projections were made of future labor market demands for white-collar jobs (sales, clerical, technical, professional, and managerial). The second part of a master plan typically involved enrollment projections, usually by major sectors of state institutional resources: private institutions, public two-year institutions, public urban institutions, public regional or residential institutions, and public doctoral-granting institutions. The third major component of a master plan usually involved some effort to define the research and public service needs of the state. In the late 1970s and early 1980s, some master plans began to give particular attention to the matter of research and development in relation to employment and economic growth in the state, whereas in the 1960s the emphasis had been on enrollment and programs in relation to jobs. Unfortunately, the relationship of research to jobs was more difficult to demonstrate in the 1980s than had been the relationship of enrollment to jobs in the 1960s.

From a discussion of state needs for enrollment, instructional programs, research, and public service, master plans usually turned to consideration of state resources for the delivery of higher education services. These parts of a master plan involved decisions about the location of institutions, institutional missions, institutional facilities, and institutional costs and financing (both for current operations and for capital improvements). In the era of substantial expansion, roughly from 1960 to 1975, the emphasis was upon building new campuses that would be geographically dispersed throughout the state, expanding existing campuses, adding new capital facilities, and increasing faculty salaries. In the years after 1975 the issues were duplication of facilities and programs, the disproportion in the size of institutions, the possibility of merging or even of closing some institutions, and the containment of cost increases. Coloring all these concerns was the continuing impact of inflation on all public service costs, as well as the slowdown in economic growth, business recession, unemployment, and reduced state government revenues.

It was far easier for state boards of higher education to outline the desirable elements of a state master plan than it was to formulate and publish a master plan. This circumstance was particularly evident in the years after 1975. Discussions with leaders of public institutions revealed a considerable gap between state government concerns and institutional interests. Public institutions continued to press for increased appropriations. In states where there was extensive faculty collective bargaining, as in New York, New Jersey, Pennsylvania, Florida, Montana, and California, faculty representatives pressed strongly for higher salaries. In other states the executive leadership of public institutions also pressed for higher salaries, partly as a means to offset the collective bargaining movement. Student lobby groups in various states, and particularly in Pennsylvania, Florida, and California, opposed increases in the charges to students for higher education. Institutions wanted improved capital facilities, little if any interference with the existing scope of their program commitments, and no projections of enrollment decline. And of course public institutions fought any plans to reduce off-campus instruction or to close or merge institutions. This institutional resistance often obtained some reinforcement from legislative representatives from the areas where particular institutions were located.

No part of a master plan encountered more resistance than the attempt by a state board of higher education to establish differential statements of mission for each public institution. The Carnegie Commission on Higher Education published a classification of institutions by major purpose in 1973 (Carnegie Commission on Higher Education, 1973a). Apart from the distinction between public sponsorship and private sponsorship, this classification structure consisted of five primary groupings: doctoral-granting institutions, comprehensive universities and colleges, liberal arts colleges, two-year colleges and institutes, and professional schools and other specialized institutions. Within these major groupings there were various subclassifications. For doctoral-granting institutions there were four subclasses: research universities I, research universities II, doctoral-granting universities I, and doctoral-granting universities II. A revised but basically unchanged classification structure was published by the Carnegie Council on Policy Studies in Higher Education in 1976. Moreover, the Carnegie Commission and Carnegie Council proceeded to assign individual institutions and campuses to the various categories.

To be classified as a research university, an institution had to receive a certain number of federal grants for research and award at least fifty Ph.D. degrees a year. Research universities I were those universities (public and private) in the top 50 among all institutions receiving federal grants for research, while research universities II were those in the top 100. Doctoral-granting universities I awarded forty or more Ph.D. degrees in at least five fields, while institutions awarding at least twenty Ph.D. degrees a year were included in group II. Comprehensive institutions in group I offered a liberal arts program, as well as "several" other programs, and enrolled at least 2,000 students. Comprehensive institutions in group II offered a liberal arts program and at least one professional program and enrolled at least 1,000 students. Liberal arts colleges were divided into two groups based either on selectivity of entering freshmen or on the number of graduates receiving Ph.D. degrees from the forty leading doctoral-granting universities as ranked by a National Academy of Sciences report published in 1967. Separate professional institutions included medical centers, schools of engineering, schools of business, schools of art and music, schools of law, schools of theology, and colleges of teacher education.

A summary of the number of public institutions listed in the two Carnegie technical papers is shown in Table 6. It is clear from this classification that the majority of public institutions are two-year institutions and comprehensive institutions. The increased number of institutions in 1976 compared with the number in 1973 reflected a more extensive identification of separate campuses by the National Center for Education Statistics rather than an actual increase in the number of institutions. Moreover, in 1981, the National Center for Education Statistics set forth a revised classification structure as the new basis for reporting of enrollment, financial, and other data (National Center for Education Statistics, 1981a).

The classification of institutions by major type was a beginning for establishing differential missions for public institutions of higher education. But it was only a beginning. There were additional factors to be considered if a useful and viable statement of mission was to be enunciated for each public institution of higher

Table 6. Types of Public Institutions as Classified by Carnegie Studies.

	1973 Classification	1976 Classification
Doctoral-Granting Institutions	108	119
Research Universities I	30	29
Research Universities II	27	33
Doctoral-Granting Universities I	34	38
Doctoral-Granting Universities II	17	19
Comprehensive Universities and Colleges	308	354
Comprehensive I	223	250
Comprehensive II	85	104
Liberal Arts Colleges	28	11
Selective I	2	0
Selective II	26	11
Two-Year Institutions	805	909
Specialized Institutions	64	70
Other	0	3
Total	1,313	1,466

Source: Carnegie Commission on Higher Education (1973a) and Carnegie Council on Policy Studies in Higher Education (1976).

education. In our study, we found a great deal of controversy about mission statements, but we did not find a single set of mission statements that adequately differentiated institutional purposes and programs. Thus, in Exhibit 1 we try to outline an adequate statement of mission.

One reason why there was not a single totally adequate master plan among the twenty-five states of this study was the controversial nature of statements of mission. Indeed, in one state the coordinating board declared that it would not attempt to establish a statement of mission for the public institutions of that state. Instead, the coordinating board asked the governing board of each public institution to define the mission of that institution and to submit such a statement to the coordinating board. It seems likely, however, that this coordinating board was making use of an implicit differentiation of mission in the exercise of its

Exhibit 1. Essential Characteristics of Mission.

Instruction: Objectives
     1.   General education
     2.   Career and professional education

       Programs
     1.   Technical education
     2.   General education
     3.   Arts and sciences: undergraduate
     4.   Professional: undergraduate
     5.   Arts and sciences: graduate I
     6.   Arts and sciences: graduate II
     7.   Professional: graduate I
     8.   Professional: graduate II
     9.   First professional: law, medicine, dentistry, osteopathic medicine, optometry, veterinary medicine, theology

Research: Major interest
       General interest

Public Service: Continuing general education
       Continuing professional education
       Clinics and hospitals
       Public broadcasting
       Museums
       Performing arts
       Consulting services

Orientation: Residential/full-time
       Urban/commuting

Access: Open admission
       Selective admission

Enrollment Sizes: Over 25,000
       5,000–25,000
       Under 5,000

Student Characteristics: Predominantly white
       Predominantly black

authority to approve new degree programs and to develop a formula for the apportionment of state support among the various systems and institutions of that state.

Differentiated statements of mission are opposed by public institutions because of faculty insistence that there be no "second-class" institutions in a state structure. Doctoral-granting institutions want to be classified as research universities. Comprehensive state universities want to be classified as doctoral-granting universities. Some specialized institutions want to be recognized as research and doctoral-granting institutions. There are even two-year institutions that want to become four-year comprehensive institutions. The author knows of at least one instance — not in one of the twenty-five states of our study — where the faculty voted censure of the president for agreeing to a statement of mission adopted by the state coordinating board that the faculty regarded as giving the university a status somewhat less than that of the "flagship" university of the state.

While we did find bits and pieces of all our concerns among the fourteen master plans that we examined, no single master plan embodied all the component elements that go to make up an adequate statement of mission. We shall therefore devote the remainder of this chapter to a discussion of the component elements of a statement of mission that do tend to provide a meaningful differentiation of mission among public institutions of higher education.

Major Purpose

We may properly begin with consideration of a statement of mission that classifies public institutions of higher education as to major purpose. Some states had begun in 1981 to make use of the new classification structure announced by the National Center for Education Statistics in April of that year. This new classification structure, apart from making a distinction between public sponsorship and private sponsorship, was divided into six major categories as follows:

A.   Doctoral-granting institutions
B.   Comprehensive institutions

C. General baccalaureate institutions
D. Professional and specialized institutions
    D-1. Medical
    D-2. Other
E. Two-year institutions

A working paper prepared by the National Center for Higher Education Management Systems (NCHEMS) in 1980 on the subject of an improved taxonomy of postsecondary institutions had proposed a somewhat more elaborate classification structure (Makowski and Wulfsberg, 1980). The principal differences between the working paper and the decision by the National Center for Education Statistics (1981a) involved a subdivision of doctoral-granting institutions into two groupings (major research institutions and other major doctoral institutions) and a subdivision of two-year institutions into three groupings (comprehensive two-year institutions, academic two-year institutions, and multiprogram occupational two-year institutions). In addition, both the NCHEMS working paper and the announcement by the National Center for Education Statistics divided professional and specialized institutions into several groupings. The center's announcement employed the following subclassification:

D- 1. Divinity institutions
D- 2. Medical institutions
D- 3. Other health institutions
D- 4. Engineering schools
D- 5. Business and management schools
D- 6. Art, music, and design schools
D- 7. Law schools
D- 8. Education schools
D- 9. U.S. service schools
D-10. Other specialized schools

Although the National Center for Education Statistics indicated that it would make use of these ten groupings within the category of professional and specialized institutions, it said that its published reports would make use of only the two groupings of specialized institutions mentioned earlier in this section. The center announced that the criterion for inclusion as a doctoral-granting institution would be the award of a minimum of thirty doctoral degrees a year in three or more doctoral-level programs. The criteria for inclusion in the category of comprehensive institutions would be the award of fewer than thirty doctoral-level degrees, or the award of such degrees in fewer than three programs, and the award of at least thirty postbaccalaureate degrees in three or more programs. General baccalaureate institutions would be those awarding less than thirty postbaccalaureate degrees per year, or awarding such degrees in fewer than three fields, and awarding over 75 percent of their degrees at the baccalaureate or higher level. Two-year institutions would be those awarding less than 25 percent of their degrees at the baccalaureate level and awarding over 75 percent of their degrees for two years of course work, including formal awards for less than two years of work.

Since the new six-category classification would be employed beginning in 1982 in reporting enrollment and financial data for the Higher Education General Information Survey (HEGIS),* it was apparent that state boards of higher education at a minimum would find it necessary to classify all public institutions by major purpose as defined by the National Center for Education Statistics. State boards of higher education, especially coordinating boards and advisory boards with their interest in all higher education institutions, would be well advised to make use of the subgroupings for doctoral-granting institutions and for two-year institutions as originally proposed by NCHEMS in 1980. In addition, these boards might make use of the subcategories for specialized institutions as set forth in the National Center for Education Statistics (1981a) announcement. The NCHEMS criterion for a major research university was inclusion in the top seventy-five doctoral-granting universities in terms of the amount of separately budgeted research reported in the HEGIS data. A comprehensive two-year institution was one awarding more than 20 percent, but less

* The preliminary enrollment report for fall 1982 issued by the National Center for Education Statistics in January 1983 made use of only five categories. The category "specialized" was not divided into medical schools and other.

than 80 percent, of its degrees in occupational and vocational fields. An academic two-year institution was one awarding at least 80 percent of its degrees in academic fields. A multipurpose occupational two-year institution was one conferring degrees and awards in two or more occupational programs but granting fewer than 20 percent of its degrees in academic areas of study.

The major purpose of a public institution is important in terms of program scope. A major research university is one that has a considerable number of doctoral degree programs and carries out a substantial amount of specially funded research. Other major doctoral institutions include those that also have a fairly extensive array of doctoral degree programs but a lesser amount of separately budgeted research. A comprehensive state university is one that offers degrees in the five major areas of the arts and sciences (the biological sciences, the humanities, mathematics, the physical sciences, and the social and behavioral sciences) and degrees in three or more professional fields (such as business and management, the fine and visual arts, nursing, and teacher education) at the bachelor's and master's degree levels, with perhaps one or two doctoral degree programs. The general baccalaureate institution primarily offers bachelor's degree programs. The two-year institution may be comprehensive in scope (it may have a college-transfer or academic program and programs in several technologies); the academic two-year institution primarily offers an associate degree program in the arts and sciences; and the occupational two-year institution primarily offers associate degree programs in various technologies.

The principal categories of the new classification structure for instructional programs published by the National Center for Education Statistics in 1981 are shown in Exhibit 2. The first part of the classification scheme provided for a categorization of programs by level; for higher (or postsecondary) education these levels were certificate programs, associate degree programs, baccalaureate programs, master's degree programs, intermediate (or specialist) degree programs, doctoral degree programs, and first professional degree programs (dentistry, medicine, optometry, osteopathic medicine, pharmacy, law, and veterinary medicine;

theology was omitted as not relevant for public institutions). The level of program offerings constitutes a major differentiation of the missions of public institutions. This distinction constitutes the fundamental difference among doctoral-level state universities, comprehensive state universities, general baccalaureate state colleges, and two-year institutions.

The second part of the classification structure was a taxonomy of instructional programs by fields of study. The revised classification structure of 1981 contained fifty principal fields of study, with various subgroupings for the disciplines, the professional fields of study, and the technologies. Because of the varied nature of the subcategories in the health field, as well as because of their generally high cost, the primary subgroupings of this field have been included in the listing.

One may quarrel with the revised classification structure as being unduly elaborate and requiring more details at the state government level than can be reasonably handled. Some generalization will undoubtedly be observed at both the institutional and the state government level. Obviously, to maintain a program inventory institution by institution is a fairly complicated process and requires a considerable amount of data about enrollment by levels (including lower-division and upper-division enrollments in bachelor's degree programs), about degrees and awards granted, and about faculty staffing and faculty compensation. Similar data are needed at the state government level in terms of program activities and costs.

In terms of subject matter specialization, the same fields of study are offered at the two-year level, the baccalaureate level, and the graduate level. This circumstance is apparent for both technological and professional studies, as well as for studies in the arts and sciences. Thus it becomes especially important to identify levels of program offerings. This need is apparent also in the arts and sciences and in many professional fields where there may be as many as three or even four levels of study (undergraduate, master's, specialist, and doctor's). In actual practice, it is not always clear what level of student will be permitted to enroll in a particular course, which further complicates the use of informational systems.

Exhibit 2. Classification of Instructional Programs.

Program Purpose

1.0   Elementary/Secondary Programs
    1.1   Elementary School Program
    1.2   Junior High School Program
    1.3   High School Diploma Program

2.0   Postsecondary Certificates/Diplomas/Degrees
    2.1   Postsecondary Certificate or Diploma
        (less than one year)
    2.2   Postsecondary Certificate or Diploma
        (one year or more but less than four years)
    2.3   Associate Degree
    2.4   Baccalaureate Degree

3.0   First Professional Certificates/Degrees
    3.1   First Professional Degree
    3.2   Postprofessional Certificate

4.0   Graduate Certificates/Degrees
    4.1   Graduate Certificate
    4.2   Master's Degree
    4.3   Intermediate Graduate Degree
    4.4   Doctoral Degree
    4.5   Postdoctoral Award

5.0   Nonformal Award Programs

Program Categories

Agriculture
    01.   Agribusiness and Agricultural
        Production
    02.   Agricultural Sciences
    03.   Renewable Natural Resources

Architecture and Environmental
Design
    04.   Architecture and
        Environmental Design

Area and Ethnic Studies
    05.   Area and Ethnic Studies

Business
    06.   Business and Management
    07.   Business and Office
    08.   Marketing and
        Distribution

Communications
    09.   Communications
    10.   Communication Technologies

Computer and Information Sciences
    11.   Computer and Information
        Sciences

Consumer, Personal, and
Miscellaneous Services
    12.   Consumer, Personal, and
        Miscellaneous Services

Education
    13.   Education

Engineering
    14.   Engineering
    15.   Engineering and Related
        Technologies

Foreign Languages
16. Foreign Languages

Health
17. Allied Health
18. Health Sciences
    18.01 Audiology and
          Speech Pathology
    18.02 Basic Clinical Health
          Sciences
    18.03 Chiropractic
    18.04 Dentistry
    18.05 Emergency/Disaster
          Science
    18.06 Epidemiology
    18.07 Health Sciences
          Administration
    18.08 Hematology
    18.09 Medical Laboratory
    18.10 Medicine
    18.11 Nursing
    18.12 Optometry
    18.13 Osteopathic Medicine
    18.14 Pharmacy
    18.15 Podiatry
    18.16 Population and
          Family Planning
    18.17 Predentistry
    18.18 Premedicine
    18.19 Prepharmacy
    18.20 Preveterinary
    18.21 Prosectorial Science
    18.22 Public Health
          Laboratory Science
    18.23 Toxicology
    18.24 Veterinary Medicine

Home Economics
19. Home Economics
20. Vocational Home Economics

Industrial Arts
21. Industrial Arts

Law
22. Law

Letters
23. Letters

Liberal/General Studies
24. Liberal/General Studies

Library and Archival Sciences
25. Library and Archival Sciences

Life Sciences
26. Life Sciences

Mathematics
27. Mathematics

Military Sciences
28. Military Sciences
29. Military Technologies

Multi-Interdisciplinary Studies
30. Multi-Interdisciplinary
    Studies

Parks and Recreation
31. Parks and Recreation

Personal and Social Development
32. Basic Skills
33. Citizenship/Civic Activities
34. Health-Related Activities
35. Interpersonal Skills
36. Leisure and Recreational
    Activities
37. Personal Awareness

Philosophy, Religion, and Theology
38. Philosophy and Religion
39. Theology

Physical Sciences
40. Physical Sciences
41. Science Technologies

Psychology
42. Psychology

Public Affairs and Protective
Services
43. Protective Services
44. Public Affairs

Social Sciences
45. Social Sciences

Trade and Industrial
46. Construction Trades
47. Mechanics and Repairers
48. Precision Production
49. Transportation and
    Material Moving

Visual and Performing Arts
50. Visual and Performing Arts

Source: National Center for Education Statistics (1981a).

The disciplines of the arts and sciences are generally considered to be the foundation stones of knowledge upon which applied technologies and professions develop. Moreover, the concept of general education at the two-year or four-year level of study requires the offering of courses embracing most, if not all, disciplines. While general education requirements in an associate degree or a bachelor's degree program are usually fulfilled by having a student distribute his or her courses across several broad fields (biological sciences, humanities, mathematics, physical sciences, and social and behavioral sciences), it is necessary for both the two-year and the four-year institution to offer courses in all these areas in order to meet the variety of student interests.

In this review of the complications of program identification for purposes of coordination at the state level, reference to one classification area in the structure established by the National Center for Education Statistics has been omitted: personal and social development. The extent to which formal courses for degree credit have been developed in such fields as basic skills, citizenship activities, health-related activities, interpersonal skills, recreational activities, and personal awareness is uncertain. One of the arguments for the residential institution has been that the student acquired this kind of personal development through extracurricular activities rather than through the formal curriculum. And, undoubtedly, the social and behavioral sciences, psychology, and physical education and health courses have explored various phases of personal and social development. It is evident that most, if not all, institutions have found it necessary in recent years to offer skills development programs because of inadequacies in the secondary school preparation of students. Often this skills development activity is offered as a student service rather than as an instructional program.

Identifying degree program offerings, making an inventory of them, and receiving information about their output and costs are activities essential to a statewide governing board, a state coordinating board, and a state advisory board. Program coordination, the elimination of program duplication, and ensuring that programs meet state and student needs depend upon program information. Program review and the approval of new programs depend on criteria about needs, quality, and costs. Indeed, a major reason why a specialized agency in higher education is necessary at the state government level is the complicated nature of program management.

We may summarize this discussion by indicating in general terms the program distribution to be observed by public institutions of higher education. The two-year institution will offer an academic program, as well as programs in selected occupational fields and technologies. The general baccalaureate institution will primarily offer a program in the arts and sciences and in certain professions at the bachelor's degree level; it may also offer one or two programs at the master's degree level. Usually the general baccalaureate institution will add some courses in business management to its curriculum in economics, some courses in computer programming to its curriculum in mathematics, some courses in social work to its curriculum in sociology, and some courses in recreational leadership or coaching to its curriculum in physical education. In addition, the general baccalaureate institution will probably include some courses in education as part of its offerings in the social and behavioral sciences and some courses in art and music as part of its offerings in the humanities.

The comprehensive state university will offer programs in the arts and sciences and in several professional fields (often business management, computer science, nursing, teacher education, and the fine and visual arts) at the bachelor's degree and the master's degree level. Some comprehensive state universities may offer one or more programs in engineering and may even offer a first professional degree program (as in law). There may also be one or two programs at the doctoral level.

The doctoral-granting state universities will offer programs in the arts and sciences and in various professional fields at the bachelor's, master's, specialist, and doctoral degree levels. They may also offer one or more first professional degree programs. The major state research university may offer much the same array of programs but in addition will be heavily involved in separately budgeted research. When the data are available, we shall probably find that there are thirty-eight to forty major state research universities. They will probably be distributed as follows:

Massachusetts (one), Connecticut (one), New Jersey (one), Pennsylvania (two), Maryland (one), North Carolina (one), Georgia (one), Florida (one), Alabama (one), Tennessee (one), Kentucky (one), Ohio (two), Michigan (two), Indiana (two), Illinois (one), Wisconsin (one), Minnesota (one), Iowa (one), Missouri (one), Louisiana (one), Kansas (one), Texas (two), Colorado (two), New Mexico (one), Arizona (one), California (five), Oregon (one), Washington (one), and Hawaii (one).

California was the only state in our study that had defined the major purpose of its three-tiered structure of higher education by law. The master plan legislation of 1960 provided that only the University of California in the state system could award the Ph.D. degree. The California State University System could award degrees through the master's and specialist levels; and, in some instances, campuses of the system had entered into cooperative doctoral degree programs with units of the University of California system. The community college system could award the associate degree.

In all but one or two other states, if major purpose was defined, it was defined by a master plan or by action of a coordinating board or a statewide governing board. State legislatures preferred to leave this kind of decision to an administrative body.

Research Emphasis

An institution could not achieve the status of a leading research university simply on the basis of federal research grants; such status depended equally on state government support, which made possible the faculty salaries, the work loads, and the enrollment of graduate students essential to the pursuit of research as a major program emphasis. This state support might be provided in several ways: by an appropriation formula that favored graduate student instruction at the doctoral level, by special appropriations for research activities or general research support, and by sizable undergraduate enrollments that provided jobs for graduate students as teaching assistants and funds that could be allocated by a governing board for graduate instruction.

Master plans in various states sought to limit the extent of graduate education at the doctoral level, and such provisions could be enforced by decisions on program approval made by governing boards or coordinating boards. In other states, the appropriation process was relied upon to give greater financial support to the state universities having status as major research universities. One reason why a formula approach was rejected in some states was the fear that it would result in some equalization of support for the major research university (or universities), the other doctoral-granting universities, and the comprehensive state universities. Such equalization might well have had the effect, as it probably would have in Indiana and Illinois, or reducing state government support essential for maintaining a university's status as a major research institution.

Faculty members in other than major research universities tended to be unhappy in the 1960s and early 1970s about their limited opportunities to participate in the conduct of doctoral degree programs and to engage in research activity. This unhappiness was alleviated in some part in the late 1970s and early 1980s by the realization that the market demand for recipients of the Ph.D. degree had subsided and that higher education institutions in the 1980s would at best absorb only about one half of all the individuals receiving the doctoral degree as of 1981 and 1982. Even so, faculty members in general tended to prefer research rather than teaching and graduate students rather than undergraduate students. Faculty members admired the process that had made them faculty members and were inclined to want to replicate themselves. And it is hardly surprising that faculty members in other than major research universities tended to resent the implication that they were not competent to carry on meaningful research activity.

As a consequence of these attitudes, master plans, as well as governing boards, coordinating boards, and advisory boards, tried not to make invidious comparisons among state universities insofar as research activity was concerned. Rather, research activity was recognized as a major emphasis in some state universities and as a general emphasis in other state universities. The allocation formula adopted by the statewide governing board in Mississippi recognized this distinction. Thus, a larger allocation for research activity was made to the three doctoral-granting universities than to the other five comprehensive institutions in the system.

Even this kind of contrast was not altogether satisfactory for many state universities. The most that could be said for this approach was that it acknowledged research activity as an appropriate part of the work load of all faculty members at the university level in a state system of higher education. At the same time, it simply was not feasible in the light of the economic circumstances that existed in most states in 1981 and 1982, and indeed in the light of the economic circumstances that had existed generally after 1973, for state governments to endeavor to support a major research emphasis in all state universities. Some distinctions in research emphasis had to be made, and state governments generally were making such distinctions and were endeavoring to enforce them.

Public Service Activities

Another problem in the determination of institutional missions was that of the emphasis to be given to public service activities. In certain situations the public service mission of a state university was determined by circumstance. State governments had since 1914 appropriated matching funds to the 1862 land-grant institutions for the support of agricultural extension services. State universities with a health science center received financial support from state governments for teaching hospitals. During the 1960s many states began to provide some financial support for statewide networks of public broadcasting. All these operations constituted forms of public service. The problem was how far state governments, and local governments, were willing to go in the support of these activities.

In the 1950s there was considerable pressure for the enactment of federal legislation that would authorize grants for the establishment of an urban extension service. Eventually, Title I of the Higher Education Act of 1965 authorized grants to the states for continuing education projects. Although these grants were curtailed in the late 1970s and early 1980s, some state governments continued to provide support to one or more urban universities to undertake projects for the benefit of municipal governments or urban populations. Community colleges receiving a portion of their support from local governments were inclined to spend some part of this support for public service activities to assist local citizens; these projects generally took the form of daycare centers and nondegree courses for homemakers and others in the community.

Institutions of higher education tended to be quite interested in public service projects that brought the expertise of faculty members to bear upon the problems created by poverty and by the lack of employment skills, homemaking skills, and craft skills. The effectiveness of these public service projects depended on the amount of funds available for them and on the competence of faculty members in helping citizens through demonstrations and short courses.

Governing boards, coordinating boards, and advisory boards were hard pressed to determine the desirable emphasis to give to public service activities in their master plans and in their recommendations for state financial support. Governors and legislatures were inclined to believe that all but a few public service projects should be financed by charges to beneficiaries and by private gifts. Only in a few instances were they inclined to offer tax support for public service activities. Indeed, the operation of individual public broadcasting stations was increasingly dependent on private gifts rather than state funding as of the late 1970s and early 1980s.

In Ohio the master plan approved by the board of regents in 1982 called for "dramatically expanded and intensified" public service activities by higher education. The master plan mentioned the activities already under way in the technology transfer organization, the area health education centers, the labor education and research service, the cooperative extension service, and the urban universities grant program. The board asserted that public service projects should be more closely focused on the need to solve the state's economic problems. More specifically, it declared that Ohio's colleges and universities, business leaders, labor leaders, and government officials should join in a new social compact to meet the problems of reindustrialization and economic growth in Ohio.

Subsequently, the board of regents submitted a formal proposal to the General Assembly in response to a legislative request for advice about the development of a business and industrial extension service. The board proposed legislation that would establish an Ohio Business, Education, and Government Alliance to pool the state's resources in a program of economic renewal. The proposal was primarily concerned with the kind of organizational structure to be established and with state financing rather than with a substantive set of activities to be undertaken by the new organization. The board asked for an initial appropriation of nearly $5 million to launch the alliance and for an appropriation of $7 million in the second year of the 1983–1985 biennium. It remained to be seen what response the Ohio General Assembly would make to this recommendation in 1983.

The Ohio master plan and special proposal in 1982 were, on the one hand, a commitment of higher education to work effectively with business, labor, and government to the end of economic renewal and, on the other hand, an indication of the major thrust that the public service activities of state institutions would probably take in the decade of the 1980s. Which universities in Ohio would be involved in this effort and what the effort would actually consist of would be determined if and when the concept of an alliance of business, education, and government was accepted and implemented. But it seemed probable that master plans in other states would more and more focus on problems of economic growth as a public service emphasis as the 1980s proceeded.

Residential and Urban Missions

Another concern in defining the mission of public institutions of higher education was that of geographical orientation. This concern had several aspects: the geographical dispersion of public institutions, the carrying out of an urban mission by institutions in a major urban environment, the enrollment of a commuting as distinguished from a residential student body, and the provision of programs and services based upon geographically perceived needs.

The geographical characteristic of institutional mission was clearly apparent in the instance of two-year institutions. The comprehensive community college, the academic institution, and the multipurpose occupational institution were urban located and were oriented to meeting the higher education and other needs of the district they served. The problem of duplication arose for coordinating and advisory state boards of higher education when there were two of these types of institutions serving the same or a similar geographical area.

Urban-located comprehensive state universities and urban-located doctoral-granting universities were usually intended to meet the higher education needs of the urban or metropolitan area that they served. Some major research universities were also located in large urban areas but were primarily oriented to the service of residential students and to the performance of research and other services for the state, the region, and the nation rather than for the local area. Given these differing missions, there might be two different public universities in the metropolitan area. Thus, the state university system in Georgia maintained Georgia Institute of Technology and Georgia State University in Atlanta. Minnesota maintained the University of Minnesota in the Twin Cities, and the state university system maintained Metropolitan State University in the same area as an upper-division institution. In addition to the University of California campuses in Berkeley, Los Angeles, Irvine, and San Diego, the California State University System operated a state university campus in San Francisco, three campuses near San Francisco, six campuses in the Los Angeles area, and one in San Diego. For the most part, the campuses of the University of California were not urban oriented, and the campuses of California State University were.

An important difference between an urban-oriented campus and a nonurban-oriented campus was the matter of commuting, as opposed to residential, students. Commuting students were often part-time students; they often attended courses in the late afternoon, in the evening, or on Saturday when they could get away from work. Commuting students tended to be older than residential students and to be particularly interested in advancing their employment skills. In contrast, residential students were usually full-time students and often were younger and more affluent than commuting students. Residential students tended to have considerable academic ability, and they required and expected more services than did commuting students. Not only did residential students require housing and food service but they also required extensive health, social, and recreational services.

Of the twenty-five states included in this study, twenty-two had located their flagship state university in a place not destined to become a major center of population in the state. In nine of the twenty-five states a separate land-grant state college had been created after the federal Morrill Act of 1862. In only one instance was this land-grant college (eventually all became state universities) located in the major urban center.

After World War II, however, public higher education finally had to recognize the existence of the American city. The response was to locate branches in major urban centers, as in Massachusetts, Indiana, Illinois, Alabama, and California; to take over municipal universities and to make them into state universities, as in New York, Ohio, Kansas, and Texas; to establish new state universities and to take over private institutions in urban centers, as in New York, Pennsylvania, Florida, Georgia, Ohio, Illinois, and Texas; and to change teacher's colleges into urban universities, as in Pennsylvania, Illinois, and Texas. The development of urban universities occurred simultaneously with an increased demand in the labor market for technically and professionally educated talent.

The urban commuting student was place bound. It was not possible for the student who was employed full time or part time to move to a campus in another part of a state in order to obtain graduate education or first professional education. As a consequence urban communities placed pressure on state governments to authorize a full array of graduate and first professional programs in the new urban state universities, even though these programs were already available at the flagship state university or the land-grant university in another location. These pressures, which have been especially evident in California, Pennsylvania, Ohio, Georgia, Florida, Indiana, Illinois, Missouri, and Texas, were exerted in the name of student need and urban economic growth.

Geography continued to be a major complication in the authorization of programs, especially at the graduate and first professional levels. No state had successfully resolved this problem. Even in California, which seemed to have gone farthest toward a solution, there had been pressures to merge the University of California and the California State University System and then to divide the merged university into two parts, one multi-campus university in the north and another in the south. The Academy for Educational Development at legislative request prepared a report early in the 1970s to describe how such a geographically arranged system might be organized.

Student Access

All twenty-five states in this study practiced open admission in some parts of their systems of higher education. But looking at all fifty states, we find that only six had specified open admission to all public institutions by law. Otherwise, open access was a policy adopted by governing boards of individual institutions or of multicampus systems.

In California the 1960 master plan legislation specified admission requirements for the three components of the state structure of higher education. The University of California system was directed to admit as undergraduate students those individuals who ranked in the upper 12.5 percent of their high school graduating class. The California State University System was directed to enroll all high school graduates who ranked in the upper third of their high school class, and the community colleges were directed to admit all high school graduates who applied.

While some states expected the community colleges and vocational-technical schools to admit any high school graduate, many state universities, especially urban ones, also practiced open admission. The Morrill Act of 1862 gave an impetus to open admission at land-grant institutions in two respects: It was intended to make higher education more generally available to the so-called working class and to offer programs of practical rather than classical education. This emphasis on open admission and practical or professional courses of instruction remained a guiding heritage for many land-grant institutions into the 1970s and early 1980s. A report at the University of Maryland in 1981 entitled *The Post-Land-Grant University* emphasized the need for selective admission at the land-grant university that was or aspired to be a major research university.

Open admission versus selective admission involved difficult questions of educational quality and educational justice. It was apparent in this study that coordinating boards and advisory boards were generally content to leave the resolution of these issues to institutional governing boards. Neither kind of board was inclined to recommend legislation to determine the admission practices of public higher education institutions, although both coordinating and advisory boards assumed that two-year institutions would practice open admission.

The advantage of open admission was that it gave all high school graduates the opportunity to enroll in a public institution and to demonstrate in actual classroom settings that they had the ability and perseverance to complete a degree program. The disadvantage to open admission was that institutions practicing such admission found it essential, particularly in the 1960s and 1970s, to assist students to overcome deficiencies in their learning, reading, and computational skills and to provide degree courses that would permit the slow learner to match learning ability with learning expectation.

The advantage of selective admission was that access to higher education could be provided primarily to students of academic ability as indicated by rank in their high school classes, by scores on standardized tests, by recommendations from high school teachers and counselors, and by personal interviews. The disadvantage in selective admission was that rank in high school class and test scores did not always correlate with the subsequent academic achievement of a student, while recommendations and personal interviews could sometimes be misleading. Moreover, black and other minority group leaders insisted that test scores tended to favor whites and to discriminate against blacks and students from impoverished families.

A major factor in favor of selective admission was its relationship to institutional quality. While institutional quality was at best difficult to define and was depended upon many variables (faculty qualifications, physical facilities and campus environment, learning resources, and expenditures per student), no variable was more closely related to an institution's reputation than the quality of its entering students. The most prestigious private colleges and universities in the United States practiced selective admission, and public universities that aspired to equal the standards of private colleges and universities did the same. A study in 1978 by the Higher Education Research Institute listed the twenty most selective public institutions alongside the twenty-five most selective private institutions based upon a selectivity index. The private institutions were led by the California Institute of Technology, Amherst, Harvard, and M.I.T.; the public institutions were led by the State University of New York at Albany, the University of Virginia, the University of California at Santa Cruz, Iowa State, and Michigan. The twenty most selective public institutions were distributed by state as follows: Massachusetts (one), New York (two), New Jersey (one), Virginia (one), North Carolina (one), Ohio (one), Michigan (one), Wisconsin (one), Illinois (one), Iowa (one), Colorado (one), Washington (one), and California (seven). The selectivity index for the twenty-five private institutions was higher than for the twenty public institutions.

The statewide governing boards had the responsibility for determining the selectivity standards for all the individual campuses under their authority. In Mississippi, for example, the Board of Trustees of State Institutions of Higher Learning had fixed a minimum American College Test (ACT) score as a floor for admission to the eight universities enrolling undergraduate students. This floor varied from a score of 15 to a score of 10. With a standardized median of 18, a score of 15 would provide access to nearly two thirds of all applicants, while a score of 10 would provide access to about 80 percent of all applicants. The junior colleges were expected to provide higher education opportunity for all other students. But each university was permitted to provide admission to some students (5 percent of a freshman class) who did not meet these minimum requirements.

Other governing boards also tried to establish differential

access standards to the various parts of their higher education systems. Coordinating boards and advisory boards generally deferred to governing boards in the determination of admission standards. National studies clearly indicated that public institutions practicing selective admission had a much higher rate of freshman retention than did open-admission institutions; selective admission four-year public institutions retained 76 to 80 percent of a freshman class, while open-admission public universities retained only 60 percent of a freshman class (Lenning, 1982).

Enrollment Size

As we noted earlier, the Carnegie Commission on Higher Education (1973c) set forth the desirable minimum and maximum enrollment sizes for institutions of higher education. The minimum effective size for both doctoral-granting and comprehensive universities was fixed at 5,000 full-time equivalent student enrollment, and the minimum effective size for a community college — presumably a comprehensive community college — was fixed at 2,000 full-time equivalent enrollment.

Because of concerns for geographical access to higher education, there were institutions of higher education in many states that did not meet these standards of effective enrollment size. In every one of the twenty-five states of this study except New Jersey, we found that, as of 1981, there were state university campuses with enrollments under 4,000 students and two-year institutions with enrollments under 2,000 students. In Texas there were eight state university campuses with fewer than 4,000 students; in Maine, New York, Pennsylvania, and Georgia there were six such campuses in each state; in South Dakota there were five; in West Virginia, Mississippi, Colorado, and Montana there were four. Other states had from one to three state university campuses with under 4,000 students. The worst situation in respect to two-year institutions was in Ohio, where there were thirty two-year campuses with under 2,000 students. There were other states with a substantial number of such two-year institutions: Maine (five), New Hampshire (seven), Connecticut (five), New York (five), Georgia (eight), Mississippi (five), Minnesota (twelve), Missouri (six), Kansas (thirteen), and Texas (nine).

The mission of these smaller state universities and two-year institutions was in each instance to provide higher education services to a sparsely populated area of the state or to some particular group of students, such as black students. In Minnesota, for example, the advisory board had been asked to make special studies of the small two-year campuses and two small state university campuses. These studies found that the major cost factor in operating a small campus was the proportion of the total operating budget required for overhead costs (academic support, student services, plant operation, and institutional administration). In each instance more than 50 percent of the institutional budget was needed for overhead. In addition, these studies pointed out that, in order to fulfill its mission, a small campus had to provide a minimum number of core courses and faculty specializations. For a four-year institution the core staffing was fixed at some 100 faculty positions, which meant in some cases a costly student-faculty ratio.

In Minnesota the state community college system responded to these studies by consolidating the overhead activities of various small campuses in order to economize on costs. In other situations, both in Minnesota and elsewhere, it was simply admitted that small campuses would cost more per student to operate than larger campuses. State legislatures interested in keeping small campuses in operation then had to find funds to ensure that these institutions would remain viable.

Both in Massachusetts and Connecticut the issue of mergers was in good part responsible for a reorganization of the higher education system. A new statewide governing board in Massachusetts moved promptly to merge two institutions, and in Connecticut in 1982 the coordinating board was given authority to propose the merger of institutions. It was likely that as costs continued to increase, the problem of mergers or closings of public institutions would become more urgent.

Enrollment size was important to the realization of the assigned mission of an institution. Special provision to meet extra costs was imperative if enrollment size was to be subordinated to the geographical or other mission of small campuses.

Enrollment Characteristics

State master plans and statements of institutional mission were very cautious in their approach to one difference among institutions of higher education, namely, the fact that some institutions enrolled a predominantly white student body and others a predominantly black student body. At one time state government law in thirteen southern states required the establishment of separate institutions of higher education for black students. Such desegregation by law has been recognized as unconstitutional for the past thirty years in the United States, and in every one of the thirteen states black students have been enrolled in predominantly white institutions during the past twenty years.

The federal government has required state governments in the thirteen states to develop master plans that would desegregate predominantly black institutions by increasing the white student enrollment. The suggested procedure for accomplishing this objective has been the elimination of some professional programs in predominantly white institutions and the introduction or expansion of these same programs in predominantly black institutions. This procedure seemed to be particularly appropriate when there were two state universities in the same urban area, one with a predominance of white students and the other a predominance of black students. Of the thirteen southern states that at one time prescribed legal separation of white and black students, five were states included in this study. Of these five states, three had developed so-called integration plans that had been officially approved by an agency of the federal government; in the other two states there were lawsuits pending that would require them to develop acceptable plans or lose federal financial support for student assistance and research activities.

In six other states of this study there were state universities that enrolled predominantly black students as a matter of urban location and as a matter of choice on the part of black students. There were even more states where community colleges and vocational-technical schools enrolled a predominantly black student body, again primarily because of location. Any campus in an inner-city area could be expected to enroll a predominantly black student body.

The elimination of legally prescribed separate institutions of higher education for white and black students was a necessary step in the direction of educational justice in the United States. The admission of black students who could meet the appropriate standards to predominantly white institutions was an accomplished fact in all twenty-five states of this study, and presumably in the remaining twenty-five states as well. But the elimination of all state universities and public two-year institutions serving a predominantly black student body involved very different questions of public policy. In at least five states of this study, there was no reason in terms of enrollment size to continue to operate certain predominantly black state universities. Their students could easily be absorbed into other state universities with largely white student bodies. These black state universities were maintained in operation because of the political pressure exerted by black political leaders in the five states.

It was argued that many black students were socially more at ease and intellectually better able to learn when associated together on a campus with a predominantly black faculty, professional staff, and executive leadership. Even if these state universities were of relatively small size, it was argued that the additional cost of operation should be borne by state governments in order to provide a satisfactory and congenial learning environment for black students.

Federal desegregation guidelines for changes in the student composition of largely black institutions did not propose the elimination of such institutions. Rather, the guidelines proposed an increase in white student enrollments, even if this action might result in enrollment loss for predominantly white state universities. In four states of this study proposals had been made to merge predominantly black state universities with predominantly white institutions, but these proposals had been vigorously opposed by black students, black faculty members, and black leaders.

It was clearly evident as of 1982 that discrimination in admission on the basis of race was not the current public policy and would not be public policy in the future. It was equally evident that in a number of states the mission of certain public institutions of higher education would continue to be for some time to serve a predominantly black student body. Master plans and mission statements would be very reluctant to avow this purpose openly and clearly, but the purpose would remain just the same.

Financial Resources

All the states in this study in 1981 and 1982 found the financial resources available for the operation and capital improvement of their public institutions of higher education to be severely limited. State governments were beginning to perceive that some adjustments might well become necessary in the 1980s and 1990s to fit the missions of public institutions to the available resources. But the whole subject of financial support is so important that we shall consider it separately in the following chapter.

If tax receipts were not adequate for the support of public institutions of higher education, these institutions had other sources of income they might utilize. One way to increase their income was to raise charges to students and others; the objection to this action, apart from the political opposition of students, was the likelihood that increased charges would result in reduced enrollments. This result seemed all the more likely in the face of federal reductions in student financial assistance. A second possible source of additional income was private gifts and benefactions. Some public institutions had done quite well in cultivating philanthropic support, but other public institutions doubted their capacity to engender much support of this kind.

There were other possible choices. One was to restrict enrollments in public institutions. No state governments were disposed to restrict open access at least someplace in a state system. Another choice was to eliminate high-cost programs or programs not integrally related to the essential mission of an institution. A process of program review instituted by public institutions and reported to state higher education boards could serve to identify high-cost programs and low-priority programs. A third choice was to work out cooperative arrangements whereby high-cost programs could be offered on a joint basis or support programs could be consolidated. But most public institutions seemed to have severe reservations about cooperation with other public institutions, primarily because such cooperation was costly in time and energy and required too many compromises.

An alternative to making programs geographically available was to offer financial assistance to students to attend institutions away from their home base. To be effective, however, such financial assistance would have to be sizable, and even then would probably not reach all the students desiring to enroll in particular instructional programs.

It was apparent in this study that state boards of higher education were only beginning as of 1982 to make in-depth studies of how to reformulate institutional missions to conform to the reality of reduced resources. Central staffs were generally somewhat small and were not prepared to undertake intensive analysis of methods for reducing costs. The generally acceptable procedure was to reduce state appropriations to individual institutions or to systems of public institutions proportionate to the overall recisions in state support. Specific reductions were then left to the discretion of the management of each institution. In Ohio, studies prepared by outside consultants in 1979 suggested various possibilities for cost containment, but the board of regents had no authority to direct the adoption of any particular action, and each public institution was expected to adopt such measures for cost reduction in the biennium 1981–1983 as it saw fit. Such a procedure left discretion in cost reduction to the executive leadership of individual institutions.

Any differential reduction in state support for institutions of higher education was a direct invitation to political infighting among them. The rivalries and political lobbying among public institutions over reductions in state support could be just as intense as the competition for increases in state support had been in the 1960s and 1970s. For this reason state boards of higher education had tasks to perform in the 1980s different from those of previous decades, but the new tasks were no less demanding.

⊰ 7 ⊱

Financing of
Institutional Objectives

IN ANY STUDY OF public higher
education, certain conclusions about the financing of higher
education will inevitably emerge. First, state governments vary
substantially in their willingness to provide for the support of
higher education. Second, state governments have different expectations about what will be accomplished by their appropriations
for higher education. Third, budgeting for higher education presents unique problems for state government budgeting, problems
different from those confronting other state government agencies.
Fourth, higher education presents special problems insofar as
financing capital improvements is concerned. Finally, there are
complications of choice to be resolved in state government financing of higher education. We will consider each of these subjects in
the present chapter. First, however, some general observations
and statistics are in order.

Table 7 presents the available financial data for all public
institutions of higher education for the fiscal year 1980. These
data include some $502 million spent on the operation of U.S.
service schools and some $60 million spent on the operation of
public institutions in the District of Columbia. Otherwise, the
state-sponsored and state-supported institutions of higher education had income of approximately $38.1 billion in the fiscal year

176

Table 7. Current Funds Income and Expenditures for
Public Institutions, 1980 (in Millions).

	Total	Universities	Other Four-Year	Two-Year
INCOME				
Tuition and Fees	$4,858	$2,012	$1,815	$1,031
State Government	17,927	6,789	7,541	3,597
Local Government	1,441	72	201	1,168
Federal Government	5,013	2,544	1,968	501
Private Gifts	974	629	315	30
Endowment	191	144	42	5
Educational Sales and Services	815	525	258	31
Auxiliary Enterprises	4,066	2,089	1,548	429
Hospitals	2,468	1,167	1,299	1
Independent Operations	111	54	52	5
Other	834	352	275	206
Total	$38,697	$16,376	$15,316	$7,005
EXPENDITURES				
Educational and General	$30,555	$12,488	$11,732	$6,335
Instruction	13,308	4,859	5,268	3,181
Research	3,378	2,420	932	26
Public Service	1,492	992	359	26
Student Aid	986	444	392	150
Academic Support	2,759	1,117	1,123	519
Student Services	1,753	470	736	547
Plant Operation	3,260	1,150	1,371	740
Institutional Support	3,126	905	1,333	888
Transfers	493	131	218	144
Auxiliary Enterprises	4,109	2,091	1,573	445
Hospitals	2,918	1,337	1,581	0
Independent Operations	94	55	29	10
Total	$37,677	$15,971	$14,915	$6,791

Note: Figures are rounded off.
Source: National Center for Education Statistics (1981b).

1980. The distribution of this income by three types of institutions is also shown. As mentioned in a previous chapter, the data for 1982 will be shown by a six-category rather than a three-category breakdown, which will be more meaningful for analytical purposes.

It will be noted from Table 7 that while public institutions of higher education had an income of $38.7 billion, only $18 billion, or 46.5 percent of the total, were derived from state governments. The other principal sources of income were distributed as follows: tuition and fees (12.4 percent), federal and local governments (16.5 percent), philanthropy (3.1 percent), sales and services (19.4 percent), and other (2.1 percent).

The important factor to bear in mind is that public institutions have multiple sources of income and that as of 1980 less than half the total income of these institutions came from state government appropriations, grants, and contracts. This fact does not deny the overwhelming importance of state government financial support of public institutions of higher education, but it does place that support in its proper perspective.

Looking at the differences among types of public institutions, we note two or three particular features insofar as sources of income are concerned. Federal funds went chiefly to universities and other four-year institutions rather than to two-year institutions. Since these funds were primarily intended for research, public service, and student aid, this circumstance is understandable. As of 1980 much of the federal financial assistance to students was not reported as governmental income since it was distributed directly to students, but there was supposed to be some change in this practice of reporting in the 1982–83 fiscal year. Local government support went principally to two-year institutions, yet even so state governments provided three times as much support to two-year institutions as did local governments.

On the expenditure side, we should observe the composition of educational and general expenditures by major program categories. The percentage distribution of these educational and general expenditures is shown in Table 8. Expenditures for research and public service activities were proportionately larger at universities than at other institutions, while expenditures for student financial aid were quite comparable at all institutions. Among support programs, expenditures for student services and institutional support were larger on a percentage basis at two-year institutions than at other institutions. This circumstance reflected the costs of the open-door admission policy of two-year institutions.

It is particularly important to observe the distribution of expenditures between output programs and support programs as given in Table 9. The first four program categories in Table 8

Table 8. Percentage Distribution of Educational and
General Expenditures by Types of Public Institutions, 1980.

	All Institutions	Universities	Other Four-Year Institutions	Two-Year Institutions
Instruction	43.5	39.2	45.3	50.8
Research	11.1	19.2	8.5	--
Public Service	4.9	8.0	2.6	1.6
Student Aid	3.3	3.2	3.4	3.2
Academic Support	8.8	8.8	9.4	8.0
Student Services	5.9	4.0	6.0	9.5
Plant Operation	10.8	8.8	12.0	11.0
Institutional Support	10.1	8.0	11.1	14.3
Transfers	1.6	0.8	1.7	1.6
	100.0	100.0	100.0	100.0

Source: National Center for Education Statistics (1981b).

represent institutional outputs: instruction, research, public service, and student aid. The remaining five program categories represent support programs or institutional overhead. Public institutions, it might be noted, have experienced a continuing increase in the costs of their support programs because of the higher energy and administrative expenditures needed to meet the requirements of various regulations, especially federal regulations.

We do not intend to focus on the financial problems of public institutions except as they affect state government responses. There have been several useful reviews of these concerns in recent years (Caruthers and Orwig, 1979; Frances, 1982). But the literature on financial analysis has ignored the technique of component

Table 9. Percentage Distribution of Expenditures.

	All Institutions	Universities	Other Four-Year Institutions	Two-Year Institutions
Outcome Programs	62.8	69.6	59.8	55.6
Support Programs	37.2	30.4	40.2	44.4

budget analysis. The financial report of a college or university represents a composite or overall summary of its sources of income and its principal programs of expenditure. In actual practice, however, there are several component budgets of an institution of higher education for which income and expenditure must be in some particular relationship. These component budgets may include instruction, research, public service, student aid, hospital operations, independent operations, and auxiliary enterprises. Each of these component budgets has its own sources of income, which is often restricted income that under the terms of a grant or bequest cannot be used for any other purpose. Auxiliary enterprises generate their own income from charges; these charges (including the allocation of student fees) must meet the costs of operations and debt service. The costs of operating a teaching hospital are usually met by patient charges, plus such endowment, gift, and subsidy income as may be available. Separately budgeted research is usually financed from restricted income. Separately budgeted public services are met by special appropriations and grants, as well as by income from sales and services.

Finally, special note must be made of the costs of student financial assistance. The recent National Center for Education Statistics financial reports have asked institutions of higher education to report the extent to which their expenditures for student financial assistance were met by restricted rather than unrestricted income. For the fiscal year 1980 all public institutions responding to the survey reported that they spent just under $1 billion for student aid and that some $648 million of this outlay was provided by restricted funds (governmental grants, private gifts, and endowment). These data thus indicate that about 35 percent of the expenditures for student aid had to be provided from the general income of public institutions. The proportion was even larger for private institutions (nearly 48 percent). It is obvious that neither public nor private institutions consider governmental and other earmarked resources adequate to meet the financial needs of the students they enroll, and consequently some portion of the general income of the institution (unrestricted gift income, unrestricted endowment income, and even some part of student fees) must be used to help students meet the direct costs of enrollment.

The financial reports of public institutions of higher education do not include all the appropriations made by state governments on behalf of higher education. The 1980 preliminary data from the National Center for Education Statistics indicated that state governments provided $387 million to private institutions of higher education. Pennsylvania and New York have for some time had sizable programs of direct subsidy to private institutions of higher education. Other states have also adopted programs of assistance to private institutions. In addition, most state student financial assistance grants are made directly to students and appear in institutional financial records only to the extent that students use this income to pay tuition or other institutional charges. Some state governments appropriate separate contributions to a retirement fund for faculty and other personnel of public colleges and universities. Some states appropriate separate amounts for the debt service on academic facilities utilized by public institutions. The data collected by Chambers (1980, 1981, 1982) indicated that state governments appropriated over $19 billion from tax funds in support of higher education programs in fiscal 1980. Public institutions reported receiving just under $18 billion from state governments for that year. The financial reports of public institutions thus show only a part, but certainly the major part, of state government appropriations on behalf of higher education.

Funding Variations Among States

There are substantial differences in the amount of support provided by different state governments to higher education. One measure of this difference is provided by the relationship between student fee income and the total income of public institutions of higher education. These differences for the twenty-five states of the study are shown in Table 10. It must be remembered that total current funds revenues include income from all sources and for all purposes, such as income from auxiliary enterprises. Tuition income will necessarily vary depending upon the number of out-of-state students enrolled in public institutions and paying higher fees than in-state students. Differences also reflect the proportion of students who are housed by public institutions and so pay charges to the institutions for room and board.

Table 10. Total Current Funds Revenues and Tuition and Fees Income
of Public Institutions in Twenty-Five States, 1980 (in Millions).

	Current Funds Revenues	Tuition and Fees Income	Percentage
Alabama	$ 778	$ 87	11.2
California	5,190	293	5.6
Colorado	689	126	18.3
Connecticut	335	38	11.3
Delaware	150	31	20.7
Florida	1,096	144	13.1
Georgia	670	78	11.6
Illinois	1,604	203	12.7
Indiana	958	145	15.1
Kansas	527	66	12.5
Maine	142	25	17.6
Massachusetts	517	61	11.8
Minnesota	822	98	11.9
Mississippi	501	58	11.6
Missouri	630	86	13.6
Montana	114	14	12.3
New Hampshire	122	33	27.0
New Jersey	822	149	18.1
New York	2,348	413	17.6
Ohio	1,666	331	19.9
Pennsylvania	1,425	344	24.1
South Dakota	123	17	13.8
Texas	2,543	210	8.3
Washington	927	85	9.2
West Virginia	306	26	8.4

Source: National Center for Education Statistics (1981b).

With these qualifications in mind, it is still possible to identify the low-tuition and high-tuition states among the twenty-five
states. For all fifty states tuition fees at public institutions came to
12.5 percent of total current funds revenues. Among the twenty-
five states, only four states were noticeably below this average.
The state with the lowest tuition was California. There were nine
states noticeably higher than the national average. New Hampshire and Pennsylvania were the states where tuition income was
the highest in relation to total income.

The variations among state governments in their support

of higher education reflect many factors. There are differences in regional tradition and history, as well as in the attitudes and commitments of governors and other political leaders. There are differences in the economic circumstances of states and in their willingness to give spending priority to higher education. Finally, there are differences in the ability of academic leaders to persuade politicians to provide resources for higher education. All these and other circumstances have their impact on a state government's willingness to finance higher education.

The most extensive analysis of state government financial support of higher education has been undertaken by Halstead (1983) of the National Institute of Education. Making use of the state appropriation data regularly collected by Chambers, Halstead developed a model to measure the principal factors that influence state government support of public higher education. The model used seven independent factors:

1. Resident student source
2. College attendance ratio
3. System cost index
4. Tax capacity
5. Tax effort
6. Allocation to higher education
7. Tuition factor

The use of these seven factors in a series of process relationships enabled Halstead to determine various derived or dependent factors: adjusted student enrollment, state and local appropriations per student, estimated tuition per student, and finally a state support figure as the output of the formula process.

Halstead collected data on the enrollment mix by type of institution for each of the fifty states. He employed a different classification system from the one officially announced by the National Center for Education Statistics (1981a). In fact, his classification was somewhat more elaborate than the one used by the Carnegie Commission and the Carnegie Council. He divided the component institutions of a state public higher education system into several types; Table 11 shows the national average

Table 11. Enrollment, Appropriation, and Tuition Data
by Type of Institution.

Type	Enrollment Distribution (Percentage)	Appropriation per Student	Tuition Revenue per Student
Research university with teaching hospital	10.8	$ 4,987	$1,373
University	14.9	3,863	1,163
Small university	5.1	2,909	1,222
Comprehensive institution	25.8	2,883	832
Baccalaureate institution	4.5	2,399	905
Two-year institution, academic	29.2	2,031	468
Two-year institution, occupational	8.0	2,266	576
Health professional institution	0.8	26,220	1,729
Other professional institution	0.8	3,242	1,140

Source: Halstead (1983).

distribution of enrollment and appropriation as of the 1980–81 academic year.

Table 12 shows for each of the states in this study the enrollment distribution as of the 1980–81 academic year. Enrollment distribution has a major impact upon expenditures and appropriations. In the absence of data on enrollment by program categories and levels of instruction for each state, Halstead used enrollment distribution by major types of institution in order to suggest differences in program costs and costs by level of instruction.

Halstead found the national average appropriation by state governments per student to be $3,102 as of the 1980–81 academic year, and he found the average revenue from tuition for that year to be $836 per student. The data for each of the twenty-five states included in this study are shown in Table 13. We may simply observe here that among the twenty-five states there was great variation in enrollment by type of institution. Thirteen states had no research university with a teaching hospital, while one state had 39 percent of all its public enrollment in such an institution. Seven states did not have a university as classified by

Table 12. Enrollment Distribution in Twenty-Five States by Type of Institution (in Percentages).

	Research University with Hospital	University	Small University	Comprehensive	Baccalaureate	Two-Year Academic	Two-Year Occupational	Health Profession	Other Profession
Alabama	8.9	27.9	0	36.3	0.7	22.0	3.4	0	0.8
California	10.7	2.1	0.7	26.4	0	55.8	3.8	0.4	0.2
Colorado	0	34.3	9.1	12.7	17.6	22.0	0.6	1.2	2.5
Connecticut	0	28.3	0	36.5	0	26.8	7.5	0.8	0
Delaware	0	69.3	0	0	7.8	0	22.9	0	0
Florida	13.7	16.6	0	14.4		55.3	0	0	0
Georgia	0	27.8	12.2	26.1	4.5	24.7	0.9	1.7	2.1
Illinois	11.0	12.2	11.0	13.3	0	51.1	0	1.4	0
Indiana	21.0	19.8	11.5	28.2	2.6	3.5	10.7	0	2.8
Kansas	0	42.2	0	26.9	4.7	23.5	0.4	2.2	0
Maine	0	0	0	63.4	8.2	6.6	12.2	0	9.6
Massachusetts	0	17.5	0	32.1	14.5	28.8	4.9	0.3	1.9
Minnesota	39.3	0	0	36.1	3.6	19.5	1.6	0	0
Mississippi	0	14.5	24.9	13.7	6.0	34.0	4.8	2.1	0
Missouri	18.3	0	6.4	39.8	5.0	24.9	0.2	0	5.5
Montana	0	0	0	68.5	12.0	6.4	0	0	13.1
New Hampshire	0	0	54.8	0	28.1	0	17.0	0	0
New Jersey	0	16.4	0	37.0	5.3	30.6	6.9	1.1	2.6
New York	0	12.1	2.8	30.4	5.0	33.0	12.4	1.5	2.8
Ohio	26.5	0	33.6	12.5	1.0	12.4	13.7	0.2	0.1
Pennsylvania	11.5	24.2	0	29.3	3.9	22.8	8.0	0.2	0.1
South Dakota	0	0	27.9	30.8	26.0	1.2	4.0	0	10.1
Texas	16.3	9.2	5.7	29.1	1.0	31.6	5.4	1.7	0
Washington	21.2	11.1	0	15.3	1.6	39.3	11.5	0	0
West Virginia	0	33.5	0	16.3	38.2	1.4	8.0	0.4	2.1

Source: Halstead (1983).

Halstead; in the other states university enrollment varied from 9 percent to 69 percent of all state enrollments. In the other classifications there were further variations in enrollment.

It has long been known in a general way that, apart from the effect of very small enrollment, programs differ considerably in their instructional costs (including overhead). Two-year academic programs tend to cost less per full-time equivalent student than do two-year technical programs. Baccalaureate programs in such professional fields as agriculture, engineering, fine arts, and nursing tend to cost more than baccalaureate programs in the arts and sciences. Master's degree and doctoral degree programs in the biological and physical sciences tend to cost more than such programs in the humanities and behavioral sciences. And health science programs, especially those for the doctor of medicine degree, tend to be the most costly programs of all. It was concern for these kinds of cost factors that underlay Halstead's efforts to present an enrollment distribution by type of institution for each state.

For the 1982–83 academic year, Halstead presented tabular data for each of the fifty states and the District of Columbia. He enumerated seven factors in state support of higher education: (1) high school graduates for 1981, (2) full-time equivalent enrollment in public higher education, (3) a system cost index based upon enrollment mix, (4) tax capacity, (5) tax effort, (6) allocation of tax revenues to higher education, and (7) tuition per student. From these factors Halstead derived a figure for each state that combined the appropriation per student and the tuition per student. He also presented an average for the fifty states and the District of Columbia.

The concepts of tax capacity and tax effort had been developed in an earlier study (McCoy and Halstead, 1979). Tax capacity was the potential of state and local governments to raise revenues for public purposes if each state were to apply national average tax rates to its tax base. Tax effort was the actual amount of state and local taxes collected in each state as a percentage of tax capacity.

The first column of Table 13 indicates the tax capacity for each of the twenty-five states of this study, as well as the national average. Tax capacity ranged from a high of nearly $1,200 per

Table 13. Critical Factors in State Support of Higher Education in Twenty-Five States.

	Tax Capacity per Capita 1981	Tax Effort (Percentage) 1981	Tax Revenues per Capita 1981	Allocation to Higher Education (Percentage) 1982–83	Appropriation per Student 1982–83	Appropriation and Tuition per Student 1982–83
Alabama	$ 767	90.6	$ 694	14.6	$3,229	$4,092
California	1,186	100.3	1,190	12.5	3,666	4,688
Colorado	1,161	83.6	970	12.5	3,254	4,649
Connecticut	1,132	102.7	1,162	6.8	3,756	4,590
Delaware	1,142	86.8	992	13.0	3,336	4,598
Florida	1,041	73.3	762	10.9	3,663	4,951
Georgia	838	97.3	815	11.8	4,582	5,231
Illinois	1,070	105.0	1,124	8.5	3,224	3,965
Indiana	932	88.5	825	10.8	3,368	4,029
Kansas	1,125	87.0	979	14.7	3,800	4,103
Maine	816	113.2	923	6.9	2,906	4,747
Massachusetts	989	134.0	1,325	4.5	2,716	4,105
Minnesota	1,031	108.8	1,121	9.2	3,350	3,854
Mississippi	737	94.6	698	16.4	3,566	4,370
Missouri	948	81.2	770	9.3	2,824	3,651
Montana	1,168	92.4	945	11.4	3,580	4,697
New Hampshire	982	73.9	725	5.2	1,663	3,953
New Jersey	1,078	111.7	1,204	7.1	3,764	5,150
New York	916	171.0	1,567	6.9	4,578	6,185
Ohio	972	88.7	862	8.2	2,666	3,766
Pennsylvania	931	104.8	975	7.5	3,777	5,777
South Dakota	888	92.9	825	9.5	2,456	3,657
Texas	1,360	64.6	878	16.2	4,588	4,931
Washington	1,021	92.1	940	11.2	2,764	3,419
West Virginia	926	83.1	770	12.1	3,351	3,811
U.S.A.	$1,029	100.0	$1,029	10.4	$3,655	$4,605

Source: Halstead (1983).

capita in California to a low of $737 in Mississippi. Tax capacity
exceeded the national average in twelve states and was below the
average in thirteen states. The second column shows the tax effort
of the twenty-five states, ranging from 71 percent higher than the
national average in New York to over 25 percent below the average in Florida and New Hampshire. The third column presents the
tax revenues per capita for 1981, the fourth column shows the
percentage allocation of tax revenues to higher education, the
fifth column shows the appropriation per student, and the final
column shows the total of appropriations and tuition payments
per student.

It is noteworthy that while appropriations per student
varied substantially among the states, from a high of $4,819 in
New York to a low of $1,957 in New Hampshire, no such varia-
tion occurred in the total of appropriations and tuition. Thus in
New Hampshire, which had a low appropriation per student,
there was nearly $2,000 per student in tuition income. Other
states with tuition income above $1,000 were Colorado,
Delaware, Indiana, Maine, New Jersey, New York, Ohio, and
Pennsylvania. Public higher education has clearly had the option
of countering relatively low appropriations per student with relatively higher tuition charges to students.

The total of appropriation and tuition income per student
in a state reflects various factors: the kinds of instructional programs provided, the number of students enrolled in these programs,
and the cost per student of these programs. The cost per student
reflected not only enrollment but also the level of faculty compensation, the nature of faculty work loads, and institutional overhead expenditures.

Halstead presented a comprehensive analysis of state
financing of higher education on a comparative basis. The strength
of the analysis was to be found in the calculations of appropriations
and tuition per full-time equivalent student and in the effort to
adjust expenditure data to enrollment mix. In the absence of more
extended information on enrollment and costs by program, this
analysis was as precise as could be undertaken. The comparison,
of course, was made state by state and not public institution by
public institution.

Chambers has for many years collected data from each of the fifty states about appropriations from tax revenues in support of higher education. His data have provided information about appropriations to individual universities and to various multi-campus systems; they have also included information on support for private institutions and for state student financial assistance programs, as well as for state boards of higher education.

The great advantage to the data provided by Chambers has been their timeliness. Their disadvantage, especially recently, has been their concentration on appropriations. In many instances, especially in 1981 and 1982, these appropriations had to be reduced by subsequent action of the governor or the legislature when tax revenues fell below estimates. Nonetheless, the Chambers data provide the most readily available information about state government support of higher education.

Table 14 presents the data about state government appropriations in the twenty-five states of this study for two time periods: the academic year 1971–72 and the academic (or fiscal) year 1981–82. It is known that in several instances the actual state support in 1981–82 was somewhat less than that reported by Chambers because of necessary recisions. In every instance, the dollar increases are impressive, ranging from 210 percent in Illinois to 456 percent in Texas. The Chambers data provided information about total dollars. But they did not offer a basis of comparison based on number of students or scope of program offerings. And obviously the dollar increases in state support between 1972 and 1982 reflected the impact of inflation more than the impact of higher enrollment or increased support of qualitative change.

The Carnegie Council on Policy Studies in Higher Education (1980) proposed that state governments should maintain at least the current level of funding per capita of state population in constant dollars. This suggestion was intended to provide a yardstick for a period when student enrollments might decline. In Table 15 the state appropriation data have been calculated on the basis of population for the two time periods. The 1972 data have been divided by the 1970 population as reported by the Bureau of the Census, and the 1982 data have been divided by the 1980 population count. Once again, the figures suggest con-

Table 14. Appropriations from Tax Funds for Higher Education
in Twenty-Five States (in Thousands).

	1971–72	1981–82	Percentage Increase 1982 over 1972
Alabama	$106,807	$ 417,757	291
California	853,623	3,328,706	290
Colorado	113,463	305,791	170
Connecticut	111,695	259,971	133
Delaware	23,091	72,125	212
Florida	247,540	802,316	224
Georgia	162,953	498,919	206
Illinois	475,179	996,810	110
Indiana	201,345	482,494	140
Kansas	84,313	278,662	231
Maine	30,741	66,871	118
Massachusetts	130,212	364,500	180
Minnesota	164,566	515,000	213
Mississippi	84,112	300,524	257
Missouri	149,109	352,770	137
Montana	30,635	83,693	173
New Hampshire	12,419	39,323	217
New Jersey	184,679	464,787	152
New York	803,913	1,855,429	131
Ohio	285,677	739,309	159
Pennsylvania	347,483	825,491	138
South Dakota	21,844	52,143	139
Texas	418,369	1,905,000	355
Washington	190,467	497,821	161
West Virginia	69,388	192,092	177

Source: Chambers (1981, 1982).

siderable growth in state government support between 1972 and
1982.

The record changes, however, when allowance is made for
the impact of inflation. The third column translates the 1982 per
capita dollar amounts into dollars with the purchasing power of
1972 dollars. In terms of real support, we find that among the
twenty-five states tax support actually declined in three: Colorado,
Illinois, and Maine. The increases per capita were relatively
modest (under 10 percent) in six other states: Connecticut, Florida, Indiana, Missouri, South Dakota, and Washington. In the

Table 15. Appropriations for Higher Education
per Capita of Population in Twenty-Five States.

	1971–72	1981–82	1981–82 in 1972 dollars
Alabama	$31.01	$107.39	$50.42
California	42.78	140.64	66.03
Colorado	51.41	105.85	49.69
Connecticut	36.84	83.65	39.27
Delaware	42.14	121.22	56.91
Florida	36.46	82.37	38.67
Georgia	35.50	91.31	42.87
Illinois	42.75	87.30	40.99
Indiana	38.76	87.89	40.99
Kansas	37.52	117.93	55.37
Maine	30.99	59.49	27.93
Massachusetts	22.89	63.53	29.83
Minnesota	43.25	126.32	59.31
Mississippi	37.94	119.21	55.97
Missouri	31.88	71.74	33.68
Montana	44.14	106.48	49.99
New Hampshire	16.83	42.70	20.05
New Jersey	25.76	63.12	29.63
New York	44.08	105.68	49.62
Ohio	26.82	68.47	32.15
Pennsylvania	29.46	69.56	32.66
South Dakota	32.80	75.57	35.48
Texas	37.36	133.89	62.86
Washington	55.87	120.54	56.59
West Virginia	39.79	98.51	46.25

remaining sixteen states, however, state support in real terms per capita increased more than 10 percent betwen 1972 and 1982.

The Chambers data offered basic information about state support of higher education. But the data required interpretation not only in terms of the impact of inflation but also in terms of instructional programs provided by fields and levels, full-time equivalent student enrollment, the scope of research support, the extent of public service activities, and the magnitude of student financial assistance at both public and private institutions. The Chambers data did permit the very important observation that state government support was concentrated on the operation of public institutions of higher education. It has been estimated that for the fifty states as a whole, 95 percent of state government appropriation support each year was directed to the operating costs of public institutions, including costs of research and public service. No doubt this proportion varied somewhat state by state.

One other comment must be made about the Chambers data. Chambers endeavored to obtain information from each state on tax appropriations in support of higher education programs. He sought to eliminate from his data the reappropriation of student fees and other income. This effort was vital to the data base on state support of higher education. At the same time, the Chambers data focused on appropriations to institutions (or systems of institutions) and did not include information about research or other grants that state government agencies might make to state universities. Data from the National Center for Education Statistics indicated that state government grant and contract income received by public institutions in 1980 amounted to about $600 million, compared to $17.3 billion in appropriation support. Moreover, the Chambers data did not provide information about institutional finance. They provided information only about what a state government appropriated from tax resources in support of higher education programs. Nevertheless, the Chambers data were an invaluable source of information about what state governments were willing to spend for higher education.

The Chambers data collected each year were presented in terms of ten-year growth and two-year growth. These data have in turn been analyzed according to changes in aggregate state personal income by Hines, McCarthy, and Cronan (1982). The results of this analysis for the twenty-five states of this study, presented according to regions, are shown in Table 16. For the United States as a whole, appropriations for higher education increased 200 percent between the academic years 1970–71 and 1980–81. In this same period, personal income increased 169 percent. In fifteen of the states of this study appropriations increased percentagewise by more than the ten-year increase in personal income. These states were concerned to improve their higher education systems in order to advance their economic performance or to demonstrate their general commitment to higher education as a force for social betterment.

Table 16. Appropriations for Higher Education and Personal Income for Twenty-Five States, 1980–81 (in Millions).

	State Appropriations for Higher Education	Ten-Year Change in Percentage	National Rank	Aggregate State Personal Income	Ten-Year Change in Percentage	National Rank
New England						
Connecticut	250.4	157	38	36,510	145	43
Maine	62.6	125	46	8,940	172	31
Massachusetts	322.5	178	33	58,232	135	49
New Hampshire	32.9	201	25	8,429	201	16
Mideast						
Delaware	63.8	215	23	6,172	149	42
New Jersey	434.2	181	32	80,724	137	48
New York	1,644.4	120	48	180,646	111	50
Pennsylvania	742.1	140	43	112,220	142	44
Great Lakes						
Illinois	964.6	102	50	120,434	140	47
Indiana	459.6	164	36	49,117	153	41
Ohio	719.9	176	34	102,410	142	45
Southeast						
Alabama	427.5	471	1	29,199	192	19
Florida	705.4	192	27	88,675	243	5
Georgia	432.0	191	28	44,217	189	22
Mississippi	261.3	262	11	16,626	193	18
West Virginia	169.8	189	29	15,243	187	25

Table 16. Appropriations for Higher Education and Personal Income for Twenty-Five States, 1980–81 (in Millions) *(continued)*.

	State Appropriations for Higher Education	Ten-Year Change in Percentage	National Rank	Aggregate State Personal Income	Ten-Year Change in Percentage	National Rank
Plains						
Kansas	259.9	217	22	23,648	179	29
Minnesota	478.0	233	18	39,744	168	32
Missouri	353.3	168	35	44,273	155	38
South Dakota	51.2	141	42	5,408	158	36
Rocky Mountain						
Colorado	264.0	139	44	29,029	236	7
Montana	66.5	128	45	6,732	182	26
Southwest						
Texas	1,464.9	326	5	136,146	243	6
Far West						
California	3,158.9	287	8	259,551	187	24
Washington	467.7	145	41	42,677	209	15
United States	20,873.3	200		2,155,237	169	

Source: Hines, McCarthy, and Cronan (1982).

State Expectations

It seems evident that state governments expect different outcomes from their appropriation support for higher education. In the absence of an empirical basis for determining exactly what these different expectations might be, we can only repeat various opinions on the subject. In some states it appeared that the ablest students, or at least the most advantaged students in terms of family income and social status, were expected to enroll in private colleges and universities. In other states the most prestigious and demanding programs of higher education were offered by public universities. Universal access to higher education was generally expected to be made available by public institutions of higher education. Access to higher education of high quality at low cost to the student was an objective in some states at some institutions, but was not accepted as a primary objective in all twenty-five states of this study.

All but four state governments studied here had made a major commitment to high-quality medical education and seemed willing to meet the costs associated with that commitment. These states, moreover, had developed area health education centers in an effort to expand the clinical and residency experience of medical students and new recipients of the doctor of medicine degree on a geographical basis. These states also aided various teaching hospitals in providing medical and hospital care to patients, some of whom were not able to pay for such care.

State governments seemed to be favorably disposed toward engineering education and research and public service in the biological and physical sciences. They seemed, in fact, to be generally disposed to favor technical education programs, while sometimes regarding other fields of study and other fields of public service activities with only moderate enthusiasm.

It has sometimes been said that state governments undertook to provide universal access to higher education in order to remove substantial numbers of young people from the labor market. We found no state government officials who mentioned this as a factor in state support of higher education. There was a general understanding that higher education did contribute to social mobility, and making it possible for young people to achieve status of the basis of "talent and virtue"—to borrow a phrase from Thomas Jefferson—was generally perceived as a major objective in the financing of higher education.

The problem for state government officials as of 1982 was to decide just what constituted an "appropriate" expenditure for higher education under current economic circumstances. In the 1960s appropriation support for public higher education expanded because the demand for educated talent exceeded the available supply. This circumstance had changed by the 1970s, and state governments were puzzled about how they should respond to this change. Faculty members and administrators still pressed for increased appropriations, that is, for appropriations that would keep pace with or exceed the rate of inflation. Public colleges and universities insisted that they were educating young people, and older people as well, for intellectual satisfaction and personal development, not necessarily for jobs. But faced by declining revenues, state government officials were doubtful about how far they could go in financing intellectual satisfaction and personal development.

To the extent that state government officials had any interest in providing additional funds for higher education as of 1982, it tended to center on quality and economic development rather than on instruction as such. In 1979 the New England Board of Higher Education, an interstate consortium of higher education and state government officials, established a special commission to explore the relationship between higher education and the economy of the six-state region. This Commission on Higher Education and the Economy of New England, composed of thirty-three government officials, college and university officials, and business leaders, issued a report in 1982. The report pointed out that institutions of higher education had both a direct and an indirect role in the economy of the region. Through their own expenditures they contributed directly to the economic base of the area, and they were also among the region's largest employers. Indirectly, a "good" higher education system attracted people to the area. But the vital indirect effect was the contribution to the region's labor force of technologically oriented and skilled individuals.

Between 1975 and 1980 employment in high-tech industries accounted for 21 percent of the increase in employment in New England, while job growth in all services amounted to some 40 percent of the employment increase, or over 330,000 new jobs. The growth in high-tech industries and in services accounted for two out of three of the region's new jobs. Moreover, in Massachusetts the unemployment rate in 1981 was well under the national average. Data of this kind encouraged state government officials to expect that the appropriations they provided for higher education would have a positive impact on future economic trends in their states. It was this expected economic connection that constituted a particular challenge for higher education leaders as they faced the 1980s and 1990s.

Unique Status of Public Universities

There were three different approaches to the support of higher education in the states of this study. One approach was to consider the public university as a government corporation, that is, as a body politic and corporate, and to appropriate an operating subsidy to the individual institution or to a system of institutions. A second approach was to consider the public university as simply another administrative department of state government and to appropriate support for it in the same way or in the same format as for other government agencies. The third approach, which fell somewhere between the other two, was a modified state appropriation practice that partially recognized the peculiar financial characteristics of public universities.

These peculiar characteristics, in fact, deserve special emphasis. Ever since my experience as an administrator of a state university in 1953, I have thought that the appropriate concept of organizational status for such a university is that of the public corporation. Further, my background in political science and public administration had provided me with knowledge about city governments as municipal corporations. I had found, for example, that much of the public law concerning city governments involves their status as municipal corporations. My experience in federal government in the 1930s and 1940s had also provided me with knowledge about the government corporation in federal administration. As a result of all these experiences, I believe the state university should be regarded as a governmental corporation. And indeed the charter for Miami University enacted by the General Assembly of Ohio in 1809 had established a "body politic and corporate" to be known as the President and Trustees of the Miami University.

It was noted above that, for public institutions, only 46.5 percent of current operating revenues was obtained from state government appropriation of tax funds. If we consider the category of universities separately from other types of institutions, we find that 41.4 percent of total income was derived from state governments. Public institutions of higher education, like private colleges and universities, obtained their current operating revenues from various sources: tuition and other fees paid by students, federal grants and contracts, endowment income, private gifts and grants from alumni and foundations and other sources, and sales and services.

The public corporation in the United States is expected to generate a considerable proportion of its income from nongovernmental sources. In addition, the public corporation has considerable discretion in the use of its income, in the contraction of debt, and in the selection and retention of personnel. All these features characterize most state universities. Moreover, the governmental appropriation to a public corporation is a form of subsidy intended to enable the corporation to charge its clients less than the full cost of the product or services rendered. Here again the public university qualifies for status as a public corporation. The practice of having governing boards of lay citizens as the governance authority of the public university is also comparable to the practice of both the municipal corporation and the public corporation.

During the 1920s and 1930s, when the state government reorganization movement was flourishing in the United States, the order of the day was executive authority and organizational integration. The power of governors to provide administrative oversight of all administrative operations was greatly strengthened, primarily through the mechanism of the executive budget. The coordination of similar types of programs was attempted by means of departmental integration, that is, the merger of departments and agencies in conglomerates of supposedly like-purpose endeavors. State universities were generally exempted from governmental reorganization plans but not from executive budget plans. And many state governments in the 1930s and 1940s created central departments of administration, personnel, and public works to provide purchasing services, personnel services, and construction services to all state government agencies, sometimes including state universities.

The executive budget movement set for itself the general objective of constructing comprehensive, timely, and informative budgets for all state government activities. In many states attainment of this objective involved bringing the state universities into the executive budget and bringing most, if not all, of their income into the appropriation process. Since the prevailing budget practice of the 1930s and 1940s was to budget and appropriate by objects of expenditure (personal services, supplies and equipment, plant maintenance, travel, and contractual services), university budgets were incorporated into executive budgets on a line item basis.

Yet the executive budget movement had to make some concessions to the unique status of state universities. One concession was to incorporate student fees into the executive budget and the state treasury process but then to reappropriate the entire amount, whatever it might be, back to the state university where the fees had been collected. Another concession was to exempt from state control the income from the sales and services of auxiliary enterprises (residence halls, student food services, bookstores, and intercollegiate athletics). Other exemptions such as those for income from teaching hospitals and experimental farms followed in due course. When federal research grants began to be made on a sizable scale during World War II, this income was also usually exempted. When such exemptions were not forthcoming, however, state universities created wholly owned subordinate corporations called research foundations to receive and disburse federal and other grants.

In the course of this study we endeavored to determine the appropriation status of the state systems of higher education. We employed three primary tests or criteria of status. First, we inquired into the method of handling student tuition or instructional fees: Was the state university required to deposit tuition fees and then receive a reappropriation of this income for operating use? We found that in fourteen states all institutions had to deposit their tuition fees in the state treasury, while in eight states they did not. In three states there was a mixed practice, the state universities being exempt from the practice and the state colleges being treated as state government agencies.

The second test was that of appropriation practice: Was the appropriation to the state universities made by lump sum or by line item? We found that the lump-sum practice prevailed in ten states, while the line item practice was used in fifteen states. We even found four states that insisted on appropriating all sources of institutional income, including income from auxiliary enterprises.

The third test involved the method of financing capital improvements. We found seven states that endeavored to finance academic facilities on a pay-as-you-go basis, utilizing current tax income for the construction of instructional and general physical facilities. We found another three states that had a tax earmarked for higher education capital improvements. We found ten states that had some kind of procedure whereby institutions could borrow for capital improvement projects by pledging student fees for payment of debt service costs; in turn, the state government reimbursed the institution for the student fees thus pledged. In the remaining five states the construction of academic facilities depended on the borrowing of capital improvement funds by the state government. In all twenty-five states the state legislature had to approve the construction of academic (as contrasted with student) facilities.

Appropriation practices, then, varied widely. In only about thirteen of the twenty-five states was the state university considered to be a public corporation, and in two of these thirteen states the status applied to some, but not all, senior institutions of higher education. There was still a long way to go in clarifying the financial status of public institutions of higher education.

On recommendation of the Ohio Board of Regents—a state coordinating board—the governor and the General Assembly in

1967 recognized the state universities as governmental corporations and enacted legislation that conferred substantial management autonomy upon each university in the handling and disbursing of its receipts. Student instructional and other fees were no longer deposited in the state treasurer's office, line item appropriations were no longer enacted, disbursements were no longer made by the auditor's office, and auditing of accounts was placed on a strictly postaudit basis. The annual appropriation in the biennial appropriation bill for each university simply read "subsidy."

A unique situation arose in Colorado in 1981. The legislature and the universities entered into a compact that bestowed a new financial status on the universities. The agreement was signed by board chairmen and chief executive officers of the universities, by the chairman of the joint budget committee of the legislature, and by the executive director of the Commission on Higher Education. A memorandum of understanding for the fiscal year 1982–83 set forth the five major principles embodied in the agreement:

1. The governing boards were given increased responsibility, reflecting increased fiscal flexibility and increased "trust" in the higher education institutions.
2. Each governing board was expected to set the expenditure level at each institution for which it was responsible. Appropriations would be based upon general fund support for each Colorado resident full-time equivalent student and would be made to the governing board rather than to institutions.
3. Each governing board would have authority and responsibility to set tuition levels.
4. There would be reduced emphasis upon line item appropriations and increased flexibility to transfer appropriations as needed.
5. Each governing board might expend all cash revenues it generated and might retain them from year to year as necessary.

This understanding came about initially because the legislature considered itself unable to provide increased appropriations to the public institutions of higher education. As a kind of *quid pro quo*, the legislature left the governing boards free to fix student

tuition and to enroll as many students, including out-of-state
students, as they wanted to enroll. But state appropriations were
limited to a fixed full-time equivalent enrollment of in-state students, and no additional state support was provided for any enrollment beyond the appropriation limit. In this way the legislature
provided for enrollment limitations — a matter of considerable legislative interest — while leaving enrollment decisions to the respective governing boards. The Colorado arrangement was highly
commendable in terms of the management autonomy that it gave
to the state universities. At the same time, to some persons the
arrangement appeared to be an abdication of legislative responsibility for adequate support of public higher education.

A different kind of approach to the appropriation process
was evident in Indiana. Here there was a modified procedure that
involved appropriation of about half the total expenditures of the
state institutions of higher education. The appropriation included
student fees, federal government unrestricted revenue (overhead
reimbursement), and state tax support. Omitted from the appropriation process were federal grants and contracts, sales and services, private gifts, and endowment income. The appropriations
were made by program categories: instruction, research, public
service, and student assistance (including fee remission).

The Indiana Commission for Higher Education, under the
leadership of its commissioner, George B. Weathersby, has in
recent years developed the concept of "purchase of services" as the
basis for its recommendations on appropriation subsidies to the
six public institutions in the state. Purchase of services covers
three principal program categories: instruction, research, and
public service. The commission also recommends the appropriation
for student financial assistance. Within the category of instruction, purchase of services is based on four major calculations: programs by field of study and level of study, program costs, student
enrollment, and division of costs between state government and
student. A sophisticated and computerized information system
permits variations in these purchase factors when the legislature is
considering the higher education appropriation. Presumably the
state of Indiana might purchase higher education services from
sources other than the six public institutions and their various
campuses. In actual practice only the public institutions are pre-

pared to provide the desired kind, quantity, and quality of service at an acceptable cost. The utility of the concept of purchase of services lies in the variety of choices that it gives to both the governor and the legislature, as well as in the definition of the relationship of public institutions to state government that the concept affords.

In South Dakota in the biennium 1981–1983 the legislature insisted upon reappropriating all income from all sources by program categories rather than by objects of expenditure, except for the sales and services of auxiliary enterprises. This practice was introduced so that the legislature could express disapproval of the allocation of funds to the institutions by the central statewide governing board. Institution budget making was thus assumed by the legislature, even though the governance authority of the governing board was not otherwise modified.

It is instructive to contrast the state budget for higher education with the budget of a state university. The two documents arc, or should be, quite different. The state budget for higher education should reflect the state's interest in higher education. The state university budget should reflect the total sources of income and all the different programs provided by the university (instruction, research, public service, teaching hospitals, independent operations, student aid, and the support programs). The difference between a state government budget and a state university budget may be illustrated by the budget recommendations of the Ohio Board of Regents shown in Table 17. The principal categories of the state budget are shown as instruction, access, public service and research, health manpower, planning and coordination, business and industry extension, and facilities. These headings well express the state government interest in higher education.

State governments had a substantial way to go in recognizing the claims of state universities to special financial status. The fault was not that of state higher education boards but rather of the administrative bureaucracies, the governor's office, and the legislature of each state. Financial controls were exercised by state governments, not by state coordinating boards or statewide governing boards. Indeed, our observation was that, while these boards might press for a relaxation of state financial controls, only unusual political circumstances would produce a climate in which change could be effected.

Table 17. Ohio Higher Education Appropriation Budget (in Thousands).

| | Adjusted Appropriations | | Regents' Recommendations | |
	1981–82	1982–83	1983–84	1984–85
Instruction				
Instructional Subsidies	$ 586,712.5	$ 646,867.1	$ 792,944.4	$ 882,117.8
Civil Service Adjustment	7,710.5	18,155.7	—	—
Remedial Course Work	—	900.0	—	—
Subtotal	$ 594,423.0	$ 665,922.8	$ 792,944.4	$ 882,117.8
Access				
Ohio Instructional Grants	$ 28,487.3	$ 33,519.4	$ 37,000.0	$ 39,000.0
War Orphans Scholarships	809.3	1,054.2	1,250.0	1,576.0
National Guard Scholarships	3,031.9	2,659.5	—	—
Academic Scholarships	3,840.0	3,600.0	4,000.0	4,000.0
Developmental Education	1,181.2	1,125.0	2,500.0	2,500.0
Central State Supplement	4,725.0	4,500.0	5,360.0	5,745.9
Subtotal	$ 42,074.7	$ 46,458.1	$ 50,110.0	$ 52,821.9
Public Service, Research, and Quality				
Cooperative Extension	$ 6,872.6	$ 7,047.2	$ 8,357.9	$ 8,357.9
Agricultural Research and Development	11,752.0	12,025.2	14,267.5	14,267.5
Labor Education	865.4	865.4	1,030.7	1,104.9
Displaced Homemakers	94.5	90.0	100.0	100.0
Eminent Scholar Program	—	—	3,000.0	3,000.0
Family Life Education	28.4	54.0	—	—
Subtotal	$ 19,612.9	$ 20,081.8	$ 26,756.1	$ 28,459.3

Health Manpower

Developmental Subsidy				
MCOT	$ 3,050.9	$ 2,430.0	$ 2,280.0	$ 1,710.0
NEOUCOM	2,419.2	3,804.3	2,482.5	2,220.0
Wright	2,494.8	2,454.3	2,482.5	2,220.0
Ohio U.	2,494.8	2,454.3	2,482.5	2,220.0
Case Western				
Medicine	4,768.6	4,768.6	5,679.9	6,088.8
Dentistry	1,559.8	1,559.8	1,486.3	1,195.0
Clinical				
Medical and Research	21,412.0	21,412.0	28,000.0	30,016.0
Dental and Vet Medicine	—	—	892.5	892.5
Primary Care	2,620.3	2,620.3	3,121.0	3,345.7
Family Practice	5,411.1	5,411.1	6,455.2	6,909.2
Geriatric Medicine	946.9	946.9	1,127.8	1,209.1
Graduate Dental Residencies	330.8	315.0	100.0	100.0
OSU Dental Supplement	259.2	—	—	—
Area Health Education Centers	79.5	225.0	1,325.0	1,700.0
Paramedic Certification	19.3	25.7	68.4	84.6
Agent Orange	—	270.0	—	—
Subtotal	$ 47,867.2	$ 48,697.3	$ 57,983.6	$ 59,910.9
Planning and Coordination				
Regents' Operations				
Personal Services	$ 1,160.5	$ 1,201.0	$ 1,345.0	$ 1,437.0
Maintenance and Equipment	546.4	651.6	715.2	753.7
Subtotal	$ 1,706.9	$ 1,852.6	$ 2,060.2	$ 2,190.7
TOTAL	$ 705,684.7	$ 783,012.6	$ 929,854.3	$ 1,025,500.6

Table 17. Ohio Higher Education Appropriation Budget (in Thousands).
(continued)

	Adjusted Appropriations		Regents' Recommendations	
	1981–82	1982–83	1983–84	1984–85
Business and Industry Extension				
Administration	—	—	$ 255.0	$ 330.0
Ohio Technology Transfer Organization	$ 260.0	$ 315.0	1,300.0	1,400.0
Urban Universities	472.5	450.0	1,300.0	1,300.0
High-Tech Facilities	—	—	1,000.0	1,000.0
Research	—	—	500.0	2,000.0
Special Training–High-Tech Areas	—	—	500.0	1,000.0
TOTAL	$ 732.5	$ 765.0	$ 4,855.0	$ 7,030.0
Facilities				
Debt Service	$ 79,321.9	$ 94,035.0	$ 129,625.0	$ 150,412.0
Police and Fire Service	255.8	243.5	250.0	250.0
TOTAL	$ 79,577.7	$ 94,278.5	$ 129,875.0	$ 150,662.0

Source: Ohio Board of Regents.

Capital Improvements

The major problem in financing capital improvements at public institutions was how to get around the limitations that state constitutions placed on state debt. All the constitutions in the twenty-five states of this study had prohibited the contracting of a state debt, except for a very nominal sum. Some states as of 1981 were endeavoring to finance capital improvements at state universities on a pay-as-you-go basis. Other states, if they were to make any expenditures for capital expansion or replacement, had to provide some mechanism for borrowing funds. In all twenty-five states, primarily in the years after World War II, the governing boards of state universities and colleges had been given the authority to borrow funds for the construction of residence halls, dining halls, intercollegiate athletic facilities, and recreational and other specialized facilities. The debt service costs for these facilities were pledged from income generated by the facilities or from special fees paid by students.

If state governments were to avoid periodic referendums on amendment of the state constitution in order to borrow funds for academic facilities, then some device similar to that for nonacademic facilities was needed. The device arrived at in ten of the twenty-five states involved a special arrangement between legislatures and governing boards. Governing boards were permitted to pledge student academic fees for the payment of debt service on academic facilities. The legislature continued to authorize the actual physical facilities to be built with this debt service pledge but committed itself to appropriate a "fee replacement" to the institution in the amount needed for debt service. To be sure, a governing board might decide to build facilities not authorized by the state legislature. In such instances, however, the legislature was not committed to provide any fee replacement. We found that in order to maintain as low an instructional charge to students as possible, state universities were careful to seek state authorization for academic facilities and thus to obtain a fee replacement appropriation.

Government Options

States have become aware in the past two or three decades that they can choose various means to fund higher education. In the years before World War II, such awareness was seldom present. Public higher education enrollment was not particularly large, faculty salaries were relatively modest, and program costs were reasonably limited. The circumstances of the 1930s were unfavorable for state governments; and, in spite of enrollment increases, public higher education was in no position to obtain additional resources.

The pattern of support for public higher education before 1941 was fairly fixed. State universities and other institutions charged students a small fee for instruction and depended on the state government to provide the limited funds required for current operations and capital improvements. There were small federal grants to the land-grant institutions and for agricultural research and extension. Only a very small number of public institutions received sizable support from private philanthropy.

This fixed pattern was disrupted by World War II and its aftermath. The male student population was drastically reduced during the war by the requirements of military service; but, after the war, veterans in surprisingly large numbers sought the benefits of higher education with the assistance of federal educational grants. Higher education was asked during the war to offer military training and in some instances to provide research and development services to improve and create new weapons and new devices of communication, and this government reliance on university research and development continued after the war. The economic growth that replaced the Great Depression demanded large numbers of technically and professionally educated persons, including the persons needed to staff the education enterprise itself. Education in general, and higher education in particular, became expensive.

As a consequence of the disruption of World War II and of the changing circumstances of the postwar years, new problems arose in the financing of public higher education. The principal choices that emerged were three in number: (1) Should state governments finance institutions or should they finance students, (2) should state governments provide financial support to private or independent institutions as well as to public institutions, and (3) should state governments finance higher education for everyone who might wish to enroll or for only a selected few? These questions arose within a context of continually advancing costs and expanding enrollments and programs.

With the increase in federal and then state government student financial aid programs after 1958, and especially after 1972, state government officials started to question the large-scale appropriations needed by public institutions in order to maintain their traditional low-tuition policy. But public institutions of higher education could not benefit from federal assistance granted to students unless they increased their tuition charges. Moreover, once tuition charges did start to increase, educational leaders urged the adoption or expansion of state student aid programs in order that tuition increases would not affect enrollment by youth from families below the median income level in the state. State governments thus found themselves being asked to support both institutions and students. The issue then became one of the priority to be given to these competing financial requests.

The tradition of charging low tuition at public institutions proved hard to overthrow. Many arguments were advanced in favor of the low-tuition policy, and criticisms of it by economists and others had only a slight impact in bringing about any change (Stampen, 1980). In the course of this study, we calculated the proportion of the total state appropriation for 1982 that was devoted to student financial assistance in the twenty-five states. The results are shown in Table 18. There were nineteen states where the proportion was under 5 percent, four states where the proportion was between 5 and 10 percent, and only two states — New York and Pennsylvania — where the proportion was above 10 percent. It was evident from these data that state governments for the most part continued to believe that their primary obligation was to support public institutions with relatively modest tuition charges rather than to support students directly.

The second issue of choice involved direct support to private higher education. Only four out of the twenty-five states in this study had any considerable program of assistance to private institutions; the most extensive of these programs were to be found in New York and Pennsylvania, although there were also programs in Illinois and Minnesota. In 1982 the Minnesota Higher

Table 18. Proportion of Appropriation for Higher Education
Provided for Student Financial Aid in Twenty-Five States, 1982.

	Percentage		*Percentage*
Alabama	0.4	Mississippi	0.4
California	2.7	Missouri	2.5
Colorado	2.1	Montana	4.2
Connecticut	3.6	New Hampshire	1.6
Delaware	0.8	New Jersey	9.4
Florida	1.6	New York	14.8
Georgia	0.9	Ohio	4.0
Illinois	9.2	Pennsylvania	10.2
Indiana	6.1	South Dakota	0.6
Kansas	1.6	Texas	4.4
Maine	0.8	Washington	1.3
Massachusetts	4.1	West Virginia	2.6
Minnesota	5.9		

Source: Chambers (1981, 1982).

Education Coordinating Board recommended that the program of assistance to private institutions be ended in favor of a somewhat enlarged program of student financial assistance that would provide increased benefit payments to students enrolling in private institutions of higher education. The primary method of assistance to private institutions in twenty-three out of the twenty-five states was through a student financial aid program.

The third issue of choice was whether or not state governments should continue to finance open admissions. In spite of the financial difficulties of state governments, we did not find a single state where any serious proposal had been made to lower state government costs by reducing or eliminating the commitment to open access to public higher education. But there was a general interest in improving high school course requirements for college admission.

Formula Budgeting

Finally, some brief mention must be made of the issue of formula budgeting for public higher education. There has been a good deal of debate in various states about the relative merits of formula budgeting in contrast with incremental budgeting. Of the twenty-five states included in this study, we found that the six states with higher education advisory boards followed the practice of incremental budgeting. Since the advisory boards were not involved in the budget-making process as a recommending body, state departments of finance or state departments of administration were the primary agencies of appropriation analysis. In California and New York the multicampus systems employed workload measurements in order to construct their appropriation requests, and there was evidence that state departments of administration tended to give some attention to these measurements in determining the appropriate increment to recommend for the annual appropriation. The prevailing practice in executive budgeting among state governments was incremental budgeting.

Among the other state boards of higher education, we found that seven of the nine coordinating boards employed formulas in the preparation of appropriation recommendations for submission to the budget agency of state government. We found that all ten of the statewide governing boards employed a formula approach to the development of the appropriation requests that they submitted to the state budget office. In turn, statewide governing boards utilized a formula in allocating higher education appropriations to individual institutions. We suspected that the two state coordinating boards that used the incremental approach to the development of their appropriation recommendations perceived that a formula might disturb the existing distribution of appropriation support among individual institutions, probably to the disadvantage of certain politically influential institutions in those states.

Incremental budgeting plays a part in all budgeting for higher education. The issue to be resolved for each succeeding year is how much shall be added to the planned expenditures for the current year. The additions depend on many factors: the allowance for inflation in the cost of personal services, additions or subtractions for changes in work loads, unusual cost increases, such as a sudden escalation of energy prices, and changes planned as qualitative improvements. The difference between a general incremental approach to these additions and a formula approach is simply one of equity. A general incremental approach assumes that at some previous point in time there was an equitable relationship in appropriations for individual institutions. The formula approach seeks to calculate an equitable distribution each year or each biennium among all the individual institutions of higher education.

Our study found that a formula approach to higher education budgeting required the accumulation of measurable data at a central point in state government for all publicly supported institutions of higher education. Insofar as current operating expenditures were concerned, these data included instructional work loads in terms of student credit hours (or full-time equivalent student enrollments) by program areas and by levels of study, student–faculty ratios or faculty work loads in terms of student credit hours by program areas and by levels of study, average faculty salaries, departmental support costs, and institutional overhead costs. To these direct and indirect instructional costs were added special appropriations for research (such as agricultural stations), public service (such as teaching hospitals and public broadcasting), student financial aid (if any) provided by the institution, remedial education activities, and debt service on academic facilities. There may be other special costs for programs in a developmental stage, programs offered at small institutions, grants for innovative experiments, and even rewards for special accomplishment.

The first objective of formula budgeting was to provide equal support for equivalent or comparable instructional programs in all public institutions. This objective involved equitable treatment by the state government of diverse public institutions, equitable treatment here meaning not equal treatment but comparable treatment on the basis of comparable programs and varying work loads. The second objective of formula budgeting was to calculate a general floor of adequacy in expenditure requirements among institutions. This calculation was needed to provide guidelines for state governments or institutions in fixing the instructional fees to be charged as a supplement to state appropriation support.

In one state of this study the program categories utilized for formula purposes were general studies, technical education, baccalaureate studies, master's studies, professional studies, doctoral studies, and medical education. Within each of these categories there was a further subdivision by disciplines and fields. Thus baccalaureate studies were divided into group I (social sciences, business administration, education, systems analysis, and mathematics), group II (humanities, foreign languages, biological sciences, physical sciences, allied health sciences, home economics, and nursing), and group III (agriculture, architecture, engineering, and fine arts). In another state the following division of expenditure components was employed: departmental faculty compensation (50 percent), departmental support (12 percent), academic support (7 percent), student services (8 percent), plant operation (13 percent), and institutional support (10 percent).

A common criticism of formulas based upon average cost per student or per student credit hour was that such formulas were advantageous to an institution in a period of rising enrollments but harmful in a period of declining enrollments. The Carnegie Council and the Sloan Commission urged caution in the use of enrollment-driven formulas in the decade of the 1980s. In Ohio in 1981 the formula was revised in two ways. First, no reduction was to be made in the institutional appropriation during the first two years of an enrollment loss. Second, instructional costs were divided into fixed costs and variable costs, so that fixed costs would not decline in a period of enrollment loss while variable costs would decline only gradually. This kind of revision was under consideration in other states as of 1982 and would undoubtedly be undertaken in most states by 1983 or 1984.

State governments vary considerably in the support they provide for their public institutions of higher education, and comparisons are likely to be misleading because of the differing circumstances involved. Halstead (1983) has endeavored to call attention to some of the important differences that affect state government support—for example, differences in the proportion of students graduating from high school; in the proportion of high school graduates who enroll in public institutions of higher education, in the kinds of institutions and programs supported, in the appropriation and tuition support provided, and in the degree of tax capacity and tax effort state by state. State governments

vary in their commitment to higher education, the higher education appropriation often being considered after welfare needs,
elementary-secondary school needs, health needs, and correc-
tional needs have received attention.

Appropriation practices also vary substantially. Some
public institutions have large sources of income apart from the
state appropriation. This circumstance is particularly applicable
to the resident institution with its income from auxiliary enterprises and the research university with its income from sponsored
research. While almost all institutions receive federal funds for
student financial assistance, some public institutions receive little
other income outside of the state governmental subsidy and student charges.

To summarize, financial support must necessarily vary
according to the mission, program offerings, and student enrollment of institutions. In all cases, however, public institutions of
higher education should be thought of as public corporations, and
state government appropriations should be considered subsidies
for the desired quantity and quality of higher education services
or as a "purchase of services" from public institutions of higher
education.

State governments confront a difficult policy choice in
striking a balance between appropriation support and student
charges to finance public institutions of higher education. They
confront another difficult policy choice in determining the amount
of funds that should go to the financing of institutions and the
amount that should go to the financing of students. And yet another policy choice is that between subsidizing public institutions
and subsidizing private institutions. Finally, there is the question
of how funds should be distributed among instruction, research,
and public service. This last choice is made all the more complicated by the changing circumstances of the American economy.
The only certain factor is that these policy choices will become
increasingly complex as the 1980s unfold.

➤⊦ 8 ⊦⊰

State Governments
and Institutional
Independence

ALL THE STUDIES AND REPORTS
mentioned in Chapter Two agreed on at least one proposition.
They uniformly declared that some kind of coordination of the state
government system of higher education is desirable. And, as a
corollary of that proposition, the studies and reports agreed that
institutional autonomy is not and cannot be absolute. The report
of the Carnegie Foundation for the Advancement of Teaching
(1982) declared: "We do not suggest that colleges and universities
can carry on their work in isolation. There is, in the strictest sense,
no such thing as autonomy on campus. Both public and private
institutions are socially engaged. They are answerable to the people
who support them and cannot be excused from explaining, and
perhaps defending, what they do" (p. 4).

The problem for state governments in the past forty years
has remained constant: How to reconcile the public stake in higher
education with the campus or institutional interest in freedom of
action. But while the problem has remained constant, the attempts
at solution have been diverse. The problem exists for a very simple
reason. Institutions of higher education wish to undertake various
programs and to commit resources to various outputs at various
levels of cost but must depend on external sources of income in

215

order to realize their wishes. State governments are called on by public institutions of higher education to provide the program resources and to accept campus priorities as to outputs with a minimum degree of control. The reconciliation of institutional aspirations and public financing has been the measure of the conflict between claims to institutional autonomy on the one hand and insistence on public accountability on the other.

The Carnegie Foundation essay of 1982 cited four essential academic freedoms. A campus should be free to decide (1) who may teach, (2) what may be taught, (3) how it shall be taught, and (4) who may be admitted to study. On first glance, these four essential freedoms need no qualification. Yet reflection soon reveals that these freedoms are by no means so absolute as campus faculty members and administrators might wish. The principle of academic freedom has been largely accepted in the United States insofar as faculty personnel actions are concerned; at least a faculty member is supposed to be protected by the institution that he or she serves against termination of appointment, failure to receive tenure or promotion, or refusal of salary increases because of the faculty member's position on matters of intellectual concern.

Nevertheless, the federal government has attached strings to its financial support of institutions and of students alike by demanding that institutions shall not discriminate in personnel actions on the basis of sex, race, religion, or handicapped status. Moreover, the absence of discrimination must be demonstrated by affirmative action and by statistical evidence of a commitment to the appointment and promotion of women, blacks and other minorities, members of various religious denominations, and handicapped persons. Thus, campus autonomy in the determination of who may teach was breached by the federal government in the decade of the 1970s.

When we turn to what may be taught, we find that state governments have found it necessary to limit institutional autonomy. Shall a public institution founded as a junior college or as a community college be free to decide on its own that it shall become a four-year college? State governments have uniformly said no. Shall a comprehensive state university be free on its own to decide to undertake instruction at the doctoral level in any program of its choosing? State governments have uniformly said no. Shall state universities be free on their own to decide to establish a college of agriculture, a college of engineering, a college of medicine, a college of veterinary medicine? State governments have uniformly said no. Decisions about what to teach have not been left solely to the discretion of public institutions because such decisions involve substantial outlays for capital facilities and current operations— outlays that must be provided by state governments.

The issue of how a program shall be taught is generally regarded as one to be resolved by an institution when it is a matter of deciding between lecture sessions or seminars, large classes or small classes, courses offered by television or by separate classroom instructors, and so on. But when the concerns about what shall be taught involve instruction versus research versus public service or involve instructional work loads and instructional costs, then there is a state government interest in what an institution may reasonably expect in terms of the financial support of these decisions.

Finally, there has been intervention by both the federal government and state governments in the question of who shall be admitted to study. The federal government has insisted that decisions about who may be admitted to study must not discriminate on the basis of sex, race, religion, or handicapped status. And again the absence of discrimination must be evidenced by affirmative action; that is, it must involve positive efforts to recruit and admit women, blacks and other minorities, persons of different religious preferences, and handicapped persons. State governments have intervened to establish or approve open-door policies at some institutions and selective admission on the basis of academic aptitude or other appropriate criteria at other institutions.

Thus, even the freedom to make such basic decisions as who shall teach, what shall be taught, how it shall be taught, and who may be admitted to study has been restricted by governments as the price of public support. It is not our intention here to contrast the relative values of social requirements and institutional autonomy in these matters. The fact is that institutional autonomy is often restricted in the name of the public interest.

In its report on *Governance of Higher Education*, the Carnegie Commission on Higher Education (1973b) presented an idealized pattern for the relation between public control and institutional independence. This distribution of authority is reproduced in Exhibit 3. In the Carnegie report there were four principal areas

Exhibit 3. Proposed Carnegie Pattern for Distribution of Authority.

Public Control   *Institutional Independence*

Governance

Basic responsibility for law enforcement.	Right to refuse oaths not required for all citizens in similar circumstances.
Right to insist on political neutrality of institutions of higher education.	
Duty to appoint trustees of public institutions of higher education (or to select them through popular election).	Right to independent trustees; no ex officio trustees with subsequent budget authority.
Right to reports and accountability on matters of public interest.	Right to nonpartisan trustees as recommended by some impartial screening agency or as confirmed by some branch of the state legislature, or both; or as elected by the public.
Duty of courts to hear cases alleging denial of general rights of a citizen and of unfair procedures.	

Financial and Business Affairs

Appropriations of public funds on basis of general formulas that reflect quantity and quality of output.	Assignment of all funds to specific purposes.
Postaudit, rather than preaudit, of of expenditures, of purchases, of personnel actions.	Freedom to make expenditures within budget, to make purchases, and to take personnel action subject only to postaudit.
Examination of effective use of resources on a postaudit basis.	Determination of individual work loads and of specific assignments to faculty and staff members.
Standards for accounting practices and postaudit of them.	
General level of salaries.	Determination of specific salaries.
Appropriation of public funds for building on basis of general formulas for building requirements.	Design of buildings and assignment of space.

Academic and Intellectual Affairs

General Policies on Student Admissions: Number of places	Selection of individual students.

Public Control	*Institutional Independence*
Equality of access	
Academic level of general ability among types of institutions	
General distribution of students by level of division.	
Policies for equal access to employment for women and for members of minority groups.	Academic policies for, and actual selection and promotion of, faculty members.
Policies on differentiation of functions among systems of higher education and on specialization by major fields of endeavor among institutions.	Approval of individual courses and course content.
No right to expect secret research or service from members of institutions of higher education; and no right to prior review before publication of research results; but right to patents where appropriate.	Policies on and administration of research and service activities.
	Determination of grades and issuance of individual degrees.
	Selection of academic and administrative leadership.
Enforcement of the national Bill of Rights.	Policies on academic freedom.
Policies on size and rate of growth of campuses.	Policies on size and rate of growth of departments, schools, and colleges within budgetary limitations.
Establishment of new campuses and other major new endeavors, such as a medical school, and definition of scope.	Academic programs for new campuses and other major new endeavors with general authorization.
Encouragement of innovation through inquiry, recommendation, allocation of special funds, application of general budgetary formulas, starting new institutions.	Development of and detailed planning for innovation.

Source: Carnegie Commission on Higher Education (1973b). Used by permission.

of concern: governance, financial and business affairs, academic and intellectual affairs, and academic innovation. The last-mentioned concern was separated from the others because the Carnegie Commission wished to emphasize public "encouragement" rather than public "control" of innovation. In our own reproduction of the Carnegie Commission pattern of authority, we have merged academic innovation with other academic affairs.

Campus Governance

The Carnegie Commission listed five areas of public control in the governance of public institutions of higher education. The first was the "basic" responsibility for law enforcement on campus. The second area was the "right" to insist on the political neutrality of all institutions of higher education. The third area was the duty to appoint or elect trustees of public institutions. The fourth area was the "right" to expect reports of activities and to insist upon accountability in matters of public interest. The fifth area was the duty of courts to hear cases alleging denial by an institution of the rights of a citizen, including the right to fair procedures in the determination of status.

As in the other areas of concern to be discussed below, the Carnegie Commission did not indicate what agency of government was to exercise public control. Nor was public control by the federal government differentiated from public control by state governments. Moreover, the commission did not provide any definition of the terms it employed or any explanation of the reasoning involved in its presentation.

In its report the Carnegie Commission recognized the authority of local government, of state government, and even of the federal government to enforce general provisions of law on campuses. Presumably this authority of law enforcement included the maintenance of law and order on an individual campus. By implication, the commission rejected the idea that a campus was a sanctuary where local and other police were not to enter to make arrests on criminal charges or to enforce order, although nothing was said about what governmental authority was to decide when and where law enforcement on a campus was to be ordered. In the

Carnegie Commission view a campus was similar to any other area of a town or city insofar as law enforcement was involved.

In its reports the Carnegie Commission generally took a strong stand in favor of political neutrality on the part of an institution of higher education. The institution was not to align itself with any particular elite or any particular interest group. Faculty members, students, and other staff personnel of a college or university might join any lawful organization as individuals. The institution was expected to associate itself with other institutions of higher education but was not expected to endorse political candidates, seek to influence elections, or lobby for causes other than the cause of the institution itself.

The Carnegie Commission recognized that state governments would necessarily select the trustees of governing, coordinating, and advisory boards. With only a few exceptions, it was the governors of our twenty-five states who appointed the trustees or regents of state universities. One exception was found in Minnesota, where members of the Board of Regents of the University of Minnesota were elected by the state legislature. But the members of two other governing boards in Minnesota were appointed. In New York the members of the Board of Regents were elected by the General Assembly, but members of the governing boards of the state university and the city university were appointed. In Pennsylvania some members of the board of trustees of the four state-related institutions were appointed, others were selected by other means. The members of coordinating and advisory boards were appointed by the governors of the twenty-five states, except where provision had been made for institutional representatives to be designated by the institutions themselves.

The public expectation of a periodic report on institutional operations was recognized as a "right," as was the obligation of "accountability" on matters of public interest. Most state governments required by law an annual or biennial report on the part of governing boards, coordinating boards, and advisory boards. Where no such reporting was required by law, the issuance of periodic reports was practiced as a matter of good public relations. The obligation of accountability, however, was another matter. The Carnegie Commission did not explain what it meant by accountability on matters of public interest, nor did it prescribe any process of enforcement.

Accountability refers to an institution's responsibility for producing results. Unfortunately, in the realm of higher education, and especially in the realm of public higher education, there is no agreement about how to identify results or to whom responsibility for results shall be rendered. The traditional measures of results are the number of students instructed, degrees awarded, research and creative projects completed, publications realized, performances accomplished, demonstrations undertaken, broadcasts made, and patients cared for. It is assumed that all these results are uniformly useful to society and worth their costs. Responsibility for the quality and quantity of these results is first of all professional (both internal and external to the academic community itself), and beyond that is exercised by the governing board of an institution of higher learning.

In this study we found almost no evidence of accountability being sought by state government officials or agencies. Statewide governing boards had the authority to require accountability, but the multicampus responsibility of such boards afforded little time or energy to assert this authority in any comprehensive way. State coordinating boards and state advisory boards prepared reports indicating the complexities of institutional accountability but advanced the art of performance assessment only marginally if at all. The New York Board of Regents possessed the authority to deregister any instructional program of a public or private institution deemed of inferior quality, but this authority was sparingly used because the criteria of inferior quality were uncertain and peer review was a costly procedure. The Carnegie Commission could declare accountability to be a proper matter of public control in the public interest, but in fact such control was essentially exercised through the budget process of state governments and tended to reflect economic and fiscal circumstances rather than cost-benefit analyses provided by state higher education boards.

The Carnegie Commission also listed under the heading of public control the duty of courts to hear cases alleging denial of general rights or unfair procedures. This statement was no more than an acknowledgment that state and federal courts had already indicated considerable inclination to intervene in such cases. The immunity of institutions of higher education from judicial oversight, if it did indeed exist in an earlier day, has certainly disappeared in the last twenty or twenty-five years. We found one multicampus system (not a statewide system) in one of our twenty-five states that in the past ten years had almost never had fewer than 100 or more cases pending in state or federal courts. Judicial accountability was a reality in public higher education, but it was an accountability largely concerned with procedural issues and with alleged forms of discrimination or denial of the equal protection of the laws. In two states of the twenty-five there had been recent judicial decisions upholding the constitutional status of the governing board as a protection against legislative action considered to be within the management discretion of the board.

On the side of institutional independence, the Carnegie Commission listed three "rights": the right to be free from the requirement of oaths not applicable to other citizens in like circumstances, the right to independent trustees, and the right to nonpartisan trustees. Insofar as the selection of trustees for public institutions of higher education was concerned, the Carnegie Commission anticipated the procedure set forth in a report from the National Commission on College and University Trustee Selection (1980). As of 1982, however, we did not find a single state among the twenty-five that observed these recommended standards and procedures.

The Carnegie Commission was critical of constitutional or legal provisions that gave elected state officials, especially governors, membership on governing boards. Although there were three states out of twenty-five where governors sat on institutional governing boards, none of these was a statewide governing board. Governors did not sit on any coordinating or advisory boards, although legislators did in several instances. The most unique board encountered in this study in terms of authority and membership was the Florida Board of Education, which was made up of seven elected officials, including the governor. In 1978 the voters rejected a constitutional amendment that would have made this board appointive.

Financial and Business Affairs

The Carnegie Commission formulation for the distribution of authority in financial affairs raised the issue of whether institutions of higher education should enjoy a unique governmental status. In essence, the commission proposed that state colleges and universities be treated as governmentally sponsored corporations rather than as state government departments. This issue was discussed in the preceding chapter.

The Carnegie Commission recommended that the appropriation of current operating income from "public funds" be made by state legislatures on the basis of general formulas that would reflect quantity and quality of output. The commission did not define the meaning of "public funds," but it may be assumed that the reference was to the appropriation of general revenue tax receipts and not to the reappropriation of institutionally generated income. There was no suggestion, either, as to how the quality of institutional output was to be measured. (It might be noted here that the Tennessee Higher Education Commission devised certain measures of qualitative achievement and used these measures to distribute additional funds to individual institutions. See Bogue and Brown, 1982.) The Carnegie Commission also advocated the appropriation of "public funds" for capital improvements on the basis of a general formula for building requirements. The commission urged a postaudit rather than a preaudit of expenditures, purchasing, and personnel transactions. The effective use of available resources should also be determined by a postaudit. The commission recognized the need for public control of accounting practices and for public determination of general salary levels.

At the same time, the Carnegie Commission insisted that governing boards should determine the allocation of resources among programs, should be free to make expenditures within the budget, should determine the work load and assignments of personnel, should determine salaries of individual personnel (presumably other than civil service personnel), and should design buildings and assign space needs.

What the Carnegie Commission failed to mention was that its proposals were directed at state departments of administration and state auditors rather than at state boards of higher education. In our study we were confronted over and over again with criticisms about costs and delays in institutional management occasioned by state departments of administration and other control agencies. The greatest degree of autonomy in institutional financial management was found to exist in Ohio. This autonomy was embodied in law *after* the Ohio Board of Regents—the state coordinating agency—had been established, and it had in fact been accomplished on the recommendation of the board of regents. The most stringent restrictions on institutional financial management were found in New York, although several other states ran a close second.

An informative report on institutional "efficiency" was prepared by Harcleroad (1975) on behalf of the American Association of State Colleges and Universities (AASCU). This study looked at both state coordination and state administrative controls. The data clearly indicated that the most onerous limitations upon the financial and personnel management of state institutions of higher education were exercised by state departments of administration rather than by state boards of higher education. Nearly two thirds of the respondents to Harcleroad's questionnaire to presidents of AASCU institutions indicated that there had been an increase in the controls over institutional financial and personnel matters by executive departments since 1969.

At the same time the Harcleroad study did not make a clear distinction between controls exercised by the central office of a multicampus governing board and controls exercised by executive departments, including the state auditor. Moreover, it was not clear whether governing board controls were subject to board discretion. In many instances these controls were mandated by state executive agencies. Presidents of state institutions were inclined to be critical of controls by central governing boards and executive departments and did not acknowledge the necessity for public control as formulated by the Carnegie Commission.

When a new chancellor for the State University of New York (SUNY) began efforts in the 1980s to decentralize controls exercised by his own office, he found that many controls were in the province of state executive agencies and could not be changed by the chancellor's office. The institutions comprising the SUNY system asserted that four basic changes were needed in order to enhance the efficiency of institutional operations. First, the "unnecessary and archaic" practice of preaudit of institutional expenditures should be ended. Second, the institutions and the system should receive a lump-sum appropriation for instruction (including overhead), supplemented by specific appropriations to support research and public service activities. Third, the institutions at the campus level should be permitted to write checks and make disbursements within budgetary limitations and subject to postaudit by a governmental agency. It was estimated, for example, that the cost of processing vouchers (disbursements) could be reduced from $8.24 to $3.80 per voucher through local management. Fourth, once appropriations were made by the legislature, they should be available for expenditure and not be subject to gubernatorial impoundment or other executive restriction.

In New York, state government controls were developed as part of the executive management movement of the 1920s. These controls have become encrusted in a sizable state government bureaucracy that has tended to view any relaxation of them as a threat to both its power and its employment. It will take substantial effort indeed to bring executive management in New York and elsewhere more in line with the decentralization and efficiency needs of the 1980s and 1990s.

Academic and Intellectual Affairs

In the Carnegie Commission formulation several important matters pertaining to academic and intellectual affairs were enumerated as proper subjects for public control. These included general policies on student admissions, policies for equal access to employment for women and minorities, policies on differential missions among systems and institutions of higher education, policies on the size and rate of growth of individual campuses, the establishment of new campuses and other "major" new endeavors (such as construction of a medical school), the encouragement of innovation through special grants, and enforcement of individual constitutional rights. The Carnegie Commission went out of its way to specify that public control should not extend to demands for secret research and to review of research results before publication. It did acknowledge that public control might extend to limitations upon patent rights for institutions or faculty members.

In connection with appropriate public control of admission policies, the Carnegie Commission referred to the number of places to be made available, equality of access, general standards of student ability among institutions, and the general distribution of students between lower and upper division. All these policy issues had been embodied in California law—for example, in the master plan legislation of 1960—and the Carnegie Commission found no reason to quarrel with these governmental practices. The commission did not state whether public control on these matters should be exercised only by law. Interestingly enough, in the twenty-four states of this study other than California, general policy decisions about student admission, including articulation between two-year institutions and senior institutions, were left largely to the discretion of state boards of higher education or to institutional governing boards. Three of the states did have laws specifying a policy of open admission to all state-supported institutions of higher education, but in Ohio this legal requirement had been modified by legislation on enrollment size.

As we mentioned earlier, no academic issue is fraught with more complexity than the differentiation of mission among institutions. In large measure we found that state legislatures were either reluctant or unable to come to grips with this problem. Faculty members and academic leaders tended to think that diffferentiation of mission meant the establishment of differential worth among institutions. Even community colleges and other two-year institutions were inclined to take this attitude. The utility of different purposes, different programs, and even different standards of performance might be understood by state government officials and by state boards of higher education. But this utility was not widely appreciated among faculty members and other persons within higher education institutions. Moreover, attempts to measure qualitative achievement in terms of the realization of specified objectives rather than in terms of the provision of particular inputs have not been popular among faculty members and others at the campus level.

Policies on equal access to employment for women and minorities have been primarily determined by federal law and enforced by federal agencies. State boards of higher education have had little if any role in the exercise of this particular form of public control.

In contrast, control of new instructional programs, of branch campuses and off-campus instruction, and of program scope in terms of enrollment has been a central element in the thrust toward state government coordination since World War II. The proliferation and duplication of programs among institutions as they expanded their enrollments and asked for increased appropriations were major factors in state government decisions to establish state boards of higher education. This proliferation and duplication were especially evident at the graduate level of instruction and in graduate professional programs, although there was also concern about the overly rapid growth of undergraduate programs in engineering and allied health fields.

The need for public control of instructional programs, branch campuses, and off-campus instruction seemed to be generally accepted in most of the states in this study as of 1980, although some problems existed. For example, there had been unfortunate conflicts over branch campuses in Alabama, and there was still some concern in several states about off-campus instruction. In Texas there was some disagreement between the coordinating board and the various systems and institutions about how to control the development of new programs.

The major issue of public control as of 1982 was no longer restriction on the establishment of new instructional programs. The major issue was the review and curtailment or elimination of existing instructional programs. In other words, the issue was what authority state coordinating boards should have to determine that particular instructional programs at particular institutions were too low in enrollment, too costly in operation, or too poor in quality to warrant continued operation. Connecticut as of 1982 had gone the farthest in conferring authority on its board of governors to make decisions of this kind. Other states were debating the desirability of public control over instructional retrenchment.

Individual institutions were inclined as of 1982 to insist that only the institution or its governing board should make retrenchment decisions. Program review and program curtailment, it was argued, were appropriate areas for the exercise of institutional self-regulation. The argument would have carried greater weight with state government officials, including state boards of higher education, if there were greater evidence that such self-regulation was in fact being exercised. Program review and curtailment were likely to arouse angry protests from faculty members and others, to lead to harsh criticism of academic leaders, and even to produce demands for faculty collective bargaining. Under these circumstances public control rather than institutional self-regulation was apt to become the order of the day in program review and curtailment.

We found very little concern as of 1982 about rates of growth or maximum campus size. These issues may have been major concerns in 1972 or 1973, but not ten years later. In 1982, however, there was concern because some campuses were declining in enrollment while others were increasing. In Colorado as part of a package of funding reform certain limits were placed on the number of students on each campus who would be subsidized through the state government appropriation. But state governments were reluctant to guide enrollment decline, and the Carnegie Council on Policy Studies in its reports at the end of the 1970s advocated that student choice rather than governmental intervention be the determinant of such decline (see Carnegie Council on Policy Studies in Higher Education, 1980). This position was one generally acceptable to state government officials as of 1982.

There was little in the way of state government encouragement of institutional innovation as of 1982. Financial constraints upon state governments were such as to discourage any concern but with the financing of essential ongoing operations. Undoubtedly some financial encouragement of institutional innovation would have been desirable. For example, state governments would have been well advised to participate in an activity such as the Fund for the Improvement of Postsecondary Education authorized by the Education Amendments of 1972. But state governments were inclined in the 1970s to leave improvements and innovations to institutional initiative and to such funding as institutions might be able to generate from private or federal sources.

Insofar as institutional independence was concerned, the Carnegie Commission set forth a number of activities that should be entirely within the decision-making authority of higher education institutions. These activities included the selection of students, the selection and promotion of faculty members, the approval of individual courses and course content, the management of research and public service projects, the determination of student grades and of qualifications to receive a degree, the selection of administrative personnel, the determination of policies on academic freedom, the determination of policies on the size of departments, schools, and colleges within budget limitations, and the development of plans for innovative activities.

On the subject of new academic programs and other new endeavors the Carnegie Commission was ambivalent. On the one hand, it recognized the need for public control of new campuses and other "major" new endeavors. Yet it also asserted that institutions should determine on their own authority "academic programs" for new campuses and other "major" new endeavors "within general authorization." It appeared that the commission favored public control of decisions to establish new campuses and public definition of their "general scope" but also favored institutional approval of individual degree programs undertaken by existing and new campuses. The commission did not attempt to reconcile these somewhat conflicting positions.

As we have just observed, the approval of new degree programs has been a major concern in the attempt of states to achieve coordination of higher education. The Carnegie Commission did not explain what it meant in speaking of the "definition of scope" for new campuses and for new endeavors. In practice, the approval of new degree programs at existing and new institutions has been at the heart of the state government concern with defining the scope of institutional operations. The Carnegie Commission, it seems, was opposed to giving state governments this authority to approve new degree programs, but it offered no other approach to the public control of institutional scope. In any event, the commission was fighting a lost cause.

All nine coordinating boards identified as such in this study had the authority to approve new degree programs. It may well be that an important consideration in the decision of the Carnegie Commission and the subsequent Carnegie Council to oppose the work of state coordinating boards and to favor state advisory boards was this matter of authority to approve new degree programs. Indeed, throughout the Carnegie reports these is a strong undercurrent of support for the idea that state government control should be exercised by governors and legislators but not by administrative agencies. Although this position was never explicitly stated by either the Carnegie Commission or the Carnegie Council, it was strongly implied in several different reports.

The report on governance issued by the Carnegie Commission on Higher Education (1973b) was silent on the subject of the exercise of authority by the various constituent groups of the academic community. Nowhere is this silence more evident that in the failure to elaborate upon the exercise of institutional authority in matters academic and intellectual. The commission identified student admissions, the differentiation of institutional mission, policies on research and public service projects, the establishment of new campuses and new "endeavors," academic innovation, the determination of courses and course content, the selection of faculty members and of academic administrators, the determination of degree requirements, the evaluation of students, the commitment to academic freedom, and the size of academic departments as matters coming within the scope of academic and intellectual affairs. Yet, in discussing institutional independence to make decisions about these matters, the commission said nothing about the distribution of authority within an institution among governing board, institutional leadership, faculty, students, professional support staff, other support staff, and alumni.

It must be assumed that the Carnegie Commission recognized the final or ultimate authority of governing boards in the decision-making process on academic and intellectual affairs. Presumably, the commission also recognized that there were appropriate faculty, student, and administration roles to be observed in resolving academic and intellectual issues. At the same time, however, the Carnegie Commission and the Carnegie Council refrained from any discussion of internal institutional governance; that is, it refrained from any prescription of the appropriate roles of faculty, students, presidents, and governing boards in the resolution of academic and intellectual issues.

The reconciliation of public control with institutional autonomy is not a simple problem. It may well be that any reconciliation acceptable to both state government officials and institutional constituencies is impossible. It may well be that a condition of dynamic tension is the best that can be expected in the relationship of state governments to publicly sponsored and supported institutions of higher education.

The problem of public control versus institutional independence is further complicated by the presence of multicampus systems of public institutions with various individual institutions or campuses that share a single or common governing board. In this study there were ten states with a single governing board for all senior public institutions of higher education, except for the municipal university in Kansas. Among the remaining fifteen states, twelve included one or more multicampus systems of senior institutions under a single governing board. Only in three states (Delaware, Ohio, and Washington) were all senior public institutions under separate governing boards.

In its presentation of a desirable pattern for the distribution of authority between public agencies and academic institutions, the Carnegie Commission specifically referred to multicampus systems as coming within its definition of academic institutions. Nothing was said about the distribution of authority between a chancellor or president in a central office and the individual campuses of the system. Although this distribution of authority was not the object of concern in our study, we nonetheless encountered a good deal of criticism from campus administrators about the loss of institutional independence to system offices. Indeed, much of the criticism of state government that we picked up in an anecdotal fashion from campus officials was directed at multicampus central offices rather than at state coordinating boards. From the campus perspective, the problem of institutional independence has a special meaning in the context of a multicampus governing system.

In the nine states of this study with coordinating boards, we found that the autonomy of multicampus systems and individual institutions was a major value that these coordinating boards sought to protect and, on occasion, even to enhance. We concluded that coordinating boards were not enemies of institutional independence. State government departments of administration, governors' offices, state legislatures, and state legislative agencies were far more evident as enemies of institutional independence that were coordinating boards.

To be sure, coordinating boards review and approve budgets and new programs and carry out master planning from the point of view of state needs and state government interests. Coordinating boards are instruments or agencies of state government. Yet coordinating boards as we observed them were well aware of their lack of governing or management authority in relation to multicampus systems and individual institutions. When the authority of coordinating boards was extended by law to certain aspects of institutional governance, this fact reflected state government dissatisfaction with the coordinating process as lacking sufficient vigor or sufficient authority.

State advisory boards were, of course, only too well aware of their lack of authority in relation to multicampus systems and individual institutions. Statewide governing boards did not lack authority in relation to individual institutions, but they sometimes failed to exercise that authority. The failure could lead to legislative retribution, as it did in South Dakota in 1981 and in Florida in 1979.

We do not conclude that institutional independence in the twenty-five states of this study was alive and well in 1982. On the contrary, institutional independence was under substantial threat. The first threat was the chronic economic stagnation in America that had existed since late 1973 and was particularly evident in 1982. The second threat was the precarious financial condition of state government finances, especially in states such as California and Massachusetts where taxpayer revolts had been successful. A third threat was the loss of public concern with higher education as a major economic asset and as a major contributor to economic welfare. The growing state government control of higher education was a reflection of these forces.

Institutions of higher education — in multicampus systems or singly — would do well to address basic causes in the winter of their discontent rather than to seek scapegoats by attacking the essentials of state coordination.

❧ 9 ❧

Future Relationships

THERE IS SAID TO BE AN OLD Chinese proverb that declares that it is dangerous to prophesy, especially about the future. It is no simple matter to suggest the probable course of human events. Straight-line projections may or may not reflect the reasonable expectation of the future. There are many possible discontinuities in human affairs: war, revolutions, technological changes, social changes, economic changes, political changes, individual or behavioral changes. No one can say with certainty how rapidly these various changes are likely to occur or what their possible consequences may be.

More particularly, there is no way of knowing exactly what relations between state governments and higher education will be in the decades of the 1980s and 1990s. The most that any thoughtful person can do is to anticipate, on the basis of experience, various problems and various possible solutions to them. Moreover, a large element of subjective judgment is involved. No two persons will necessarily evaluate the past in the same way or anticipate the same set of future circumstances. Yet none of this gives us warrant to avoid making some predictions about future events.

State Government Concerns

It is evident that state governments will continue to reflect various social concerns in regard to the performance and cost of higher education. Moreover, the state government perception

of social concerns will not necessarily coincide with the perception
of these concerns on the part of the leadership, faculty, staff, and
students of individual colleges and universities. There will continue to be different responses to different perceptions of needs
and values.

The future of the American economy and the role of higher
education in relation to economic expectations will undoubtedly
continue to be the single most important issue for state governments and institutions of higher education in the remaining years
of the twentieth century. In the aftermath of World War II, the
American economy experienced nearly thirty years of healthy
growth. There were occasional warnings about a finite set of raw
materials, about exhaustible energy resources, about the disparate
distribution of economic welfare among the peoples of the world,
as well as among classes of people within particular societies, about
contamination of the environment, and about limitations on economic growth. In spite of these warnings, however, the essential
mood of the United States was optimistic. But then came the war
in Vietnam, followed by the oil embargo of 1973 and the economic
recession that began in that same year. Thereafter circumstances
changed. Economic growth slowed down; international tensions
increased; the future of developing nations became clouded; international competition challenged American industry; inflation was
rampant; unemployment was persistent; and governmental intervention in the American economy took an uncertain form.

It was inevitable that higher education would be affected by
these circumstances. Moreover, a further complication was the
prospect of a substantial decline in the number of persons of traditional college age. Plagued by voter criticism of tax levels and high
expenditures, state governments began to reconsider the benefits
and costs of higher education.

Colleges and universities, both public and private, have been
ambivalent about their economic role. On the one hand, faculty
members and others have been loud to proclaim that their purpose
is not to prepare individuals to function in the prevailing economy
but to prepare individuals to live intellectually and socially satisfying lives. On the other hand, no one has answered the question of
how a satisfying life is to be lived without useful and rewarding

employment. And, in actual practice, a substantial part of the higher education endeavor has been directed toward professional or paraprofessional employment.

Indeed, the major economic role of higher education is to prepare individuals of "talent and virtue" for vital professional and other services in the economy and society. This role will continue to be the primary purpose of higher education in the years ahead. But many troublesome issues arise here: how to identify talent and virtue in individual students and in their academic performance, how to balance the number of degree recipients with the number of positions needed in the economy, how to provide the needed kind of educational experience, how to determine what should be spent on higher education, and how to finance the costs of higher education.

A second role of higher education involves the advancement of technology in the economy. A major purpose of higher education institutions is to advance knowledge and to support creative activity. From the faculty point of view, research and creative activity provide their own reward. From the point of view of the economy, research is justified insofar as it produces a knowledge base for new products and new production processes that will materially and physically benefit mankind. All production processes from growing crops to teaching school to practicing medicine involve the current state of technology. Improvements in these processes to advance output, curtail environmental pollution, and enhance society's health and well-being are useful. In addition, creative activity helps to enhance humanity's cultural awareness. Higher education has played a major role in advancing technology and stimulating creative activity.

Given the probable economic environment of the 1980s and 1990s, state governments will want to ensure that research will contribute to economic growth and the economic betterment of their citizens. New products and new production processes will be needed to increase employment, to improve the physical and mental well-being of all persons, and to achieve a more healthful and satisfying environment. The alternative to economic growth will be continuing social warfare over the distribution of such stable or declining output as the economy can provide. If higher education can demonstrate a contribution to general economic growth, as it has in the more limited area of agricultural output, then higher education will be regarded politically and socially as deserving state government support.

A third purpose of higher education is that of technological transfer or public service. Here again the record has been particularly outstanding in agriculture and in health care, but helpful contributions have likewide been made in other areas from public education to public broadcasting. Business, industry, and many professions in America have tended to rely primarily on educated talent for their advancement rather than on a university connection. It is still to be demonstrated whether such a connection, once achieved, would be helpful to business, industry, or the professions.

Apart from this general concern with the state of the economy, state governments have other interests in respect to higher education, as mentioned in Chapter Two: planning for enrollment decline, ensuring program quality and coordination, encouraging private higher education, providing student financial assistance, working out the desirable relationship between vocational-technical education and higher education, and financing higher education. Embedded in these concerns are troublesome problems that involve the size, location, and program scope of higher education institutions, the access of students to higher education, the recognition and reward of academic achievement, and the quality of academic performance represented by the award of academic degrees. None of these issues is simple to resolve in a liberal democracy, a mixed economy, and a pluralistic society.

Of course, these issues are also of concern to the leadership, faculties, staffs, and students of higher education institutions. But these various constituencies of academic communities are limited in the responses they may be willing to make in trying to resolve or mitigate these concerns. Higher education institutions must depend upon others for financial resources; in the case of public institutions they are especially dependent upon the resources provided by state governments and by the federal and local governments. Higher education institutions take on certain characteristics of all organizational entities: a concern with self-perpetuation, a concern with self-protection, and a concern with organizational or constituent well-being. These limitations serve to restrict the range of responses that higher education institutions can and will make to urgent economic, political, and social needs.

State governments must continue to provide resources to higher education that will stimulate the desired responses to urgent public needs, and higher education institutions must continue to perform their essential tasks in ways that are sensitive to these urgent public needs. On the one hand, state political leaders are disposed to say that all they ever hear about from higher education representatives is the need for more financial support and that they hear almost nothing about the cost-benefit derived from these expenditures. On the other hand, representatives of higher education institutions are disposed to say that all they ever hear about from state political leaders is the need for immediate results from processes that inevitably require time and patience.

From these divergent points of view arises the organizational context in which state governments and higher education institutions must undertake to resolve their mutual concerns. In the 1980s the organizational context is made more complicated by an economic and financial environment quite different from that of the 1960s. The unfavorable economic and financial environment constitutes a new challenge, and a new opportunity, for higher education. That same environment places a new imperative on state governments.

Governance Structures

For public institutions of higher education the state government involvement begins with the determination of how campuses are to be governed. The choices are three or four in number: (1) a governing board for each senior institution and each two-year institution; (2) a governing board for a system of senior institutions and a system of two-year institutions; (3) a statewide governing board for all senior institutions and all two-year institutions; and (4) various possible combinations of these arrangements, such as separate governing boards for senior institutions but not for the two-year branches of state universities. In some fashion each state government has provided for a governing board for its various public institutions of higher education.

The prevailing practice of campus governance observed in this study was the multicampus structure. Among the twenty-five states we visited there were ten with statewide governing boards (four boards included only senior institutions) and twelve with one or more multicampus systems of senior institutions. Among these twelve states only five had multicampus governing structures for all senior institutions; the remaining seven states had multicampus governing boards for some campuses and separate boards for other campuses. There were only three states that had separate governing boards for each of their senior campuses.

We did not undertake in this study to contrast the multicampus governance structure with that of the separate campus governing board. The two studies of the multicampus governing structure by the Carnegie Commission and the Carnegie Council made no comparative analysis of the two structures. The first study (Lee and Bowen, 1971) declared that the multicampus structure did promote differential missions among campuses, did assist substantially in creating new campuses, did promote program expansion at the graduate level, and did improve higher education budgeting. The acknowledged shortcomings had to do with uncertainties about the relative roles of the state government, the coordinating agency, and the governing board; inadequate delegation of fiscal authority by state governments; insufficient innovation in academic plans and programs; and the tendency of the governing board to think of its role in relation to particular campuses rather than to the system as a whole.

Among the twenty-two states with multicampus systems we found only four where in the past ten years serious attention had been given to the restructuring of campus governance. In one state we were told that the legislature was opposed to the creation of separate governing boards for each campus because such action would give the governor too many appointed positions to fill. In the other states there was evidence of legislative dissatisfaction with multicampus boards, but there was no agreement about acceptable alternatives. The dissatisfaction tended to reflect geographical differences about relative rates of development and support among the campuses of a system. We did not find any example among the twenty-two states of an actual restructuring of the component campuses of a multicampus system.

We are forced to accept the conclusion that the multicampus system for the governance of public higher education is unlikely to be abandoned or to be modified substantially in the foreseeable future. Governors seem to be generally satisfied with multicampus systems and to fear that increased competition for students, programs, and funds would result from a governance structure that emphasized the unique aspects of each separate campus. Legislators who represent urban areas with state universities that lack the status of the flagship state university may be dissatisfied, but in the economic environment of the 1980s they are unlikely to succeed in their efforts to alter institutional missions.

The single-campus governing board appears to be much more on the defensive than does the multicampus governing board, and the multicampus governing board that is less than statewide in scope appears to be more on the defensive than does the statewide governing board. Governors in particular see in the multicampus governing board an organizational arrangement that can be used to curtail or restrict institutional and local aspirations, and they are likely to view the statewide governing board as even more disposed to achieve order among competing campuses. The restructuring of higher education institutions in Massachusetts in 1980 vividly illustrated this tendency. When governors and legislative leaders share dissatisfaction with the existing governance arrangements for the higher education campuses within a state, change is fairly certain to occur.

Statewide Multicampus Systems

At the level of state government, one organizational choice is the statewide multicampus system of senior institutions. Among the twenty-five states of this study, there were ten with such statewide multicampus structures. One of these was quite new, while three others had been established since 1965. The remaining six had all been in existence since World War II, and three were founded before 1900.

One of the important observations of this study was that the older the statewide multicampus system, the greater was the disillusion of state government officials with this organizational arrangement. There were several factors operating here. In half of

the ten states either two-year community colleges and/or
vocational-technical institutes did not operate under the governance authority of the multicampus system. Thus, in spite of the
statewide multicampus system for senior institutions, statewide
coordination by no means existed. In addition, there was the
problem of where to locate the planning function that included
private institutions in the state and the administrative functions
that involved student assistance, federally supported statewide
programs, and certain other general activities. Six of the ten states
had established postsecondary education commissions to exercise
these other functions; only four of the states had designated the
statewide multicampus system as the state agency for general
higher education activities.

But the most important factor in state government disillu-
sionment was the perception that statewide multicampus governing boards were more closely attuned to campus than to state
interests. State government officials wanted statewide governing
boards to address the issues of duplication of programs among
institutions, the small size of some campuses, the uncertain quality of some campuses and programs, and the high cost of various
programs. State governments wanted statewide governing boards
to order presidents to behave differently and to tell them not to
expect ever-increasing state financial support. The statewide
governing boards perceived that they were being asked to make
unpopular political decisions that state government officials, especially state legislatures, were unwilling to make. This reluctance
of governing boards to attack critical political as well as higher
education issues led state officials to complain that the boards
were not doing their job. Legislative dissatisfaction with statewide
boards was expressed as threats to reduce appropriations or to
curtail appropriation increases and to restructure the state government organization for higher education. Thus in one state dissatisfaction with the statewide boards led to an increase in the role
of the state advisory board for higher education.

In Massachusetts legislative leaders came to see the coordinating board as ineffectual in its relation to the component parts
of the state higher education system. After 1965 there had been a
period of rapid expansion in the programs and locations of state

institutions of higher education. The period was seen as one in which there had been inadequate planning and budgeting by the Massachusetts Board of Higher Education. Then came a period of belt tightening after 1974 — a period of conflict, fiscal stringency, and even some enrollment declines. In this environment the statewide multicampus governing board was seen as the means whereby state government concerns could be met. In time, however, it may well turn out that the political expectations that were expressed in the 1980 law will not be realized, in part because the political expectations themselves were unrealistic.

We hazard the guess that the attraction of the statewide governing board will become less evident as experience with this arrangement grows. We do not expect any statewide systems to be abandoned, although such a proposal was made in two of the ten states of this study. We don't doubt but that some other states where the state coordinating board is perceived as a political failure will be tempted to establish a statewide governing board. We do expect that state governments after considerable experience with statewide governing boards will begin to experiment with additional arrangements for planning, budgeting, and coordination. These additional arrangements may well be centered in advisory boards or in other agencies of state government.

The fault of the statewide governing board from the viewpoint of state government is also the virtue of the statewide governing board from the viewpoint of higher education: its identification with institutional interests. The statewide governing board tends to see its role in terms of the interests and aspirations of individual institutions, even though it must in some instances restrict the aspirations of particular institutions to expand programs for which there is inadequate funding and no evident need. The statewide governing board seeks to satisfy to some extent the various constituencies of the campus community, the alumni, the local community, and such publics as express a special interest in a particular institution. This effort is more fully understood by the governing board than it is by governors and legislators.

The most conspicuous defect of the statewide governing board lies in its failures to formulate and articulate a state government interest in higher education. This defect may be inherent in

the institutional governance responsibility of the board. The statewide governing board is only too cognizant of the urgent and
unmet needs of state universities. Accordingly, it is difficult for the
governing board to take an impartial look at the circumstances of
private institutions, of community colleges not in the system, and
of vocational-technical education. These other institutions are
seen as a threat to the "adequate" support of the institutions for
which the statewide governing board is responsible.

Another problem for the statewide governing board is its
relationship to campus presidents. Campus presidents necessarily
have to express and advocate the interests of their campuses. They
have to maintain some semblance of order and civility among
campus constituencies. They have to cultivate cooperative relationships with their local communities. They have to maintain
friendly relations with local legislators and with various external
publics. Yet at the same time the campus president is expected to
be loyal to the system. The statewide governing board can always
remove an uncooperative or disloyal president, but it has also to be
alert to the possible political repercussions of such action.

The chancellor of a statewide system finds it difficult to
define his or her role. Is the chancellor in effect the president of
each campus, or is the chancellor a coordinator of systemwide concerns and a representative of the system to the political leadership
of a state? We found chancellors to be somewhat ambivalent about
the definition of their role. If they acted as coordinators and political representatives, they were likely to be criticized on the grounds
that they were not sufficiently involved with institutional needs.
But if they acted as campus presidents, they were criticized for trying to centralize the management of campuses with varied needs
and interests. Chancellors had to walk a narrow path between
campus autonomy and systemwide management.

Somewhat to our surprise we found that chancellors in
statewide governing systems had difficulties with campus presidents not too unlike the difficulties encountered by coordinating
board executive officers. At any rate, the statewide governing
board was no magic solution to the problem of systemwide unity
and loyalty or to the problem of state government relationships.

We are disposed to believe that one of two courses of action will emerge in the 1980s and 1990s in those states where statewide governance of at least all senior public institutions has been established. One course of action will be the development of higher education advisory boards in addition to the statewide governing board. The advisory board will be responsible for a state master plan; for policy development in relation to private higher education; for the recommendation of coordinated relationships among state universities, community colleges, and vocational-technical education; for advice about program needs and costs; and for the management of statewide programs such as student financial assistance. The other possible course of action is for statewide governing boards and chancellors to understand their role primarily in state government terms and to behave increasingly like state coordinating boards. In states with relatively small populations a statewide governing board may successfully combine the two roles. In states of larger population we believe that statewide governing boards should perform their governance role and leave the state government role to an advisory board.

Coordinating Boards

By definition, state coordinating boards exercise three primary functions: (1) developing and publishing master plans, (2) reviewing and making recommendations about the current operating and capital improvement needs of higher education programs, and (3) reviewing and approving degree programs in terms of state needs and the costs of the programs to the states. This third function in the 1960s was restricted to *new* degree programs. In the 1980s and 1990s increasing attention will undoubtedly be given to the review and approval of existing programs. The coordinating board in Connecticut was given authority as of 1983 to review and to terminate existing programs. It is probable that similar authority will be conferred on other coordinating boards in the years ahead.

Another troublesome issue will be that of the elimination or merger of campuses with small enrollments. When the author was chancellor for a state coordinating board, he decided that the minimum enrollment size for a comprehensive state university should be 5,000 full-time equivalent students, for a comprehensive two-year institution 2,000 full-time equivalent students, and for an academic two-year institution with only a college-transfer program 1,500 full-time equivalent students. (The enrollment standards subsequently recommended by the Carnegie Commission were not too far different from these figures.) When a campus was smaller than these limits, there were two choices. One choice was to fund the campus as if it did in fact have these minimum enrollments. The other choice was to close it or merge it with another campus. In the 1960s it was not too difficult to persuade a governor and legislature to provide extra funding for small campuses. In the 1970s such extra funding became more difficult to obtain, and in the 1980s and 1990s such extra funding will be provided with considerable reluctance.

The 1982 law in Connecticut that created the board of governors as the coordinating agency provided that as of 1983 the board might direct the closing or merger of small campuses. The definition of small campuses was left to the determination of the board. Orders to close or merge a campus were subject to legislative veto. This arrangement has considerable merit and might well be emulated in other states. It must be made clear that the only alternative to closing or merging a small campus is to provide extra funding for the operation of the campus.

Coordinating boards have in the past often had the authority to approve the establishment of branch campuses by a state university or community college and to approve the offering of off-campus courses. In the future, the elimination of branch campuses and off-campus courses will be even more important functions of such boards. In Alabama in 1979 the Commission on Higher Education was given the authority to order state universities to eliminate off-campus courses of questionable need and high cost. Such authority might well be conferred on coordinating boards generally.

Coordinating boards have often had the authority to operate special statewide programs, such as student financial assistance programs and federal grant programs. Of the nine coordinating boards in this study, seven administered the state's student financial assistance program. In another state the coordinating board reviewed the appropriation request of the student assistance agency but asked the legislature that it not be given administrative author-ity for the operations of the agency. It seems appropriate for the coordinating agency to administer statewide programs.

The master-planning authority was given careful attention by all state coordinating boards. The statement of role and scope or of mission for each campus was an important, indeed critical, feature of these master plans. As succeeding plans were prepared, the definition of mission tended to become both more comprehen-sive and more precise. The most recent master plan prepared and adopted in New Jersey is an especially informative and definitive document. We found that master plans were essential to the actions of the coordinating boards in reviewing instructional and other programs and in providing guidelines for state financial support of higher education.

The scope of authority of coordinating boards extended to all aspects of higher education, including state relationships to private higher education. Possession of this wide-ranging author-ity was one of the notable strengths of state coordinating boards. Their authority, however, usually did not extend to vocational-technical education, and this exception is so important that it deserves special mention later. Each of the nine state coordinating boards in this study served as the 1202 commission of its state. When federal grants for these commissions were terminated, the co-ordinating boards continued to perform the specified planning func-tion as an integral part of the master-planning operation. Consulta-tion with private institutions and with public systems or institutions continued to be an essential aspect of the master-planning process.

Both the Carnegie Commission and the Carnegie Council referred in their reports to the "heavy hand" of state regulatory agencies, by which they meant the state government coordinating boards. The two Carnegie bodies never specified, however, what authority of the coordinating boards they considered to be exer-cised in a "heavy-handed" way. Presumably the reference was to the authority to review and approve new degree programs and to review and recommend current operating and capital improve-ment requests of the various campuses. The further implication must be drawn that the Carnegie study groups were opposed to program review and preferred that budget requests be reviewed by the governor's office rather than by a coordinating board.

This study, however, has found the program review and budget authority of coordinating boards to be vital factors in the implementation of state master plans and to be conducive to their careful preparation. If a coordinating board no longer enjoyed such authority, not only would the board cease to be a coordinating board but the coordinating function would fall upon the governor's budget office and the state legislature. There may be differences of opinion as to the desirable agency for the exercise of program review and budget authority, but I have no hesitancy in stating my preference for the coordinating board.

The principal problems for the coordinating board confirmed by this study have been two: (1) its relationship to multicampus systems or campuses of public higher education in a state and (2) its relationship to the governor and legislature. We shall comment about the second of the two problems later. Here we may observe that the attitude of governing boards and campus presidents toward coordinating boards tended to be about as hostile at the beginning of the 1980s as it was in the 1960s. Governing boards and presidents believed that coordinating boards should be advocates of institutional interests, and they expressed dissatisfaction that coordinating boards should think of their role as that of furthering the interests of the state government. Reconciliation of divergent points of view about the role of coordinating boards depends on the realization on the part of governing boards and presidents that there is a state government interest in higher education that may be different from what institutions perceive as their interests. Continued hostility toward coordinating boards can only be harmful to campuses in the decades of the 1980s and 1990s. Perhaps it is too much to hope that this prospect will come to be generally understood by the leadership of state universities and community colleges.

Advisory Boards

One unexpected conclusion of this study — unexpected by me at least — was the vitality and influence of state advisory boards. Among the six states of this study with advisory boards, we found those in California, Minnesota, and Washington to be especially vigorous and to exercise considerable impact upon the legislative deliberations of their respective states. We found that the New York Board of Regents had substantial master-planning authority for higher education, although its authority was nonexistent in budget matters and was exercised somewhat spasmodically in the registration and deregistration of instructional programs. The work of the Pennsylvania Council of Higher Education may have been inhibited by several adverse circumstances. In Delaware the future of the advisory board was still uncertain.

It was impressive to observe in California, Minnesota, and Washington the extent to which the state legislatures made use of the advisory boards. Not only were numerous questions addressed to these advisory boards but a considerable number of actions resulted from the studies submitted by the advisory boards. We were not able to construct any quantitative data about the impact of advisory boards, but our impression was that the boards helped to discourage legislation that was likely to be harmful to institutions of higher education and encourage careful legislative attention to complex issues of quality, cost, and program duplication.

All the advisory boards had authority to prepare master plans of state educational needs. The prevailing practice among the advisory boards examined in this study was to prepare reports about discrete issues rather than to prepare elaborate presentations of general needs. Advisory boards generally lacked the personnel resources to undertake extensive master plans, although such plans had been prepared in New York and Pennsylvania. The highest priority of advisory boards was to respond to issues reflecting current legislative interests.

Although advisory boards lacked the statutory authority to review and recommend appropriation support for a state's public system of higher education, we found that advisory boards were increasingly being asked to comment on the appropriation needs of higher education: The one state in our study where this development appeared not to be happening was New York, and this situation probably reflected the long-standing hostility between governors and the board of regents in that state. Since members of the board are selected by the legislature and since the board has often asserted its independence from the executive office, it is little wonder that governors going all the way back to Alfred E. Smith in the 1920s have been inclined to ignore the board. The one successful onslaught upon the New York Board of Regents was that of Governor Thomas Dewey; it resulted in legislation in 1948 that created the State University of New York and removed the system of teacher's colleges in the state from the governance authority of the board. The bureaucratic strength of the executive budget office in New York was another factor that prevented the board of regents from playing an effective budget role in relation to higher education.

The advisory boards also accumulated a considerable array of miscellaneous functions. One such function was the administration of state student financial assistance programs. Another function was the management of federal programs involving state action, such as those involving facility and public service assistance. And of course the role of the New York Board of Regents in professional licensure was not only unique but also most impressive. The New York board was also involved in the granting of institutional accreditation.

Advisory boards tended also to have considerable impact on the behavior of public institutions of higher education. Although the boards generally lacked authority to approve degree programs and other activities of these institutions, the institutions were cautious about incurring any critical or adverse comment from the boards. Such comment could lead to questioning during appropriation hearings and might even result in restrictive legislation. As a result, public institutions tended to take the work of the advisory boards seriously and endeavored to influence their advice in the interest of preventing or modifying public criticism.

It appeared as of 1982 that most of the advisory boards were tending to become more and more like coordinating boards. In Pennsylvania the staff of the Council of Higher Education had also served as the staff of the former Board of State College and University Directors. With the formation of a new governance structure for the newly designated State System of Higher Education, it was possible that the council might become more active as a general planning and coordinating agency. The role of the New York Board of Regents depended on future relationships with a new governor and with the leaders of the state legislature. In Delaware the Postsecondary Education Commission might increasingly become a factor in the state government budget process. In California, Minnesota, and Washington it appeared that cutbacks in state government revenues might well force the advisory boards into more active roles in appropriation issues. It was possible that in these three states in particular governors and legislative leaders would depend increasingly on the expertise that the staffs of these boards provided.

One of the interesting factors about the advisory boards in five of the six states was that there was no question about the place of the board in the structure of state government. The boards were obviously agencies of state government. The governing boards and presidents of public institutions could make no claim that these boards were somehow tied to institutional interests. The five advisory boards served governors and legislative leaders; the decisions made upon the advice of these boards were political decisions arrived at through the political processes of the state governments. The decisions were matters of state law; only in special circumstances could even those universities with constitutional status afford to ignore them. Advisory boards spoke for the state government interest in higher education in all the ramifications of an enlightened public interest.

At the same time, the advisory status of state advisory boards had the result of involving these boards to a substantial degree in state politics. The advisory boards could not implement master plans on their own authority. Every recommendation of an advisory board was a recommendation subject to legislative action or inaction. The advisory board and its staff were enmeshed in the political process; it was little wonder that the executive directors of advisory boards often became tired and disillusioned by the constant political strife to which they were subjected. On the one hand, the advisory board had governing boards and presidents to contend with, and on the other hand it had governors and legislators to contend with. Moreover, it had almost no leverage with either set of actors.

All higher education boards — statewide governing boards, coordinating boards, and advisory boards — were involved in state government politics. But the advisory board was located in the very middle of the state government political process. This location was anything but enviable. And there did not appear to be any ready solution for the political complexities confronting the state higher education advisory board.

Vocational-Technical Education

No question in the area of higher education was more intractable, we found, than that of vocational-technical education. The problem resulted from the growth of a strong bureaucracy of vocational educators — a bureaucracy reinforced by federal grants that by law had to be apportioned by a single state government agency. That state government agency in twenty-two states of this study was the state board of education. Within these twenty-two state governments, however, five had established a joint or liaison committee to bring together representatives of elementary-secondary and higher education for preparation of the state vocational-technical education plan and for allocation of federal funds. In three states — Colorado, Indiana, and Washington — special agencies bringing together representatives of elementary-secondary and higher education had been established to prepare vocational-technical education plans. In Ohio, legislation drew a sharp distinction between vocational education as a secondary school program and technical education as a higher education program, but the state board of education remained as the sole state government agency responsible for the vocational-technical education plan.

Vocational educators in state systems of public school education had been quick to extend the scope of their programs to postsecondary education in the 1950s. Hence, as community colleges and even state universities began to develop two-year programs in technical education, they found themselves in competition with area vocational schools, often labelled area vocational-technical schools. Some duplication of programs inevitably resulted. But in state after state in this study, vocational educators were adamant in their refusal to leave technical education to the jurisdiction of community colleges and state universities. As a result there was often a lack of coordination and some costly duplication in postsecondary technical education.

The Board of Regents in Georgia appeared to have made considerable progress in attacking this problem of duplication of effort, as did the coordinating boards in Colorado, Illinois, and Texas. In Indiana a delivery system not connected with the secondary schools or the universities offered technical education, subject to the coordinating authority of the Commission for Higher Education. Among states with advisory boards, California and Washington appeared to have moved the farthest in resolving the problem of duplication.

Apart from the unique organization of the Indiana Vocational-Technical Education system, the most promising solution for state governments to the problem of vocational-technical duplication was to restrict technical education to community colleges. The second most promising solution was to make all offerings of technical (postsecondary) education subject to the authority of state higher education coordinating boards. But both solutions would continue to encounter strong opposition from the vocational education bureaucracy.

State Higher Education Boards and Politics

Political judgment in the United States prescribes that education, both elementary-secondary and higher education, shall be governed and administered by boards. This political judgment is founded on a long tradition of boards of education at the local and state levels and of governing boards for institutions of higher education. When state universities and state colleges were established by law or constitutional provision, their governance was vested in a governing board variously designated as a board of regents, a board of trustees, a board of governors, or a board of curators. When state governments undertook to create state agencies for higher education, in every instance the board form of organization was utilized.

The governing board for public institutions of higher education served a twofold purpose. First, the board was an insulating device to protect public institutions from the more crass forms of political pressure in the appointment of personnel, the acquisition of land, the construction of buildings, and the purchase of supplies. Although not without faults, the board was the only device that presented some hope of separating public institutions of higher education from external political pressures. The second purpose of the governing board of lay citizens was to achieve some form of linkage between the general interests of society in the conduct of higher education and the professional interests of presidents and faculty members.

When state governments established statewide governing boards for higher education, this device was the only possible choice of structure, given the long tradition of governing boards for institutions of higher education in America. When state governments established coordinating and advisory arrangements at the state level, the board device was uniformly adopted. State governmental officials realized that a single administrator appointed by the governor and subject to service at the governor's pleasure would not be an acceptable arrangement to all those persons who believe that higher education is a particularly fragile enterprise.

In this study we found no particular criticism of the board form of organizational structure at the state government level. In relation to all three kinds of boards—governing, coordinating, and advisory—we did encounter occasional complaints that governors failed to give sufficient attention to the desirable characteristics of board members: community status, professional or other demonstrated abilities, commitment to public service, a sympathetic attitude toward the purposes of higher education, and representation of differing groups in a pluralistic society.

A problem in the composition of coordinating and advisory boards was the inclusion of institutional representation in their membership. In the ten states with statewide governing boards, all board members were representatives of the general public. Among the nine coordinating boards, three included institutional representatives, although in each case members from the general public were in the majority. Three of the six advisory boards included institutional representation. The coordinating and advisory boards that did not include institutional representation had advisory committees of institutional representatives. We concluded that this last arrangement was the most satisfactory one.

The customary practice on higher education boards is to have staggered terms. Among the ten statewide governing boards, we found four with fifteen members, two with thirteen members, two with ten members, and two with nine members. The nine coordinating boards varied in membership size; there were four with nine members, two with eighteen members, and one each with sixteen, twelve, and eleven members. Among advisory boards, the one in California had twenty-three members, in Washington sixteen members, in New York fifteen members, in Delaware fourteen members, in Minnesota eleven members, and in Pennsylvania nine members. The terms of service for governing boards ranged from four to twelve years, with the most common period being six or seven years. Two coordinating boards had terms of nine years, five had terms of six years, and two had terms of four years. Three of the advisory boards had terms of four years, two had terms of six years, and one had terms of seven years.

The length of the term of board members raises the question of the desirable relationship of board membership to the term of office of a governor. Governors now generally serve four-year terms, usually with the possibility of being re-elected once. Only one of the twenty-five boards in this study was elected by the legislature; otherwise the public members were appointed by the governor and approved by the senate. Altogether seven of the twenty-five boards had terms of four years; thus a governor in one term could alter the entire composition of the board. One board had terms of five years for its membership, nine boards had terms of six years, and four boards had terms of seven years. In these instances a governor elected for two terms could alter the entire composition of a board. In the remaining three instances (I omit New York), a governor serving two terms might name a majority of the members of the higher education board, but not necessarily all of them.

The critical issue in state government operations is how the higher education board and its executive or administrative officer is to relate to the political leadership role of the governor and to the law-making role of the state legislatures. A doctrinaire response to this issue would be that the higher education board makes its best judgment on an issue, and the governor and legislature then dispose of the issue. This response at best is unrealistic; at its

worst it is even mischievous. The political process of state government involves an interplay of leadership attitudes and commitments, professional and administrative judgments, political
pressures from interest groups (including the bureaucracy of
public employees), and general public attitudes as they are inter-
preted by the leading political actors. The political process involves
controversy about who will be benefited and who harmed by any
particular course of action. The political process continually
endeavors to determine the public interest. In this process governors and legislators identify groups and persons who are sympathetic to their goals and others who are not.

It would be reassuring to declare that higher education
issues are beyond the maneuvers and coalition building of the regular state government consideration of public problems. Such
is not the case. Public higher education is a public problem. Public
higher education involves many public issues, including program
needs, location of institutions, and financing. These public issues
must be ultimately resolved by a political process in which governors and state legislators are key participants. Public higher education is inextricably entwined in the politics of state government.

As a consequence of this situation, state government higher
education boards have to relate in some way to governors and
state legislatures. To be sure, higher education boards can express
their best judgment about how state needs can best be met by
public and private institutions of higher education. But unless
such judgments are acceptable to governors and legislative leaders, they are no more than expressions of opinion; even worse,
such judgments may be regarded by governors and legislators as
inadequate or even hostile. To avoid open political warfare,
higher education boards have to find some way in which to engage
in political dialogue with state government officials.

The problem of relations between higher education boards
and governors becomes particularly evident when a new governor
is elected to office. If the new governor is of a different political
party or different party faction, then he or she may tend to be
especially distrustful of the board members appointed by his or
her predecessor and by the staff head selected by that board.
Much of course depends upon the personality and attitude of the

new governor. In this study it was evident that some governors began their tenure in office with a favorable disposition toward higher education and quickly found a way to work effectively with the higher education board. Other governors were narrowly partisan in their point of view and distrustful of higher education boards and their staff heads. When this last situation existed, higher education boards tended to be ignored or to be confronted with the possibility of legislation that would change their composition and role.

Governors can influence higher education boards by their appointments. Governors can decide to what extent they want to exert political leadership in implementing the master plans of coordinating boards and advisory boards. Governors can make recommendations about current operating appropriations and about capital improvement appropriations that will have a profound influence upon access to higher education, the scope and quality of higher education programs, the number of persons who receive the benefit of higher education, and the effectiveness of higher education research. Governors can also seek legislation to change the form of higher education boards. In all these actions, of course, governors must have the consent of the state senate in appointments (except in Massachusetts) and of both houses of the state legislature in enacting legislation.

In several states of this study, particular efforts had been made to find effective ways to relate higher education boards to the governor's office. In Massachusetts there had been a secretary of education in the governor's office who exercised some supervision over the state's board of higher education. This office was abolished along with the board in 1980 when the Massachusetts Board of Regents was created as a statewide governing board. The New Jersey Board of Higher Education appointed a chancellor for a five-year term subject to the approval of the governor, and the chancellor in turn headed a department of higher education with a seat in the governor's cabinet. In Pennsylvania there was a secretary of education with a vague relationship to the state board of education and to its constituent body, the Council on Higher Education. The chairman of the board and of the council was appointed by the governor and served at the governor's pleasure. In Florida the governor is chairman of the state board of education; the other six members are elected public officials of the state and include the commissioner of education. The board of regents is considered an operating unit of the Department of Education, and in 1981 the commissioner of education was made an ex officio member of the board of regents. At the same time, the Postsecondary Education Planning Commission in Florida was made an arm of the state board of education. In Missouri the Coordinating Board for Higher Education appointed a commissioner of education who was head of an executive department of higher education. In Colorado the executive director of the Commission on Higher Education was head of a department of higher education and sat in the governor's cabinet.

We did not find that in any of these arrangements there was some organizational magic that made relations between higher education boards and governors smoother and more effective than did the less formalized arrangements that existed in the case of the other statewide governing boards or of the other eleven coordinating and advisory boards. These formalized arrangements emphasized that a close working relationship between higher education boards and governors was essential. But the principal ingredients of the relationship continued to be the personalities of the governor and the board's staff head.

There was an illustrative episode of board-gubernatorial relations in New York in 1981. In 1980 the board of regents released one of its periodic master plans for higher education in the state. In 1981 Governor Carey wrote to the board complaining that his office had not been consulted in the preparation of the master plan and that the master plan did not address certain issues of primary concern to him. The governor listed four concerns that he believed should have been considered in the master plan and were not. These concerns included the role of higher education in state economic development; the balance that should be maintained between the state university, the city university, and the private sector; the extent to which remediation of poor learning skills should continue to be a cost of public higher education; and the adequacy of health services education in the state. As a result of this communication, the board of regents agreed that in the future it would work with the governor's office in the development of master plans for higher education.

What is the most effective way to relate a higher education board to a state governor? There did not appear to be any ready answer to this question. In my opinion, the board arrangement continues to be a necessary device, even though a part-time lay board is not the completely ideal way to provide continuous and effective leadership. Boards must continue to select staff heads with professional competence, personal integrity, and political sensitivity. Board size should range from a minimum of seven or nine members to a maximum of thirteen or fifteen members. Board membership should consist of public representatives. The term of members should be for a period of from six to nine years, except for one member. The exception is that one member of every higher education board should have a four-year term coinciding with that of the governor. In this way, the governor can name one member to a higher education board at the beginning of his or her term.

There remains the question whether or not the member whose term coincides with that of the governor should be appointed chairman by the governor. My associates and I have concluded that the board should select its own chairman and should be free to accept or reject as chairman the individual named to the board by the governor.

As far as the staff heads of higher education boards were concerned, the prevailing practice we encountered was for them to serve on annual contracts at the pleasure of the boards. In two or three instances we did encounter a multiyear contract between a board and its staff head. The year-to-year arrangement appears to be the preferable one, even though it may result in something less than the desirable continuity in working relationships between the board and the staff head.

A Summing Up

There have been two principal theses to this account of state governments and university governance. One thesis has been that the state government interest in higher education is not the sum total of the interests of the various public institutions of higher education and their internal constituencies. The second thesis has been that state government issues in higher education are extensive and complex. These issues cannot be subsumed under the heading of budget analysis, even though higher education appropriations largely determine what a state government can and cannot expect from its public institutions of higher education.

State governments are representative of society's interest in and concern with higher education. To be sure, it has been the federal government in the past thirty-five years that has fostered research activities at some 100 or more universities, that has enlarged student access through financial assistance, and that has furthered nondiscrimination in access and employment. Yet it must not be forgotten that state governments have built and supported public research universities, that they have been committed to increasing access to higher education through open-door admission and low tuition policies, and that those few state governments that once segregated students by race have ceased to do so by law in the past twenty years.

State governments continue to expect certain major contributions from public institutions of higher education. These contributions include the education of a technically and professionally competent work force to meet the needs of the American economy, the education of a community leadership concerned with the general welfare, the performance of research conducive to economic development and to public betterment, the encouragement of creative activities that will advance public culture, the transfer of technological and scientific innovation to business and the professions, the demonstration and encouragement of new and better ways to assist families and groups in advancing their welfare, the provision of equal opportunity for education among all individuals regardless of socioeconomic status, and the promotion of social mobility on the basis of talent and virtue. To this listing of society's expectations, we should add what is perhaps the most important one: the cultivation by higher education of an individual's commitment to a free society and attachment to the essentials of liberal democracy and social pluralism.

State governments, moreover, are concerned with both public and private higher education. They are concerned with public higher education because it enrolls an overwhelming proportion of all students. They are concerned with private higher education because it prevents public domination of the educational endeavor and because in many instances it establishes standards of performance vital to public higher education and to all of society.

There is, of course, another social expectation that must be mentioned. Society and state governments are concerned about the costs of the higher education enterprise: the costs of instructional and other programs and the costs of providing equal educational opportunity. There are few if any state government officials who do not accept the grand design of higher education, but there are many who question the cost effectiveness of higher education. There are also many who question whether the multiple outputs of higher education can or should be accomplished in the same mix by all public institutions of higher education.

Of course, the constituent groupings of public higher education institutions have their own expectations. Governing boards, presidents, and presidential associates have concerns about the mission assigned to their particular institutions or sets of institutions, about the programs they may undertake, about the financial resources available to them, about enrollment sizes, and about the adequacy of physical facilities. Faculty members of public institutions have a natural interest in salary levels, employment security, instructional work loads, the amount of time available for research and public service, standards of tenure and promotion, the quality of instructional and other outcomes, participation in institutional governance, and control of degree programs and courses. Students of public institutions have interests and concerns about access to particular institutions, the amount of tuition and other charges, the availability of financial assistance, student services, the quality of instruction, participation in institutional governance, and job opportunities.

The problem is how to reconcile the expectations of society with those of the varied constituencies of institutions of higher education. The expectations of society can never be fully realized, nor can those of institutions. Somehow social expectations and institutional expectations must be adjusted, somehow a compromise must be struck. But the grand design of higher education must not be lost and the interests of the institutions must not be sacrificed in this process of adjustment and compromise.

In its final report, the Carnegie Council on Policy Studies in Higher Education (1980) offered a checklist of imperatives for state governments: to maintain the current level of support on a per-capita basis in constant dollars, to provide tuition grants to all needy students, to support private higher education, to assist institutions in adjusting to changing needs, to avoid "excessive regulation," to employ flexible funding formulas, to encourage institutional cooperation, to ensure statewide coverage of open-access institutions and of area health education centers, and to expend public funds with maximum institutional autonomy. The Carnegie Foundation for the Advancement of Teaching (1982) offered a somewhat different set of recommendations to state governments: to plan and provide basic support for a comprehensive system of higher education, to encourage "good" institutional management, to appropriate funds in broad categories of expenditure rather than by line item, to call upon institutions to review academic programs and to report the results, to work with regional accrediting agencies to evaluate the performance of each campus, and to give special priority to the maintenance of diversity among public institutions.

The Carnegie Foundation essay went on to declare that state governments should work to accomplish these objectives primarily "through statewide coordinating boards" (p. 81). While the Carnegie Foundation did not clearly define what it meant by a coordinating board, one implication was at least certain: State governments require a specialized administrative agency in the field of higher education. Our study confirmed that need.

The state government agenda for higher education is extensive: open access and selective access, increased quality in educational outputs, renewed attention to the demands of state economic development, support of students as well as support of institutions, support of research and technological transfer within the system, support of cultural enrichment, development of a comprehensive system of public higher education, assignment of differential missions among public institutions, encouragement of private higher education, coordination of programs and elimination of high-cost and limited-need programs, closing or merger of institutions with low enrollment and high overhead, distribution of financial support among institutions on the basis of adequacy and equity, and encouragement of institutional management autonomy and accountability. If a state government is serious about this agenda, it will be serious in its support of a state board of higher education.

Morever, campus presidents need the assistance of state boards of higher education. Given the conflicting aspirations of the varying constituencies of the academic community, institutional leadership must be reinforced, must be offered encouragement and recognition, must be supported in carrying out the priorities and making the hard choices that reflect state needs and the state's ability to finance higher education.

State government concerns with higher education must be expressed through the political process of executive, legislative, and judicial power. In turn, the political process must be aided and abetted by administrative machinery. State governments have looked to executive and legislative agencies and to higher education boards to assist them. All these higher education boards, whether statewide governing boards, coordinating boards, or advisory boards, will be called upon for even greater help in the decades of the 1980s and 1990s.

The final organizational question is which kind of board will be most helpful: a statewide governing board, a coordinating board, or an advisory board. Most organizational studies of the past have avoided any specific answer to this question. By implication at least, the Carnegie Commission on Higher Education and the Carnegie Council on Policy Studies indicated a preference for advisory boards and a second preference for statewide governing boards. The 1982 essay of the Carnegie Foundation for the Advancement of Teaching advocated institutional self-regulation of institutional interests, combined with oversight by a statewide coordinating board.

The author can do no more than to express certain conclusions reached from experience and study:

The statewide governing board is not an effective device for reconciling institutional interests and state government interests unless it purposefully undertakes to emphasize its state government role and to deemphasize its institutional attachments. In states that have statewide governing boards, there will be an increasing tendency to supplement their role by developing and encouraging advisory boards with broad scope in relation to all the higher education interests of the state.

Coordinating boards will need to exercise their authority for planning, for approving and reviewing programs, for budgeting, for information collection and analysis, and for administration of assistance programs with increasing sophistication and care. Coordinating boards will find themselves more and more occupied with the problem of campus size and of the effective and efficient operation of campuses. The guidelines set forth for coordinating higher education for the 1970s (Glenny and others, 1971) will continue to be valid in the 1980s and 1990s. Coordinating boards will continue to be resisted by institutional governing boards and presidents, even though such resistance is shortsighted and may eventually be self-defeating.

Advisory boards will come to act more and more like coordinating boards, and state boards will tend to delegate more authority to them or to incorporate their recommendations into legislation by reference.

All types of boards — governing, coordinating, and advisory — will improve their ties to the executive branch of state government, while resisting crude and highly partisan executive and legislative pressures.

State governments will increasingly recognize the need for effective coordination of higher education, whatever the organizational arrangement they may adopt to this end.

Public institutions of higher education will gradually come to recognize and accept the proposition that university governance must be reconciled with state government concerns about higher education.

Administrative machinery, however, is not the bottom line in public higher education. Institutional effectiveness, social responsibility, governmental accountability, and the preservation of a free society are the true goals of such education. Let us hope that they will always remain its goals.

References

Berdahl, R. O. *Statewide Coordination of Higher Education*. Washington, D.C.: American Council on Education, 1971.

Berve, N. M. *Major Issues of Concern to State Higher Education Agencies and State Policy Issues*. Denver: Education Commission of the States, 1981.

Bogue, E. G., and Brown, W. "Performance Incentives for State Colleges." *Harvard Business Review*, Nov.–Dec. 1982, pp. 123–128.

Bowen, H. R. *The Costs of Higher Education: How Much Do Colleges and Universities Spend Per Student and How Much Should They Spend?* San Francisco: Jossey-Bass, 1980.

Breneman, D. W. *The Coming Enrollment Crisis: What Every Trustee Must Know*. Washington, D.C.: Association of Governing Boards of Colleges and Universities, 1982.

Carnegie Commission on Higher Education. *The Capitol and the Campus: State Responsibility for Postsecondary Education*. New York: McGraw-Hill, 1971.

Carnegie Commission on Higher Education. *A Classification of Institutions of Higher Education*. Berkeley, Calif.: Carnegie Council on Policy Studies for Higher Education, 1973a.

Carnegie Commission on Higher Education. *Governance of Higher Education*. New York: McGraw-Hill, 1973b.

Carnegie Commission on Higher Education. *Priorities for Action: Final Report*. New York: McGraw-Hill, 1973c.

Carnegie Council on Policy Studies in Higher Education. *Low or No Tuition: The Feasibility of a National Policy for the First Two Years of College*. San Francisco: Jossey-Bass, 1975.

Carnegie Council on Policy Studies in Higher Education. *A Classification of Institutions of Higher Education*. (Rev. ed.) Berkeley, Calif.: Carnegie Council on Policy Studies in Higher Education, 1976.

Carnegie Council on Policy Studies in Higher Education. *Faculty Bargaining in Public Higher Education*. San Francisco: Jossey-Bass, 1977a.

Carnegie Council on Policy Studies in Higher Education. *Selective Admissions in Higher Education: Comment and Recommendations and Two Reports*. San Francisco: Jossey-Bass, 1977b.

Carnegie Council on Policy Studies in Higher Education. *The States and Private Higher Education: Problems and Policies in a New Era*. San Francisco: Jossey-Bass, 1977c.

Carnegie Council on Policy Studies in Higher Education. *Three Thousand Futures: The Next Twenty Years for Higher Education*. San Francisco: Jossey-Bass, 1980.

Carnegie Council on Policy Studies in Higher Education. *A Summary of Reports and Recommendations*. San Francisco: Jossey-Bass, 1981.

Carnegie Foundation for the Advancement of Teaching. *The States and Higher Education: A Proud Past and a Vital Future*. San Francisco: Jossey-Bass, 1976.

Carnegie Foundation for the Advancement of Teaching. *The Control of the Campus*. Washington, D.C.: Carnegie Foundation for the Advancement of Teaching, 1982.

Caruthers, J. K., and Orwig, M. *Budgeting in Higher Education*. AAHE-ERIC Higher Education Report, No. 3. Washington, D.C.: American Association for Higher Education, 1979.

Chambers, M. M. *Grapevine*, October 1980.

Chambers, M. M. *Grapevine*, November 1981.

Chambers, M. M. *Grapevine*, January 1982.

Commission on Financing Higher Education. *Nature and Needs of Higher Education.* New York: Columbia University Press, 1952.

Commission on Higher Education and the Economy of New England. *The Competitive Strength of Our Knowledge-Intensive Region Is a Matter of Concern.* Boston: New England Board of Higher Education, 1982.

Committee on Government and Higher Education. *The Efficiency of Freedom.* Baltimore: Johns Hopkins University Press, 1959.

Dressel, P. L. (Ed.). *New Directions for Institutional Research: The Autonomy of Public Colleges,* no. 26. San Francisco: Jossey-Bass, 1980.

Education Commission of the States. *Challenge: Coordination and Governance in the 1980s.* Denver: Education Commission of the States, 1980.

Education Commission of the States. *Higher Education in the States, 1981, 7* (1) (entire issue).

Education Commission of the States. *Higher Education in the States,* 1982, *8* (2) (entire issue).

Education Commission of the States, National Center for Higher Education Management Systems, State Higher Education Executive Officers Association. *State Postsecondary Education Profiles Handbook, 1981.* Denver: Education Commission of the States, 1981.

Eulau, H., and Quinley, H. *State Officials and Higher Education.* New York: McGraw-Hill, 1970.

Frances, C. (Ed.). *New Directions for Higher Education: Successful Responses to Financial Difficulty,* no. 38. San Francisco: Jossey-Bass, 1982.

Glenny, L. A. *Autonomy of Public Colleges: The Challenge of Coordination.* New York: McGraw-Hill, 1959.

Glenny, L. A. *State Budgeting for Higher Education.* Berkeley: Center for Research and Development in Higher Education, University of California, 1976.

Glenny, L. A., and others. *Coordinating Higher Education for the '70s.* Berkeley: Center for Research and Development in Higher Education, University of California, 1971.

Halstead, D. K. *Tax Wealth in Fifty States.* National Institute of Education. Washington, D.C.: U.S. Government Printing Office, 1978.

Halstead, D. K. *How States Compare in Financial Support of Higher Education 1982–83.* Washington, D.C.: National Institute of Education, 1983.

Harcleroad, F. F. *Institutional Efficiency in State Systems of Public Higher Education.* Tucson: Higher Education Program, College of Education, University of Arizona, 1975.

Hines, E., McCarthy, J., and Cronan, E. *State Support of Higher Education: Appropriations Viewed in Relation to Personal Income.* Normal: Illinois State University, 1982.

Lee, E. C., and Bowen, F. M. *The Multicampus University: A Study in Academic Governance.* New York: McGraw-Hill, 1971.

Lee, E. C., and Bowen, F. M. *Managing Multicampus Systems: Effective Administration in an Unsteady State.* San Francisco: Jossey-Bass, 1975.

Lenning, O. T. "Variable-Selection and Measurement Concerns." In E. T. Pascarella (Ed.), *New Directions for Institutional Research: Studying Student Attrition,* no. 36. San Francisco: Jossey-Bass, 1982.

McConnell, T. R. "Autonomy and Accountability: Some Fundamental Issues." In P. G. Altbach and R. O. Berdahl (Eds.), *Higher Education in American Society.* Buffalo: Prometheus, 1981.

McCoy, M., and Halstead, D. K. *Higher Education Financing in the Fifty States.* Washington, D.C.: U.S. Government Printing Office, 1979.

Makowski, D., and Wulfsberg, R. M. "An Improved Taxonomy of Postsecondary Institutions" (working paper). Boulder, Colo.: National Center for Higher Education Management Systems, 1980.

Millard, R. M. *State Boards of Higher Education.* AAHE-ERIC/Higher Education Research Report, No. 4. Washington: American Association for Higher Education, 1976.

Millett, J. D. *Financing Higher Education in the United States.* New York: Columbia University Press, 1952.

Millett, J. D. "State Governments." In P. G. Altbach and R. O. Berdahl (Eds.), *Higher Education in American Society.* Buffalo: Prometheus, 1981.

Moos, M., and Rourke, E. F. *The Campus and the State.* Baltimore: Johns Hopkins University Press, 1959.

Mortimer, K. P., and McConnell, T. R. *Sharing Authority Effectively: Participation, Interaction, and Discretion.* San Francisco: Jossey-Bass, 1978.

National Center for Education Statistics. *A Classification of Instructional Programs.* Washington, D.C.: U.S. Government Printing Office, 1981a.

National Center for Education Statistics. *Current Funds Revenues and Expenditures for Colleges and Universities.* Washington, D.C.: National Center for Education Statistics, 1981b.

National Commission on College and University Trustee Selection. *Recommendations for Improving Trustee Selection in Public Colleges and Universities.* Washington, D.C.: Association of Governing Boards of Universities and Colleges, 1980.

National Institute of Education. *The Vocational Education Study: The Final Report.* Washington, D.C.: National Institute of Education, 1981.

O'Hara, J. W. "Trends in State Aid to Private Higher Education." Paper presented at annual conference of the American Education Finance Association, Washington, D.C., March 1983.

President's Commission on Higher Education. *Higher Education for American Democracy.* Vol. 1: *Establishing the Goals.* Washington, D.C.: U.S. Government Printing Office, 1947a.

President's Commission on Higher Education. *Higher Education for American Democracy.* Vol. 3: *Organizing Higher Education.* Washington, D.C.: U.S. Government Printing Office, 1947b.

President's Commission on Higher Education. *Higher Education for American Democracy.* Vol. 5: *Financing Higher Education.* Washington, D.C.: U.S. Government Printing Office, 1947c.

President's Committee on Education Beyond the High School. *Second Report to the President.* Washington, D.C.: U.S. Government Printing Office, 1957.

Sloan Commission on Government and Higher Education. *A Program for Renewed Partnership.* Cambridge, Mass.: Ballinger, 1980.

Stampen, J. *The Financing of Public Higher Education.* AAHE-ERIC/ Higher Education Report, No. 9. Washington, D.C.: American Association for Higher Education, 1980.

Task Force on Coordination, Governance, and Structure of Post-secondary Education. *Coordination or Chaos?* Denver: Education Commission of the States, 1973.

University of Maryland. *The Post-Land Grant University.* College Park: University of Maryland, 1981.

Van de Water, G. B. "Emerging Issues in Postsecondary Education." *Higher Education in the States,* 1982, *8,* 1–28.

Index